*Start Point Lighthouse*

# Contents

# Maps

# Welcome to
# **Devon**

# A Short History

**Devon is a large county, with two coastlines, two cities, one complete National Park and part of another.**

Cliffs, dunes, estuaries, moorland, heathland, rivers, farmland, woods, plantations, parks and quarries – all provide different habitats for an astonishing range of plants, trees, insects, birds, animals and fish. There can be no other British county with such a diversity of natural species. Perhaps only in stretches of standing water is it deficient; Slapton Ley is its largest freshwater lake. However, a number of newly-excavated trout fisheries have produced more large ponds, and the large reservoir at **Roadford**, west of **Okehampton**, opened in 1989 to solve Devon's water shortages, has also helped.

# Top Tips

**Dartmoor**
for its scale and beauty
*(Chapter 4)*

**Paignton**
Paignton & Dartmouth Steam Railway
*(Chapter 2)*

**Exeter & Plymouth**
for shopping and much more
*(Chapter 1/3)*

**Sidmouth**
for its more than 500 listed buildings or groups of buildings
*(Chapter 1)*

**Saltram House**
near Plymouth, National Trust
*(Chapter 3)*

**Morwellham Quay**
Museum and Visitor Centre
*(Chapter 3)*

**Lynmouth area**
scenic beauty and a good walking area
*(Chapter 5)*

**Rosemoor Gardens**
RHS garden near Great Torrington
*(Chapter 5)*

**Dartmouth**
especially via the railway
*(Chapter 2)*

**Paignton Zoo**
for the kids
*(Chapter 2)*

# Early Man

Human beings seem first to have colonized southern England about 200,000BC, probably using the then still-existing continental land bridge, though the evidence for their arrival so long ago is sketchy. The discovery of some primitive stone tools in river gravel on the borders of Devon and Dorset in the nineteenth century points to this era, but unfortunately, the finds were unearthed before modern archaeological techniques were sufficiently advanced to note them in their context. This era was an interglacial period. The land that is now England was subjected to further glacial advances (Ice Ages) in more recent millennia.

The next evidence of man's presence is through numerous finds in **Kent's Cavern** in **Torquay**, which probably date from between 20,000 and 30,000BC. Flint spear heads and scrapers, a bone pin and bone harpoon heads point to hunting activities, but it is not known if Kent's Cavern was a permanent refuge or a seasonal bolt-hole. Clearly the people were hunters and gatherers, but little else is known about them. This was the **Palaeolithic era**, the **Early Stone Age**.

As the ice melted for the last time, forests began to take over from the tundra-type landscape, and man – now called Mesolithic, or **Middle Stone Age** man – had to adapt to hunting the different kinds of animals which had themselves become forest species – deer, pigs and oxen. Flint scatters from this time have been found near the North Devon coast and on Dartmoor.

The **Neolithic people** seem to have come from what is now northern France, and their settlement sites so far uncovered are in south and east Devon at Hazard Hill (Totnes), Haldon, High Peak (Sidmouth) and Hembury (Honiton). All are in elevated positions.

Burial sites are further clues to Neolithic man's culture. A site was excavated at Broad Sands (Paignton) which had a passage leading to a central chamber, all this beneath a circular mound. The best-known Neolithic monument in Devon is the so-called **Spinster's Rock** on north-eastern Dartmoor between Chagford and Drewsteignton. It stands in a field, but may be visited from the lane at Shilstone Farm. It consists of three orthostats, or stone uprights, supporting a massive capstone, and the whole structure is large enough to give present-day bad weather protection to some of the cattle who graze the field. When originally erected the four stones were at the middle of an earth mound which has now entirely disappeared.

The beginnings of a lifestyle not dissimilar to our own can be recognized in the Neolithic culture. The cultivation of cereals and the possession of flocks and herds mark an enormous change from the predatory wanderings of small bands of hunters and gatherers in earlier times.

**The Neolithic people** were now submerged by the arrival of a people who, although the first representatives of the **Bronze Age** culture (they used bronze, an alloy of tin [10 per cent] and copper [90 per cent], in their weapons and ornaments) are often referred to as the **Beaker Folk**. Their beakers were distinctively waisted, decorated pots,

# Stone Monuments

Barrows, cairns and cists (small stone-lined chambers set in the ground) have all yielded objects, and are some of the more easily recognised features of the Bronze Age in the present-day landscape. Barrows tend to be found in lowland parts of Devon, around North Molton, Upton Pyne and Farway, while cairns and cists appear on the more stony areas, such as Dartmoor and, to a lesser extent, Exmoor.

On Dartmoor, cairns and cists are often found in association with the curious and inexplicable linear monuments called stone rows or stone alignments. These are single or multiple lines of upright stones extending across the moor for distances as short as a cricket pitch or as long as 2.25 miles (3.5km), the longest in the world. Carnac in Brittany has similar monuments. Although their purpose remains obscure, a funeral ritual connection seems likely, and a link with astronomical observations is possible.

Other monuments to be seen are stone circles – rings of upright stones, like a kind of mini-Stonehenge – and standing stones or menhirs. They may be found with stone rows or on their own, and can be over 14ft (4m) high (above ground level). Such a prodigious monument can be found at Drizzlecombe in the Upper Plym Valley, in a fascinating group of Bronze Age remains.

possibly used more for ritual or social purposes than for purely utilitarian functions. Although they had mastered the technique of smelting ore to produce metal, the use of stone in tools and weapons continued.

While the monuments connected with death and funeral ritual are interesting and tend to be more obvious, it is the ruined stone foundations of **Bronze Age dwellings** on Dartmoor which are of the greatest interest to the visitor, and which are most abundant.

There are about 2,000 of these hut remains – 'hut circles' on the Ordnance Survey maps – on Dartmoor. Some are found singly, others in groups, enclosed, or scattered on the open moor. As it is not known how many were occupied at once, any population figure must be guesswork. Dartmoor, however, is the finest repository of Bronze Age remains in Europe; they have survived as they were made of granite, and there has been comparatively little subsequent disturbance.

In the past 75 years or so, aerial photography has revealed a network of parallel field systems with house sites on the lower slopes of high Dartmoor. Archaeological investigation has thrown a great deal of light on this hitherto unsuspected culture, which dates from about 1500 to 1000BC. Separate territorial areas divided by rivers and watershed reaves (boundary banks) have been discovered, but little is known of the system of land tenure or agricultural economy of the people

# Devon

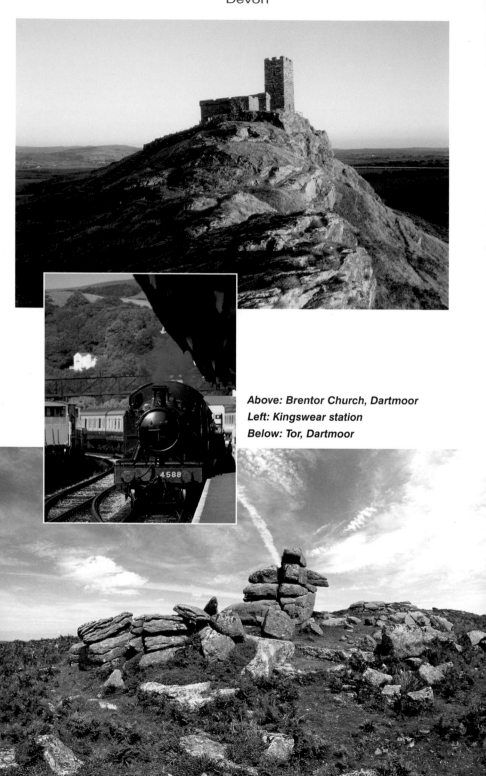

*Above: Brentor Church, Dartmoor*
*Left: Kingswear station*
*Below: Tor, Dartmoor*

*Above: Dartmouth Castle*
*Below: Ilfracombe Harbour*

11

who laid out these wide-ranging occupation patterns.

The Bronze Age gave way to the **Iron Age** (indicating the development of ferrous smelting techniques) during the last thousand years BC, probably about 750BC. As in all these eras, dates are approximate, and in any case the changeover was gradual. The Iron Age is typified by the **hillforts** that still corrugate many Devon summits and cliff tops. The building of these enormous earthworks must have occupied hundreds of people for many years, in view of the primitive tools and equipment they possessed; the cult of the tribe seems to have been well developed; and the construction of such gigantic defensive positions suggests that the people were warlike.

The hillforts are often called 'castles'; this may well confuse anyone looking for medieval masonry, and finding nothing more dramatic than concentric banks and ditches. They often contain the place-name element 'bury'

## Evidence of Roman Occupation

For many years it was thought that the Romans did not venture westwards, but archaeological work has proved the existence of interior roads pushing north and south of Dartmoor, the northerly one probably venturing down into Cornwall. Marching camps and forts west of Exeter are also known, but little remains to be seen above ground, apart from a number of Roman milestones in Cornwall.

– Cadbury Castle overlooking the Exe Valley north of Exeter, and no fewer than three Hemburys (near Honiton, Buckfastleigh and Bideford). In all, there were about fifty or sixty hillforts in Devon, but as there is no way of knowing if they were all occupied simultaneously, no prehistoric population can be postulated.

# The Romans to the Norman Conquest

The **Romans** arrived in Devon in AD49 as a conquering force, and the Second Augustan Legion was stationed at Seaton in that year. No doubt the fleet kept pace down the Channel with the advancing army (which was commanded by Vespasian, a future emperor), until the site of Exeter was reached. There may have been a local settlement at Exeter before the arrival of the Romans, but this has yet to be proved. The local people were the Dumnonii.

Here the invaders set up a base for their operations in the far west, and the situation was probably rather like a cavalry fort on the North American plains in the early nineteenth century, the Dumnonii playing the part of the Red Indians. The settlement was defended by an earth bank initially, and strengthened later by the construction of a stone wall. Supplies came from the east along what is now the A30 (still a road of Roman straightness east of Exeter Airport) and by ships up the Exe Estuary to what is now Topsham. Again, the road joining Exeter with Topsham is unmistakably Roman.

The Romans had at least two fortlets on the county's north coast: some remains are still visible at **Old Burrow** (near the Somerset border) and at **Martinhoe**.

The most spectacular discovery during the many post-war digs in Exeter was of a **legionary bathhouse** in what is now the Cathedral Close. Unfortunately, as the vast cost of roofing it was prohibitive, the exposed remains were covered with polythene and sand and the whole excavated complex back-filled.

The principal trade of early Exeter was agricultural produce; a possible stockyard was discovered. Evidence of metalworking and pottery production attests the self-sufficiency of this focus of Roman culture in a part of the country still largely uncivilized. No temples are known, but a fourth-century pottery sherd bearing the early Christian device, the chi-rho symbol, is proof of a non-pagan influence.

Towards the end of the fourth century most of the Roman garrisons had been withdrawn from Britain to defend Gaul and Italy against the attacks of barbarians. The decline of Exeter is not fully understood, but it shared the loss of the stabilizing Roman influence with the rest of the country. With the departure of the Romans, the public buildings first ceased to be maintained and then collapsed, the structure of the ordered Roman society collapsing with them. A curious effect was a reversion to pre-Roman customs by the indigenous people. Some of the Iron Age earthworks were (perhaps briefly) re-occupied, and old tribal values resurrected. Perhaps they had never been totally suppressed.

With the departure of the Romans, we enter the **Dark Ages**, those secret centuries whose enigmatic annals seem lost for ever. To fill the vacuum, and on the slenderest evidence, commentators have created the Arthurian legends, but they apply to Cornwall and Somerset rather than to Devon.

The **Saxon** invasions of south-east England did not affect the south-west for some time, but gradually the Saxons pushed westwards. Exeter became part of the Kingdom of Wessex in 680, and the Tamar was reached by 780. Devon was now a shire county, like its neighbours to the east.

Here and there a trace of these years survives – a carved stone here, an inscribed monolith there; an example is the splendid cross shaft at **Copplestone**, north-west of Crediton, its interlaced ornamental patterns as fresh now as if it had been carved fifty years ago. But although large monasteries were established at Exeter and Crediton and smaller ones elsewhere, few worthwhile traces of pre-Norman architecture have survived. The Crediton monastic foundation was responsible for the religious development of Winfrith, better known as St Boniface, who was born there about 680 and later established Christianity in central Germany; he is often regarded as the greatest Englishman.

Alfred became king in 871 and began to put the Wessex fortifications in order. The Danes carried out probing raids and occupied Exeter in 876, but Alfred put them to flight in the following summer. The burghs established by Alfred were Exeter, Pilton (now part of Barnstaple), Lydford and Halwell, although the last was later moved to Totnes.

Towards the end of the tenth century, a further flush of Danish attacks up the estuaries of the Tamar, the Teign and the Exe led to much slaughter and plunder, culminating in the sacking of Exeter in 1003. In the meantime Crediton had become the diocesan headquarters, part of the former vast Sherborne diocese. In 1050 it was decided to transfer it to Exeter, as this could be defended, its walls now erect again; and here it has remained ever since.

These were years when the natural forests of Devon were gradually cleared. Most of the villages and settlements we take for granted in the countryside were established in those far-off misty days under the Saxon kings.

**Dartmoor Pony**

# 1066 to the Civil War

The **Norman** invasion meant little to the people of Devon for over a year. Life went on and, after all, Devon was a long way from Hastings and its aftermath. However, the mother of the defeated King Harold, Gytha, fled to Exeter with her daughter, and this probably strengthened the resolve of Devonians to resist the invaders. Exeter's walls were repaired, the whole area rallied round to defend the city, and William realized that he himself would have to persuade the West Country to toe the line. So he arrived outside Exeter at the head of an army, and after lengthy negotiations peace with honour was agreed.

One of his first actions was to build a castle on the highest part of Exeter's walls, as much to subdue the local population as to defend the city, thus establishing the rule of law from this elevated site. Rougemont castle remained the seat of law for more than 900 years, housing Exeter's Crown Court in its Georgian buildings until 2003. As a result, the ordinary people of Exeter regarded the castle with something akin to awe and would venture only with reluctance within its walls — a long-standing folk memory, perhaps? The castle's new owners will be hoping that this can be overcome as they recently opened the building to the public as a centre for heritage and cultural events.

Other castles were built at Totnes, Okehampton, Barnstaple and Plympton. The descendants of the first Norman Sheriff of Devon, Baldwin de Brionne, are the Courtenays, the Earls of Devon, who now own Powderham Castle. Their family home was Courtenay, near Paris.

Nearly 20 years after he had become king of England, in late 1085, William decreed that a national survey, or census, should be carried out, the result being the Domesday Book. (Exeter is fortunate in possessing the original returns for south-west England in the Cathedral Library.) For the first time we know the structure of society in Britain; details of ownership, land, population, taxes and livestock were all written down. 1,170 places in Devon were listed, the total population being about 60,000, fewer than live in Exeter today; probably one fifth were slaves.

We have already seen that much of Devon's early history is bound up with that of Exeter, and so the trend continued into modern times. Plymouth, by far the largest place in present-day Devon, is not mentioned in records until 1211.

The third of Exeter's sieges occurred in the middle of the twelfth century, during the civil wars which dogged the reign of Stephen; the first occasion when William's castle was put to the test.

There was considerable movement through the county a few years later as the Second and Third Crusades left England from Dartmouth in 1147 and 1190. Dartmouth was really only a convenient collecting point. At that time it was little more than a splendid natural port, an advantage it still possesses. The South Devon ports came into their own at this time because of the marriage in 1152 of Henry II to Eleanor

## Perkin Warbeck

The West Country has seen the passing of a number of lost causes; the first was that of Perkin Warbeck, who claimed to be one of the princes murdered in the Tower. He landed in Cornwall in 1497, but Exeter stood firm for the king. A grateful monarch presented the city with a sword of state and a cap of maintenance, which are still carried before the mayor on all ceremonial occasions. Warbeck was later hanged.

of Aquitaine, a province in south-west France. Trade was boosted, and Dartmouth and Plymouth (as well as ports in Cornwall) grew in importance as a result.

The middle of the fourteenth century was marked by the arrival of the Black Death, that rat-flea scourge of the **Middle Ages**. It came into England at Melcombe Regis (what we now call Weymouth) in 1348 and soon reached Devon. Perhaps a quarter to a third of the population died. Recent discoveries suggest that whole settlements in the more marginal areas (on the edge of Dartmoor, for example), were wiped out.

The main industry in all these years was cloth (though tin developed later on Dartmoor) and every valley had its fulling or tucking mill. The trade was stimulated by continental links, but suffered in later years when England was at war with the Netherlands, Spain and France.

Cloth and tin supplied the necessary stability to the county when it seemed

that all around was changing with the suppression of the monasteries in the years following 1536. They had been vast landowners, but everything was taken over in the name of the king, and allotted to selected gentry. The main houses affected were Plympton, Tavistock, Buckfast, Torre, Forde, Hartland, Dunkeswell and Buckland.

Fifty years after the Warbeck uprising, the **Prayer Book Rebellion** (or the Western Rebellion) occurred. It originated in Sampford Courtenay, near Okehampton, in 1549, an unlikely place for a violent anti-establishment movement to start; large numbers of Cornish people lent weight to the rebellion against the new English Protestant Prayer Book. After much loss of life, the rebels were put down in a battle near Clyst St Mary, after another battle just west of Honiton.

The scene now shifts to Plymouth and the sea. Plymouth was obviously the best base port for the war against Spain. Dartmouth had a haven better protected from south-west gales, but the steep hills prevented easy land access and, what is more, **Sir Francis Drake** and **Sir John Hawkins** lived locally. But practically every port played its part in the sea war, by building the ships that defeated the Armada in 1588. It is said that the Spanish fleet was first sighted in Devon from the cliffs near Hope Cove, although it was earlier spotted off the Lizard in Cornwall. A system of fire beacons alerted the country to the danger. The development of the New World encouraged trade from West Country ports and Plymouth, Bideford and Barnstaple soon had strong links across the Atlantic.

In the middle of the seventeenth century there was further unrest. The Civil War ebbed and flowed across the land, and family loyalties were split. Exeter was twice besieged, in 1643 and 1645–6, but there were no major battles such as those at Naseby or Marston Moor.

# Monmouth to the Present Day

The next uprising passed through the east of the county. The ill-starred Duke of Monmouth, who proposed to depose James II, landed at Lyme Regis, just in Dorset, in 1685. He advanced through Axminster (Devon) to Taunton (Somerset), but was defeated at Sedgemoor and executed a month after he landed. The Devonshire Regiment originated as a unit raised to oppose the insurrection.

Only three years later, however, William of Orange landed at Brixham on Guy Fawkes Day 1688 with a vast army, many of them Dutch and German mercenaries; what became known as the **Glorious Revolution** was successful. James II was ousted, and William and Mary took the throne.

For half of the following 127 years, until Waterloo, England was at war with France. Plymouth developed as a naval base, but trade was thwarted and foreign travel inhibited. Road transport was encouraged by the first of the Devon Turnpike Acts in 1753. Roads were improved, and stagecoaches began to make road travel easier and more reliable.

The British fleet, finding that it could very easily be bottled up in the Hamoaze at Plymouth, began to use the sheltered waters of Tor Bay as an anchorage; until Plymouth Breakwater was built, well into the nineteenth century, Plymouth Sound was a useless refuge for sailing vessels which needed to depart quickly. It was the fleet medical officers, understanding the climatic benefits of the site, who began to recommend Torquay to their consumptive patients; thus it was as a haven for invalids that the village of Torquay became a town and, later, a holiday resort. In the 1840s the railway reached Devon, and the chosen routes soon established the holiday resorts, which have continued, although widespread car ownership has made many people independent of the railways.

World War I had little direct effect on Devon, except to cream off the pride of its menfolk, as a glance at any war memorial will show. For this was the end of an era, and things were never the same again.

In World War II the battle came to Devon. Exeter and Plymouth were blitzed out of all recognition by German bombers, and Teignmouth and Exmouth were also badly damaged. Slapton Sands was used by the US forces for invasion exercises in 1943, and 3,000 people from seven parishes in the hinterland covering 30,000 acres (12,000 hectares) were evacuated as live ammunition was used. Dartmouth became an important base for the invasion of northern France.

In the years since the war the railways have contracted, the dual carriageways and M5 motorway have arrived, caravan and camping sites have multiplied, and sailing and self-catering holidays are in vogue. Devon is now in competition with cheap overseas package tours, but, because of its heritage of history and beauty, its accessibility and hospitality, there is an enormous amount to see and do in the county.

# Local Food & Drink

Devon is the home of clotted cream and of course, sea food, having the sea to the north and south of the county. The county also produces good beers, ciders and plenty of quality meats from its farms.

## Beer

Country Life Brewery at The Big Sheep, Abbotsham, near Bideford produces over 15,000 pints of award winning ales a week. It is North Devon's largesr bottling brewer.

Devon offers a wide variety of local bottled beers, cider and wines.

*Scones with jam and cream.*

## Cider

In the north and east, look out for the Lyme Bay Winery of Axminster, producing cider, perry (from pears)

*Ancient thatched pub in Devon, dates from the twelfth century*

Coleton Fishacre

*Lobster pots on the dockside at Seaton*

and mead along with wine, spirits and hqueuers. Also Ostlers Cider from Barnstaple.

There are several producers in the south, including Luscombe Organic Drinks of Buckfastleigh; Heron & Valley Cider of Kingsbridge; Ashridge Cider of Totnes and Winkleigh Cider of Winkleigh.

## Spirits

Plymouth Gin is still made at the Blackfriars Distillery in Plymouth along with other specialities such as Plymouth Sloe Gin.

Bramley and Gage of South Brent produce fresh fruit liqueurs including Dittisham Plum; raspberry; blackberry and black current. All with no added chemicals, sweetners or preservativies.

## Cheese

Curworthy Cheese at Jacobstowe, Okenhampton produce a full-fat semi-hard cheese plus Belstone, Devon Oke and Meldon.

## Farmers Markets

### Exeter

Cromer Fore Street/South Street
☎ 01392 665 757
Every Thurs 9am–1.30pm.

### Newton Abbot

High Street
☎ 01623 353567
Every Tues except Bank Holidays, 9am–3pm.

### Paignton

Preston Down Road
TQ13 1RN
1st and 3rd Wed of the month.

### Plymouth

Amada Way
☎ 01752 306550
2nd and 4th Sat of the month.

### South Molton

Pannier Market
☎ 01769 572252
4th Sat of the month, 7am–1pm.

## Tavistock

☎ 01822 820360
2nd and 4th Sat of the month, 9am–1pm.

## Tiverton

Food Hall, General Market
Every Tue, Fri and Sat.

# Gardens & Parks

## Arlington Court & The National Trust's Carriage Collection

Arlington, nr Barnstaple, EX31 4LP
☎ 01271 850296

## Coleton Fishacre

(National Trust)
Brownstone Road, Kingswear,
TQ6 0EQ
☎ 01803 752466

## Knightshayes Court

(National Trust)
Bolham, Tiverton, EX16 7RQ
☎ 01884 254665

## Killerton

(National Trust)
Broadclyst, Exeter, EX5 3LE
☎ 01392 881345

## A La Ronde

(National Trust)
Summer Lane, Exmouth, EX8 5BD
☎ 01395 265514

## Castle Drogo

(National Trust)
Drewsteignton, nr Exeter,
EX6 6PB
☎ 01647 433306

## Sharpitor

(National Trust)
Salcombe, TQ8 8LW
☎ 01548 842 893

## Lukesland Gardens

Ivybridge, PL21 0JF
☎ 01752 691749

## Northernhay Gardens

Civic Centre Paris Street,
Exeter, EX1 1JN
☎ 01392 262630

## Bickton Park Botanical Gardens

East Budleigh, Budleigh Salterton,
EX9 7BJ

## Coldharbour Mill

Uffculme, Cullompton, EX15 3EE.
☎ 01884 840960

## Orchid Paradise

Burnham Nurseries Ltd,
Forches Cross, Newton Abbot,
TQ12 6PZ
☎ 01626 352233

## The Garden House

Buckland Monachorum, Yelverton,
PL20 7LQ
☎ 01822 854769

## Tapeley Park

Instow, North Devon

## Great Torrington

RHS Garden Rosemoor

# 1. Exeter and East Devon

Most people arriving in Devon do so through East Devon. A few come by the northern routes, over Exmoor or through South Molton, and a handful come across from Roscoff, land at Plymouth Airport or enter from Cornwall. Most visitors come by road, down the M5 or along the A30; some by rail or via Exeter Airport (the regional airport for the south-west). This is the corridor, where the peninsula narrows to about 33 miles (53km), through which nearly everyone passes.

If the visitor misses the sign announcing DEVON beside the M5 there will be little in the landscape to inform him that he has left Somerset. The main physical jolt is likely to be the red soil, which he will first see near Cullompton. This is the New Red Sandstone, and is particularly noticeable where it outcrops in sea cliffs for a few miles on either side of the Exe Estuary.

Those who know East Devon better realize that there is another kind of scenery — a landscape of flat-topped hills and deep valleys north and south

*Opposite Page: Sidmouth on the Jurassic Coast*
*Below Top: Exeter Cathedral*
*Below Bottom: Rougemont Castle*

of Honiton. The hills to the north are the Blackdowns, shared with Somerset. The main railway into Devon comes through the Whiteball Tunnel and under the county boundary, beneath a shoulder of these hills. The nearby M5 motorist, just after passing the Wellington Monument (in Somerset) will notice a small dome-like structure on the end of one of the Blackdowns' heath-topped spurs. This is Culmstock Beacon, and the little building may have had a connection with the beacon fire. It stands about a mile (1.6km) inside Devon and gives a stupendous view westwards, for despite its modest altitude at 820ft (287m), the ground falls away and there is no higher land until the Haldon Hills (their summit is 826ft [289m]) are reached beyond Exeter. Entering Devon from Somerset, unless bound for North Devon or North Cornwall, all routes lead to Exeter, reached within 15 minutes of crossing the boundary.

## Exeter

**Exeter** is the undisputed capital of the county. Communications, culture, administration, commerce, education, medicine and religion all focus here. Plymouth is much larger and, since the opening of its Theatre Royal in 1982, is now competing in the field of culture, but in no other sense, except its superb natural position beside the Sound and in its role as a port, naval and commercial, is it more important than the ancient city of Exeter. The two are so dissimilar as to make comparisons impossible.

Much has been written about Exeter's history in the introductory chapter, but its visual attractions have not been mentioned. Taking the broad view, one of the appealing aspects is its size; large enough to attract specialized shops, events and institutions, but small enough to be comfortably cosy. Looking down the main street there are green fields only a couple of miles away, and from the highest part of the city (now known as Pennsylvania, as the 1822 builder of Pennsylvania Park was a Quaker who named his terrace after the American province), and from the Exeter Bypass, the sea and the supertankers off Torbay can be seen due south; Dartmoor is visible due west.

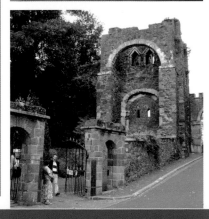

Exeter's old buildings, the cathedral and the Guildhall apart, do not make a great impact, and many of the more interesting features of its heritage have to be searched for. On a dull or wet day in August, when tourists swarm to the city and the car parks show 'Full' signs, the Cathedral Close and High Street teem with life, but few day visitors penetrate to Rougemont Gardens below the castle, walk the line of the city walls, or visit the underground passages. The latter are, in fact, misnamed. While appearing to be just that, they were built in the fourteenth and fifteenth centuries to bring water into the city from springs outside the walls.

# Town Centre Tour

Since so much of old Exeter was destroyed in May 1942, the remaining historic buildings and places of interest are slightly off-centre, and can best be linked by a walk round the walls, with a deflection here and there to see something near at hand. Visitors are always surprised at the variety of interest that lies between the ancient core and the newer Exeter outside the walls. The distance is 1½ (2.5km) and the area enclosed is 93 acres (37 hectares). Five-sixths of the city wall is still visible and the walk round the complete circuit takes between $1^1/_2$ and 2 hours.

A good place to start is in the High Street where a line of paving slabs, laid as broken pieces, marks a length of the **city wall** where it has disappeared. (This is the site of the medieval East Gate.) Although it can be followed in either direction, as one way seems to go through the front door of a shop

the other may be more fruitful! At once a corner bastion may be seen; a wall plaque states that the city walls were originally built by the Romans about AD200.

As the wall is followed, at Bedford Street one enters Southernhay East, where, on one of Exeter's elegant Georgian terraces, are some curious Coade stone keystones of moulded faces. Turn behind No. 9 to rediscover the wall and follow it to South Street where two more wall plaques, one on either side of the street, explain that the massive **South Gate**, demolished in 1819, was for many years a prison. From here it is worth deviating along Magdalen Street to see **Wynard's Almshouses**, opposite the one-time Eye Infirmary. Round a cobbled courtyard, still with its well-head, is a pleasing group of red sandstone cottages and a chapel. Founded in the fifteenth century and rebuilt several times since, the buildings were converted into offices for various voluntary organizations in the 1970s and were redeveloped as private dwellings in 2002. They are not open to the public. Now return to the site of South Gate and cross Western Way at the traffic lights and follow the wall to the back of the **Custom House** (1681), the first building in Exeter to be constructed from brick in modern times, and the **Quay House** Visitor Centre where the history of the city, particularly the river quays, is explored. This part of Exeter is also the heart of Exeter's nightlife, with discos and clubs accommodated in old warehouses.

Now resume the wall circuit. Behind the Custom House and along Cricklepit Street, on the left are the remains of

Exeter's last **watermill**, with an undershot waterwheel. This mill was first recorded in 1190 and has recently been restored to house the headquarters of Devon Wildlife Trust. The mill is open to visit on weekdays, with occasional days when the waterwheel can be seen in action. On Western Way, across the road is a ruined church, which stands on a bridge now high and dry. This was Exeter's first bridge (1240) and it crossed a much wider river. The Exe now runs in a narrower and deeper channel beyond. There is another wall plaque on the line of the walls at the site of the West Gate.

Stepcote Hill, the cobbled medieval way into the city, climbs steeply up beside **St Mary Steps church**. Until 1778 this was the main road into Exeter from the west. The church has a famous clock, of which various parts can be seen to move when it strikes the hour. Facing it is a wooden-framed Tudor building that was moved here in 1961 and is now known as *'The House that Moved'*. It was in the way of the new road, but by strapping it together and jacking it up on rollers the little building was moved to its present site and saved for posterity.

Walk up West Street to Fore Street, now the main way into Exeter from the west. The route is straight ahead up Bartholomew Street, but turn briefly up Fore Street for 50yd (46m), where on the left will be seen the Victorian façade of a 1471 building, the **Tuckers Hall**. Here the craft gild (*sic*) of the Exeter woollen trade, the weavers, fullers and shearmen met, and, in a somewhat altered form, still meet. The roof timbers are original and the panelling is Jacobean.

Return to the foot of Bartholomew Street and carry on up to a walkway along the top of the walls beside a restored chapel of 1817 with a Doric porch. This leads to a pleasant backwater known as Ash Grove where the wall turns 90 degrees right and follows along the top of the Long Brook Valley. At the corner there was once a bastion known as the Snail Tower, which was designated one of the three common jakes (lavatories) in 1568. Where the path meets the road by some iron gates on the left, enter the gates and go down some narrow steep steps to a lower level. Here one is standing outside the **Exeter catacombs**, built against the walls in the Egyptian style of 1811 then in vogue and operated in a desultory fashion until 1883. They never caught on as a way of disposing of the dead, and were sealed off for many years. Exeter's Red Coat guides now offer guided tours during the summer months.

A hundred yards away from the wall, in Mint Lane is **St Nicholas' Priory**, experience tudor life in a 1602 town house. Originally part of a medieval priory. The guest hall on the first floor is a particularly handsome room.

The walk is resumed to the foot of North Street where there was another gate, **North Gate**, and below one can see the **Iron Bridge,** an early example of cast-iron civil engineering. It was built to ease the approach to this side of Exeter for horse-drawn vehicles. Up Northernhay Street, Queen Street contains some of Exeter's best nineteenth-century architecture. The classical **Higher Market** (1838, now adapted as a shopping precinct)

- Church
- Castle
- Knightshayes Court
- Museum
- Old Blundell's School

Tiverton

Grand Western Canal

M5

Uffculme    Culmstock

Bla ck

Museum

Bickleigh Mill   Bickleigh    Cullompton

Fursdon House

Broadhembury

Hembury Fort

River Exe

Killerton House

River Culm

B3181

Crediton

River Clyst

B3176

River Tale

Honiton

- Almshouses
- Catacombs
- Cathedral
- City Walls
- Guildhall
- Rougemont Castle
- Royal Albert Memorial Museum
- St Nicholas' Priory
- University
- Quay House
- Underground passages

Broadclyst

Cadhay House   Chanter's House

A30

Ottery St. Mary

River Otter

B3180    B3176

Exeter

M5

Crealy Park   A3052

Museum

Topsham

Woodbury   Bicton Park

Salco Regis

Sidmouth

Haldon Hills

Haldon Belvedere

Powderham Castle

Hayes Barton

Mill
Otterton

East Budleigh

- Museum
- Observat

Kenton

Lympstone

Starcross

Exmouth

Fairlynch Arts Centre and M

Budleigh Salterton

0 1 2 3 4 5 miles

0 1 2 3 4 5 6 7Km

Dawlish Warren

Dawlish

- A la Ronde
- Miniature Railway
- Museum

# Exeter and East Devon

and the **Royal Albert Memorial Museum** (1865–6) in Early English revival are worth seeing, but note that the museum interior is closed until

2011. The Rougemont Hotel and the Central Station opposite were built on made-up ground in the valley of the Long Brook.

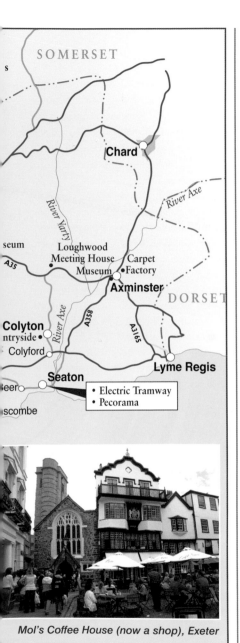

Mol's Coffee House (now a shop), Exeter

## The Guildhall at Exeter

The Guildhall is special, even if the exterior is not particularly attractive. Four great granite columns carry the weight of the Mayor's Parlour above, a room lit by five large original Tudor windows, for this frontage was added in 1592. Passing through an impressive inner door, between small porters' lodge-type rooms, which were once the city police station and the city fire station, one enters the hall itself, with a fifteenth-century arch-braced timber roof. Enormous pictures hang on the walls and the city silver fills a cabinet in the gallery. A feeling of great age pervades the atmosphere, as well it might, for this is the oldest municipal building in the country. Much altered, it's true, it is on the same site as a building mentioned in a deed of 1160.

Across Queen Street are **North-ernhay Gardens** with the walls on the right. Head towards the **Exeter War Memorial**. This attractive open area was laid out as a public space as long ago as 1612. A small door in the wall leads into **Rougemont Gardens**. The wide ditch is all that remains of the moat that separated the castle from the city (see Introduction).

At the far end of the gardens from the little door is the Regency building called Rougemont House. Opposite is the gatehouse to **the castle**, now redundant, as the present–day entrance stands alongside. Inside the castle yard are the Palladian (1774) court buildings, now accessible to the public as a music, arts and food venue. On the higher side of the 'moat' one leaves the garden through **Athelstan's Tower**, an attractive viewpoint. Athelstan reigned from 925 to 940, and this tower is part of

William's post-conquest fortifications.

On emerging from the tower, **the prison** (1790 and 1853) may be seen across the valley, and beyond, on the lower slopes of Pennsylvania, the twentieth-century West Country equivalent of the 'dreaming spires', the University of Exeter. The campus is beautifully landscaped and well worth a special visit, and includes the Northcott Theatre (plays, films and a licensed buttery) and the Great Hall (concerts). Round the north-east corner of the walls a short walk downhill brings you back to the starting point in the High Street.

The city has the narrowest street in the world, **Parliament Street**, at 25in–45in (63–114cm) wide. Its name cannot be explained it links High Street to Waterbeer Street.

# The Cathedral

Enter the Cathedral Close by Broadgate, where one of several gates into the close stood in medieval times. Violence to the clergy after dark led to this drastic action; Salisbury's gates are still *in situ*. The simple stone **Devon War Memorial** on the right, designed by Lutyens, stands on the site of the Roman bathhouse excavated in the early 1970s and now covered over. The cobbled approach to the west front is made of granite setts from Portugal. This processional way is designed to improve the rather squat west front.

The cathedral's twin towers are Norman, although perforated by later Gothic windows, and are all that survive of the cathedral built between 1133 and 1160. Bishop Bronescombe became dissatisfied with this building

and began rebuilding it in 1270, but his conception was not completed for about a hundred years.

Inside, from beneath the west window is a good view of the 300ft (105m)-long unbroken tierceron vaulting. This weighs about 5,000 tons, and stands on columns of Purbeck (Dorset) stone. Much of the cathedral is of stone from Beer in East Devon.

The roof bosses have been restored to their original medieval hues. Churches in the Middle Ages were dazzling, and where possible the brightness has been put back in Exeter Cathedral. Look especially for the complicated boss dating from 1350 in the second bay from the west, which depicts the murder of Archbishop Thomas à Becket in Canterbury Cathedral in 1170. The knights are killing him as he kneels, defended by his cross-bearer. A mirror on wheels enables the bosses to be studied without neck strain.

Other glories to look for are the Minstrel Gallery of about the same date, the Bishop's Throne (1312–17) which is regarded as the finest piece of wood carving of its age in Europe, and the tombs in the attractive Lady Chapel at the east end.

The side chapel behind the throne, St James' Chapel, was destroyed by a bomb in World War II, but fortunately the throne had been taken to pieces and removed to the country for safety; otherwise it would have become so many wood splinters. Shrapnel damage can be seen above the choir. The chapel is now restored.

Of the buildings in **Cathedral Close** the most noteworthy is **Mol's Coffee House**, its bay windows a reminder of Drake and Hawkins when they chatted over their coffee. Though there is nothing else to match Mol's, taken together the Close's buildings comprise a delightful scene. It is here, in St Martin's Lane and along Gandy Street (the other side of High Street) that the essence of Exeter's attraction is most deeply felt.

## Recent Develoments

In recent years, major developments have taken place to expand Exeter's sporting, leisure and artistic life. There are sports centres offering facilities for badminton, basketball, keep fit, gymnastics, swimming, volleyball, weight training and more informal activities; while the **Exeter Phoenix** in Bradninch Place is the place to go if you are interested in dance, folk, jazz, rock, film, theatre or cabaret. Classes and courses are always on the go and there is a bar and café.

Exeter has sprawled east and south in living memory, gobbling up the villages of Heavitree, Whipton and Pinhoe, though the residents of Clyst St Mary might object to their village being called a part of Exeter. Here, at **Crealy Park**, is one of Devon's finest sites for children, with every conceivable ride (on land and water) as well as such favourites as a pets' corner.

## Topsham

Exeter has also 'acquired' the desirable estuary port of **Topsham**, 5 miles (8km) away. Topsham is a place of individual character and this has enabled it to retain its independence despite the administrative takeover. Untouched by bombs in World War II, it has a great wealth of buildings of enormous charm. While none of them is of the highest grade in architectural terms, collectively, and as a group, they form a town that is a delight to reside in, as is reflected in house prices. Cheek by jowl the older houses stand, many of them terraced, but deep-set on their narrow sites. Monmouth Street, Higher and Lower Shapter Street, the Strand, Victoria Road and Ferry Road are some of the constricted thoroughfares that reward the explorer.

There is a walk of about half a mile to the far end of the Goat Walk, a narrow pedestrian walkway beside the estuary at the southern end of the Strand, thus passing the so-called 'Dutch' houses, attractive bow-windowed residences with flower-decked courtyards. A small **museum** entirely in keeping with the town is reached along the Strand and is well worth a visit.

Topsham developed as a port for Exeter in the Middle Ages, although it had earlier performed this function in Roman times. Small craft could reach the city by coming up the river, but following a dispute, the Countess of Devon built a weir across the river in 1282, thus cutting Exeter off from the sea. From this time, the city's merchandise had to pass through Topsham to the advantage of the treasury of the countess and her successors. A short canal – England's first pound-lock canal – was built to bypass the obstruction in 1564–6, and was later considerably lengthened. The name **Countess Wear** (or Weir) came to be attached to the hamlet (now a suburb) between Topsham and Exeter.

Topsham is no longer a commercial

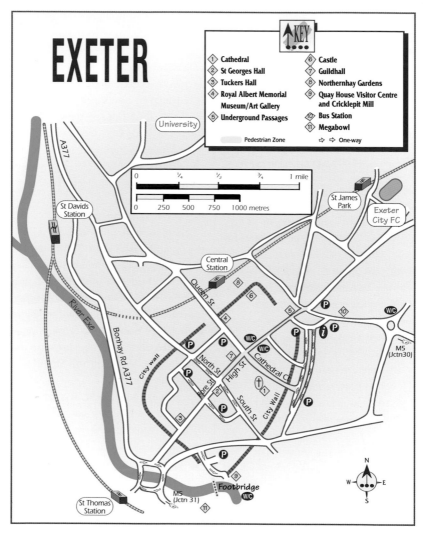

port. However, it still serves as a base for hundreds of recreational sailors. A small salmon fishery exists, and there is no more enjoyable way of passing a fine evening than standing on the cliff at the top of Church Steps with the tide flooding below, the sun setting over Haldon, and the fishermen seine-netting on the far bank of the Exe. Of the numerous public houses here, the Bridge Inn beside the River Clyst on the Exmouth road is the most unspoilt.

Perhaps the most satisfying way to experience the appeal of Topsham is to go by bus (they are very frequent) from Exeter and walk back along the canal, after exploring its narrow streets and alleys. The foot ferry across the Exe brings one to the canal, and a level walk of 5 miles (8km) to the city.

Once past Topsham, the Exe Estuary

## The Grand Western Canal

Grand Western was the rather pretentious name for a scheme which went off at half-cock. Originally intended to be part of a through route from Taunton to Topsham, as part of a plan to link the Bristol and English Channels, the Taunton–Topsham canal, with three branches to Cullompton, Tiverton and Wellington, was granted an Act of Parliament (as all canals needed in the 'Great Age' of canal building) in 1796, the projected cost being £166,724. The section of the canal from Tiverton to Lowdwells, on the Somerset border, a distance of 11 miles (17.7km), was started in 1810 and completed in 1814 at a cost of £220,000. Not for another 13 years was any further work carried out. By then the plan to extend the canal to Topsham had been abandoned. Though the section from Lowdwells to Taunton was completed, it was never profitable and was closed in 1869.

Happily, the section from Lowdwells to Tiverton was not allowed to deteriorate too much when it went out of use in 1924, and in recent years the Tiverton end was re-opened as an amenity waterway and Country Park. A **horse-drawn passenger barge** with bar and refreshments operates from the basin and the whole section can be walked, a beautiful trip through some very pretty country.

widens to admit the River Clyst (pronounced 'Clist'), and Exmouth is soon reached along a busy switchback road past the Royal Marine camp and the turning to **Lympstone**. This village has charm when the tide is in, but at low tide the expanse of mud is vast and intimidating.

As the main road approaches Exmouth, a sign (left) points to **A La Ronde**, an eccentric building of 1796, owned by the National Trust. The name suggests a circular structure, but it really has sixteen sides. Two 'ladies of quality', the Misses Jane and Mary Parminter, having travelled in Italy, modelled it on the sixth-century basilica of San Vitale at Ravenna. The rooms lead off a central octagon, which is lit by apex roof lights 35ft (12m) above.

The quirky architecture of the house is matched by the interior decoration of shells, feathers and much of the original furniture and bric-à-brac collected by the two women. Later additions to the structure, such as the gargantuan Victorian central heating, an early flush lavatory and the gas lighting, have only added to the eclectic atmosphere of this extraordinary dwelling. A little way up

## Enjoy Topsham on foot

There is only one way to enjoy Topsham – on foot. Everything is so crowded that cars are a nuisance, and this is Topsham's one drawback. Several car parks exist, but residents prefer to have their vehicles outside their houses, even if it means using the pavements. Do not add to the problem, but park in a car park and explore if possible when the tide is high, as your enjoyment will be enhanced if the slimy, dark silt of the inter-tidal zone is obscured! Not for nothing is the place disparagingly referred to as Topsham-on-mud by those who are jealous of its attractions.

the lane a small chapel and almshouses of contemporary date called **Point-in-View** are also worth a visit.

# Exmouth

**Exmouth** is the fourth largest urban area in Devon after Plymouth, Torbay and Exeter. It is the family holiday resort *par excellence* with a long sandy beach, good parks, undercover entertainments, boat trips, a busy shopping area, and attractive hinterland. At one end of its 2-mile (3.2km) seafront, the longest in Devon and Cornwall, is **Exmouth Dock**, once a busy commercial enterprise used by coasting vessels, but now a marina. Here (in summer) the ferry leaves for Starcross, a 1.5-mile (2km) trip across the mouth of the estuary.

The broad tidal waters of the Exe are very popular with sailors and waterskiers, and naturalists wax lyrical about the birds which choose to winter on the muddy flats, or use it as a migratory stopover. The Exe has international importance as a habitat for birds.

On the sea front is the **Great Exmouth '00' Model Railway**, the world's largest display at that gauge, set in attractive and realistic landscapes. **Exmouth Museum** is in Sheppards Row, Exeter Road.

**Orcombe Point** at Exmouth's eastern end marks the start of the **Jurassic Coast World Heritage Site.** Here stands the **Geoneedle**, showing the sequence of rocks along the 95 miles (153km) of coastline to Swanage in Dorset, the oldest rocks in East Devon and the youngest in Dorset. At the entrance to Sandy Bay is the **World of Country Life**, with a comprehensive collection of rural

artefacts, together with collections of vintage vehicles and classic motorcycles, farm animals and a pets' corner. There are also exotic animals such as llamas, a host of other country-related items and age-related adventure playgrounds for children. As the display is under cover this makes a fine refuge in bad weather, but a visit is always worthwhile.

# The Budleigh Salterton – Bicton Cross Area

**Budleigh Salterton** is the next place along the coast, a genteel watering place with a pebble beach and an attractive, slightly old-fashioned air. Not for Budleigh the lures of amusement arcades and discos. At the Exmouth end of the beach, hand-powered capstans are still used to haul fishing boats up the beach over wooden rollers.

Where the main street meets the promenade, the **Fairlynch Museum** occupies an attractive *cottage orné* (there are many more to be seen in Sidmouth). Children will love the imaginatively conceived smugglers' cellar.

The East Budleigh road heads north up the Otter Valley and **East Budleigh** is reached after 2 miles (3km). A signposted side road in the village near the church leads in another mile to **Hayes Barton**, Raleigh's birthplace in 1552. A fine example of a Tudor farmhouse, it is not usually open to the public, but it can be seen from the road.

East Budleigh is unspoilt and still possesses many cob and thatch buildings. Cob is a dry compacted mass of mud and straw, which will last for hundreds

## Bicton Park

On the A376 at Bicton Cross a brick direction post (dated 1743) bears a passage of scripture on each face. Bicton Park is a place which can only be described as a total experience; there is so much here to do and see. The owners' claim that it is the 'One Stop Family Day Out' is not made glibly. There are gardens, parkland, a lake, train rides, a wonderful adventure playground, and a couple of hangar-like covered exhibitions, the Hall of Transport and the James Countryside Museum. Not far away is the Bicton Arena, where equestrian and other outdoor events are promoted.

of years given a good hat (a roof) and a good pair of shoes (a stone plinth). The Sir Walter Raleigh Inn is a good place for a drink and a meal. The church, on its eminence, contains the Raleigh pew (among many carved bench ends) bearing the date 1537, and some well-restored roof bosses.

One of the roads at Bicton Cross leads to **Otterton** and **Otterton Mill**, widely advertised as 'The Museum that Works'. Here, waterpower from the River Otter is used to drive the

waterwheel, and food made from flour milled on the premises can be eaten in the restaurant and purchased in the shop. There is often an exhibition in the gallery.

Before leaving the district, the interesting area loosely called **Woodbury Common** should be visited. This is an open unproductive upland, of poor soil, partly used for commercial forestry but largely uncultivated and ungrazed. It extends from the outskirts of Exmouth to beyond the Exeter to Sidmouth road. Much used for walking and riding, it is also ideal for cross-country running and orienteering. The Royal Marines train here. A wonderfully scenic road passes along the ridge giving extensive views across to Dartmoor one way and Dorset the other, even though the altitude nowhere reaches 600ft (210m). Many walks can be devised in any direction over such open country.

# Sidmouth

**Sidmouth** is the unrivalled aristocrat of the East Devon coast; a town of distinction and character. It occupies the valley of the little River Sid, between

## The Barn

In 1896–7 the architect Edward Prior built a house in Foxholes Road, in Exmouth, called **The Barn** (now the Barn Hotel), which has been called 'the most important house of its date in Europe'. It was an expression of the Arts and Crafts Movement, an attempt to return to simplicity and a national style, while being modestly original. As its plan evokes the shape of a butterfly, the quest for simplicity is hardly satisfied, though the desire to achieve originality is eminently successful. The Barn was thatched when newly built, and was burnt down in 1905, being rebuilt the following year. Its main features are two enormous round stone chimneys flanking a central gable which links the two main house components. The structure is of local sandstone intermixed with large sea-scrubbed pebbles.

## Folk Festival

Sidmouth never developed as a family resort, as it lacked the vital natural element so necessary for the success of a holiday with children – sand. (There is some at low tide at Jacob's Ladder Beach.) However, in recent years it has hosted the annual International Folk Festival, when groups of musicians and dancers from all over the world enliven the town for a week in August. An after-dark informal procession ends the event, when the lighted torches are doused in the sea.

the mighty slopes of Salcombe Hill and Peak Hill, and extends back to its satellite Sidford.

Although it was a place of no consequence before the end of the eighteenth century, Sidmouth achieved the respectability of court patronage in 1791 when the king stayed here; in 1819–20 the Duke and Duchess of Kent and their infant daughter Victoria, later Queen Victoria, enjoyed a lengthy winter sojourn in its mild climate. Society soon caught on, and a building boom in the attractive Georgian and Regency style began. Present-day Sidmouth is therefore a product of the first forty years of the nineteenth century, sympathetically brought up to date by sensitive owners.

The best way to discover some of the architectural surprises in Sidmouth is to walk enquiringly around with open eyes. The prominent Regency row known as **Fortfield Terrace** sets the standard for the rest of the town. The Esplanade nearby is similar, for both have elegant first-floor wrought-iron balconies with tent-shaped canopies and trellis sup-

ports. The Russian double-headed eagle on No. 8 marks the visit there in 1831 of Grand Duchess Helene of Russia, sister-in law of the Tzar.

Rather later is **Coburg Terrace** (1815) and the **Royal Glen Hotel** (1810), each with a castellated parapet and Gothic windows. And peppered around the town, many of them standing in mature gardens, are such stylish residences as Powys, Hunter's Moon and Cedar Shade. Another kind of building represented locally is the *cottage orné*, an attempt to reproduce a rustic building of Romantic design, usually with a thatched roof. Examples can be seen at the foot of Peak Hill – Rock Cottage and Beacon Cottage for instance.

In the town the observant visitor will notice a number of mid- and late nineteenth-century shop fronts, delightfully rare survivals, and protected by the listing process as much as the houses themselves. Amazingly, there are over 500 buildings or groups of buildings listed as of special architectural and historic interest in the Sidmouth area. One last house must be mentioned – **Old Chancel**, near the church. This was built by a local antiquary, Peter Orlando Hutchinson, in the 1860s, using the demolished material of the 'restored' parish church, and is partly ecclesiastical in style.

The **Sidmouth Museum** in Church Street is in character with the town. There are displays of Regency prints, Victoriana, lace and the complex geology of East Devon. A curious and little-known Sidmouth connection with the world of commerce, going back a hundred years, began with a

Miss Cash, a cripple, who embroidered names and monograms on linen with dyed cotton. This developed into Cash's Name Tapes. She lived at Barton Cottage near Church House.

A very different site is the **Norman Lockyer Observatory**, founded in 1912 by the man now seen as the father of astro-archaeology for his investigations into the astronomical alignments of Stonehenge and other stone circles. The Observatory has a planetarium and several large telescopes.

Continuing eastwards, the A3052 should be taken to the top of Trow Hill, where, round the corner, a sign points to Branscombe. Just off the main road at **Salcombe Regis** is the **Donkey Sanctuary**, where infirm donkeys are nursed, and elderly animals are given a well-fed comfortable old age. Admission is free, and the visitor can wander around the buildings and paddocks.

# Branscombe

If Sidmouth is unrivalled as a town in East Devon, **Branscombe** is the most delightful village on the East Devon coast, and is perhaps the longest village in Devon. The sea is $1^1/_2$ miles (2km) beyond **The Pottery**, at the top of the scattered groups of buildings.

**Branscombe church** is on the right $^3/_4$ mile (1km) further on. Its exterior is dominated by the Norman tower, and inside there is an Elizabethan gallery (reached by outside stairs), box pews and a rare three-decker pulpit. A little further on is a thatched blacksmith's forge, and opposite is a thatched cottage set back from the road, the famous **Branscombe Bakery** (National Trust), where the ovens were heated by ash faggots. This is now a tearoom. The adjacent **Manor Mill and Forge** have been restored.

Down at **Branscombe Mouth**, the

*Sidmouth*

road ends at the pebble beach, and a car park. It is an interesting place; fishing goes on here, both from the beach and from boats. The Sea Shanty café was once a coalyard (the coal came by sea), there were lime kilns and a gypsum works here, and the coastguard cottages (now the Lookout) hint at the smuggling trade which was rife in East Devon in the eighteenth and early nineteenth centuries.

This is a good place for a walk of $2^1/_2$ miles (4km), lasting perhaps $1^1/_2$ hours. Walk up the hill to the east, the Beer side, but follow the concrete track into the cliffside caravan site. These caravans occupy the level patches used by generations of Branscombe people to grow early potatoes. The route follows the higher of the tracks between the caravans and soon reaches a good signed path entering the scrub. This is the **Hooken Landslip** which broke away from the cliff in 1790, and the Pinnacles, great turrets of white stone, are the major manifestations of this collapse. The path climbs steeply to the clifftop. Now turn left and follow the path back to Branscombe.

The stone from this area was used for building from Roman times and is known as Beer stone, after the village just beyond. Exeter Cathedral has thousands of tons in its structure, brought by sea and river from Beer. When first taken from the workings, it can be cut with a saw, but it hardens after exposure to air. **Beer Quarry Caves**, part of the Jurassic Coast, Dorset and East Devon World Heritage Site, are open to the public and are enormously exciting to penetrate.

# Beer and Seaton

**Beer** is now a holiday and fishing village. A stream bustles down the main street. Beer and Seaton are often spoken of together as they almost merge. Seaton presents two faces to the world: a quiet retiring ambience at the Beer end, and a more gregarious outlook near the mouth of the Axe. A holiday camp and limited boat anchorage opportunities no doubt contribute to this ambivalence.

Together the two places have much to offer the holidaymaker. At **Seaton** the disused railway track has been rebuilt into **a tramway**. Open top tramcars (closed trams in bad weather) shuttle along the **Axe Valley** between Seaton, Colyford and Colyton. Children of all ages head for **Pecorama** where a wide range of attractions including an outdoor model railway and the **Beer Heights Light Railway** will keep everyone happy for hours; lunch can be taken in a Pullman car.

Built-up Devon ends at the east end of Seaton seafront. Beyond is the main landslip area stretching away to Lyme Regis in Dorset, a tortuous tumble of unstable cliff, tangled with wood and scrub, and a haven for wildlife. Naturalists regard it as the last and largest wilderness on the coast of southern England. **The South Devon Coast Path** passes along its length, but there are no escape routes. Either the walker treks all the way from Seaton to Lyme Regis – a distance of $6^1/_2$ miles (10km) – or you come back the way you went. At the time of writing the approach from Seaton is over Axe Cliff golf course and through a few fields, and it is well worth attempting a short distance into the landslip to get its atmosphere. But one may have to back-track. The path goes on, and on... There are buses back from Lyme Regis, but check their times first!

There have been many landslips here over the centuries, but at Christmas 1839 a cataclysmic slip occurred after heavy rain. For naturalists the interest lies in seeing what plants develop from a given point in time, and the area is a National Nature Reserve. The Devon county boundary is crossed just before Lyme Regis is reached. The area was used by John Fowles in his book *The French Lieutenant's Woman*, and subsequently used as the location for the film.

# West from Axminster

**Axminster** is a name known throughout the world on account of its product – carpets. They are manufactured here in a modern computerised factory. There is a **museum** in the town, which includes the making of Axminster carpets. Another old trade can be viewed at the tannery at **Colyton**, a small market town not far away. This particular tannery uses oak bark to produce high quality leather, the only remaining tannery in England to do so.

To the north of Colyton is **Loughwood Meeting House**, built in 1653 and used by dissenters. This tiny chapel lies just below the busy A35, but is seemingly far more remote and well worth a visit for a few peaceful moments.

A few miles to the north is **Honiton**, on the southern route into Devon; here the A30 and A35 roads unite. The town is bypassed, and the wide street with market stalls on Tuesdays and Saturdays is busy all day with unhurried activity. The local museum, called the **Allhallows Museum** after the building in which it is housed, specialises in Honiton lace, a craft still actively pursued.

**Broadhembury** is the kind of place people think of when Devon is mentioned; a great deal of cob and thatch and a picturesque church. The 'Hembury' of the name refers to the very large earthwork on a spur of the Blackdown Hills, **Hembury Fort**, above the village. When the Iron Age people fortified it, the site was already old; it had been a causewayed camp in Neolithic times.

The old road from Honiton to Exeter leaves no one in doubt as to its origin. The Romans laid it down about 1,800 years ago. Going from Honiton westwards, just before the dual carriageway is reached, on the right is a thatched building of some antiquity. This stands on the site of the St Margaret's leper hospital. In medieval times lepers were not encouraged in towns; this hospice is nearly 1 mile (1.5km) outside Honiton. subsequently it became an almshouse.

**Ottery St Mary** is a thriving little town. The church is the showpiece, a miniature Exeter Cathedral, and like its exemplar, a squat structure. Westwards from the church, and past the college, is **Chanter's House**, the house of the Coleridge family, made famous by the poet Samuel Taylor Coleridge, the author of *The Ancient Mariner*. Chanters was a temporary home for Oliver Cromwell in the Civil War (closed to the public). Two other buildings worth

*Otterton*

*Above: Branscombe*

*Left: Knighthayes Court*

*Below: The South West Coast Path is one of the longest routes in Britain and includes both coasts of Devon*

seeing in the college are the Warden's House and the Vicar's House.

In **Cornhill**, the pleasant terrace just below the churchyard, are two shops restored by the Devon Historic Buildings Trust from ignominious dereliction. Round the corner in **Paternoster Row** are several good examples of eighteenth-century town houses with dated rainwater heads (1759 and 1779). Lower down the town, in Jesu Street, is a nonconformist church built of brick in 1664, one of the earliest in England.

To the west of the M5 lies the enormous **Killerton** estate of the National Trust, given to the Trust in 1944 by Sir Richard Acland, and centred on the garden and park of Killerton House. Killerton House is not particularly attractive in itself, but the fascinating Paulise de Bush costume collection is here. The gardens are a delight, gradually merging into the wooded clump of Dolbury, an Iron Age hillfort on the summit of Killerton's sheltering eminence.

Much of nearby **Broadclyst** is owned by the Trust including **Budlake Old Post Office Room**, **Clyston Mill** and **Marker's Cottage**. These three properties recall a simpler lifestyle than Killerton House and the mill is still in working order.

Easily reached on the other side of the M5 is **Ashclyst Forest** and **Paradise Copse**, also National Trust, an extensive woodland where one can wander all day and not see another human being. Roe deer are there in abundance and may be spotted during the day if all is quiet, but one frequently sees them near the roads through the forest as dusk falls.

# The Cullompton Area

**Cullompton** bestrides the B3181 and revels in its freedom from traffic following the construction of the M5. Motorway and railway users should look for its fine church tower (1549), a notable landmark. The interior is completely perpendicular in style. Its two most noticeable features are the bright and beautifully carved roof which extends from end to end, and the rood screen, also coloured, which spans the width.

Beyond Cullompton the highly-regarded **Coldharbour Mill** project at **Uffculme** is worth visiting. Until 1981, it was a working wool mill, and when it closed because of the economic recession, it was converted to a working museum of the woollen trade. An 18ft (6m) waterwheel provides some of the power. These old industrial enterprises are a fascinating feature of the British countryside. Not far from here is the Grand Western Canal.

At **Hemyock**, near Culmstock, to

## Cadhay & Escot

A mile north-west of Ottery St Mary is **Cadhay**, a beautiful Tudor manor house built in 1550 by John Haydon, a successful lawyer. The house is approached along an avenue of lime trees, and is open to the public at certain times. Nearby is **Escot Park and Gardens** with an arboretum and rose garden, and collection of wildlife including wild boar, pot-bellied pigs beavers and birds of prey.

the north-east of Uffculme, **Hemyock Castle** is an interesting medieval building, delightfully set in the Blackdown Hills. The castle, which saw action in the Civil War, is open on Bank Holiday Mondays in summer.

# Tiverton

**Tiverton**'s life has always revolved around its rivers. It stands at the confluence of the Exe and the Lowman (Tiverton means 'two ford town'). For hundreds of years, woollen mills were powered by water from the rivers, but when the woollen industry declined, John Heathcoat set up his lace factory here in 1816, after he had been forced out of Leicestershire by the Luddite machine wreckers. Much of Tiverton's life still focuses on the Heathcoat factory, now diversified and modernised.

Tiverton has some interesting buildings. **Old Blundells School** at the foot of Canal Hill can be viewed from outside. The school, founded in 1599, is one of England's great public schools, and straddles the A373 a mile east of the town, a site to which it moved in 1880. **The Old Police Station** in St Andrew's Street was restored by the Devon Historic Buildings Trust and converted into two modern dwellings. Also in St Andrew's Street is **Tiverton Museum**, a most enterprising collection that has won the Museum of the Year award.

The church should be seen for the Greenway aisle, and Castle Street has the town leat – Tiverton's medieval water supply – running along its length. **Tiverton Castle,** which is frequently open, is much altered from medieval times, and today serves as a private residence. Originally built in 1106, it last suffered attack in 1645, when Sir Thomas Fairfax, Cromwell's general, captured and slighted its defences.

A grandson of John Heathcoat built **Knightshayes Court** (National Trust), 2 miles (3km) north of Tiverton. The architect was William Burges, whose wildly fanciful decorative whims set him apart even among the extravagant nineteenth-century practitioners of his profession. His dilatoriness in not completing the interior of the house led to his being superseded by J D Crace. The gardens are splendid, and like those at Killerton, gradually merge into informal woodland. There are some fine topiary animals on the box hedges of the formal garden. The house looks proprietorially down on the town that brought the family so much wealth.

# Bickleigh and Crediton

The Exe Valley is now followed down to **Bickleigh**, where the road crosses the river by a narrow bridge in the midst of the kind of pretty scenery for which Devon is famous. Even if this is quintessential England, there is a successful vineyard here on the western slopes overlooking the bridge. Public houses and thatched dwellings crowd in upon the river, making it the sort of place to linger, and there is plenty of interest for everyone, especially the **Bickleigh Mill Craft Centre**, with old-time machinery and farming methods, shops, a restaurant.

**Bickleigh Castle**, downriver and detached from the honeypot around the bridge, is a charming relic of stirring times past. Apart from the thatched Norman chapel – probably the oldest complete building in Devon – the chief survival is the three-floors-high gatehouse containing the most impressive room, the great hall, occasionally open for special events.

From Bickleigh, the hill road to Crediton is worth taking as a journey into deepest Devon. Up and down and round swoops the A3072 with expansive views north to Exmoor. To the south, the looming tree-topped Raddon (Red Down) Hills block the view to Exeter.

After $2^1/_2$ miles (4km) take a turning left signposted to **Fursdon House**, which is 1 mile (1.5km) south of the A3072. Here generations of the Fursdon family have lived for over 700 years. The house is small, not particularly attractive, but a warm, lived-in atmosphere pervades the panel-lined rooms. There are walks on the small estate, and delicious teas.

Just before Crediton a visit to **Shobrooke Park** to see the flock of Canada geese on the lake will set them honking excitedly as the visitor approaches along the public footpath.

**Crediton**, mentioned in the introductory chapter as being the head of the Exeter diocese until 1050 and the birthplace of St Boniface, has not in modern times equalled or surpassed these Dark Age achievements. Some disastrous fires, common in Devon towns in medieval times, have swept away historically important buildings, and their replacements make little impact on the visitor. Only the splendid church, a towering edifice like a small cathedral and unlike any other church in the county, is worthy of Crediton's lustrous past; but one wishes it were set on a more prominent site, a hilltop perhaps, or at least above the main road, where it would be better appreciated.

# South-West of Exeter

As one travels south-west from Exeter the view is blocked by the **Haldon Hills**, a flint-topped plateau of greensand and sandstone, similar in many ways to the Devon hills inland from Sidmouth. Being flat-topped and not dipping below 600ft (210m) except in the saddle between Great and Little Haldon and with a modest maximum altitude of 826ft (289m), this range cries out for an artificial eye-catcher. One was provided in the late eighteenth century when Sir Robert Palk built the three-sided **Lawrence Castle** (often called **Haldon Belvedere**) on Penn Hill as a memorial to his great friend Major-General Stringer Lawrence. We should now call it a folly.

Away to the south stretch the coniferous plantations of the Forestry Commission and a number of walks of different lengths have been laid out through the forest, starting from the Commission's information point on **Buller's Hill**. There are directions from the ridge road, and indeed it is signposted from the A38 dual carriageway. Fallow deer can often be seen, and forty-nine resident bird species are known, as well as thirty-six species of butterfly.

Where the A38 passes over the ridge is **Haldon Racecourse**, home of the Devon and Exeter Races since 1769, and the similar hilltop, 1 mile (1.5km) away on the A380, carried an Admiralty telegraph station during the Napoleonic Wars. The name **Telegraph Hill** has been applied to the road ascent on the Exeter side.

The best route to Kenton is the Starcross road going south then east and dropping steeply off the plateau to the rich red Devon soil. A lane leads down to the magnificent red sandstone church of **Kenton**. Inside is the well-restored rood screen (with coloured figure paintings), rood loft and pulpit. It is said that the grooves rubbed in the Beer stone dressings of the porch were caused by the village archers sharpening their arrow points.

**Starcross** is a short distance away along the west bank of the Exe Estuary. Here the railway travels along the 'sea' wall, blocking off the fine views of the tide-riding boats from the ground floor rooms of the nineteenth-century terrace houses.

The Italianate sandstone tower near the station marks a pumping house of **Brunel's 1846 atmospheric railway**. This well-known engineer decided to power his trains on atmospheric principles. A continuous pipe with a longitudinal slot on top was laid between the rails in which ran a piston fitted to the leading vehicle of a train. Stationary steam engines pumped out air from the pipe in front of the piston, forming a vacuum, while air coming in behind the piston pushed the train along. The system was not successful, as Brunel did not have the materials to match his idea, and after spending £426,368 installing what became known as the 'atmospheric caper', he cut his losses and began running conventional locomotives.

The mouth of the estuary is marked by **Dawlish Warren**, a popular resort which has developed beside the sandspit which protrudes towards Exmouth. The plants and birdlife are of national importance, and there is a visitor centre open in the summer where information on the natural history of the area can be found.

## Powderham Castle

The estate should be entered from the south of Kenton on the A379. Powderham Castle, the home of the Courtenay family, the Earls of Devon, since 1390, stands in one of the finest parks in the county; it still has a large herd of fallow deer, and a strange amalgam of architectural styles. Perhaps the most interesting rooms in the house are the marble hall and the staircase hall. The former contains a 13ft (4.5m) longcase clock, by Stumbels of Totnes (1740), which plays a tune at 4, 8 and 12 o'clock. Various events are held at Powderham Castle and in the park throughout the summer and times of opening are widely advertised.

# Places to Visit

## In and around Exeter

### The Catacombs

A nineteenth-century attempt to solve the problem of burial space in the city by stacking coffins in a stone mausoleum. Can only be visited on a Red Coat guided tour which normally take place three times a week between Apr and Oct. Contact the TIC for further details.

### Crealy Park

Off J30 of M5 on A3052
☎ (01395) 233200
www.crealy.co.uk
Adventure play for children of all ages, pets corner, restaurant. Open:10am–6pm daily, Easter to early Sep.

### Cricklepit Mill

Commercial Road
☎ (01395) 279244
Mill with 2 waterwheels. Headquarters of Devon Wildlife Trust. Open:9am–5pm Mon-Fri.

### Exeter Cathedral

☎ (01392) 285983
www.exeter-cathedral.org.uk
Gothic nave between massive Norman towers. The Bishop's Throne is notable. Open: 9.30am–4.45pm, Mon-Sat.

### Exeter Red Coats Guided Tours

Evit, Dix's Field, Exeter EX1 1GF
☎ (01392) 265203
www.exeter.gov.uk/visiting
Open daily except 25–6 Dec. Wet weather gear essential.
♿ ♅<FREE

### The City Walls

Five-sixths of the wall is still visible. Built on a line determined by Roman engineers and rebuilt and restored after every siege.

### Exeter Phoenix

Bradninch Place, Gandy St, Exeter
☎ (01392) 667080
www.exeterphoenix.org.uk
Dance, jazz, rock, films, theatre. Bar and café.
♿ ♅<Child Rate ☂

### The Guildhall

The oldest municipal building in the country. The hall itself, with a fifteenth-century arch-braced timber roof, stands behind a Tudor pillared front of 1592. The Guildhall is still a working building but is open for viewing whenever possible.
☎ (01392) 665500 to arrange a free tour or check opening times.
www.exeter.gov.uk also gives details of this and other places to visit.

### Sports facilities

Exeter
☎ (01392) 265372 for details and opening times

### Quay House Visitor Centre

46 The Quay EX2 4AN
☎ (01392) 271611
www.exeter.gov.uk
An exhibition explaining Exeter's maritime heritage. Open: 10am–5pm

# Places to Visit

| | |
|---|---|
| ℗ | Parking Available |
| ♿ | Disabled Facilities |
| 🚻 | Family Attraction |
| <№ | Concession for under certain ages |
| ☂ | Suitable in Wet Weather |

daily, Apr to Oct; 11am–4pm Sat and Sun rest of the year.

℗(Nearby) ♿ 🚻<FREE ☂

## Rougemont Castle

The shell of William the Conqueror's castle, now a heritage centre.

## Royal Albert Memorial Museum

Castle Street EX4 EPQ
☎ (01392) 665858
Specialist displays of silver, costume, clocks and watches, paintings, flora and fauna.Closed for redevelopment until 2011.

℗(Nearby) ♿ 🚻<FREE ☂

## Spacex Art Gallery

Preston Street
☎ (01392) 431786
www.spacex.co.uk
Contemporary art gallery hosting exhibitions, workshops and special events. Open: 10am–5pm Tue to Sat. Admission free to exhibitions.

☂

## St Nicholas' Priory

The Mint, Off Fore St EX4 3BL
☎ (01392) 665858
www.exeter.gov.uk/priory
Tudor life presented in a 1602 townhouse. Open: 10am-5pm Sat (also Mon-Fri in Devon school hols).

♿ (Limited access) 🚻<18 FREE ☂

## Tuckers Hall

Fore Street
☎ (01392) 412348

A medieval building, the only Exeter trade guild to survive with its headquarters intact. Open: 10.30am–12.30pm Tue, Thu and Fri from Jun to Sep; Thu only from Oct to May.

## Underground Passages (Aqueducts)

Paris Street
A medieval civil engineering solution to the lack of water within the old city.
☂

## Wynard's Almshouses

Magdalen Street
Medieval houses for the elderly, now converted into private dwellings.

## Topsham Museum

25 The Strand, Topsham EX3 0AX
☎ (01392) 873244
www.devonmuseums.net/topsham
A small museum largely devoted to the sea and shipping. Open: 2–5pm Mon, Wed, Sat and Sun from Apr to Oct.

♿ 🚻<FREE ☂

# In & around Exmouth and Sidmouth

## A La Ronde (N.T.)

Summer Lane, Exmouth EX8 5BD
☎ (01395) 265514
An eccentric sixteen-sided house decorated with shells and feathers, and full of bric-a brac of many kinds. Open: 11am–5pm Sun to Wed, late Mar to Oct; Sat-Sun only, Feb to Mar.

♿ (Limited) 🚻<Family Ticket ☂

## The Barn Hotel

Exmouth
☎ (01395) 224411
www.barnhotel.co.uk
The most important house of its date in Europe.

## The Great Exmouth '00' Model Railway

Queens Drive, Seafront, Exmouth, EX8 2AY
☎ (01395) 278383
www.exmouthmodelrailway.co.uk
Fun for both parents and children with model trains. Open: From 10.30am daily from Easter to the end of Oct; 10am-3pm Sat-Sun Nov to Mar.
Ⓟ (Nearby)  ♿  ŤŤŤ <Child Rate  ☂

## The World of Country Life

Sandy Bay, Exmouth, EX8 5BU
☎ (01395) 274533
www.worldofcountrylife.co.uk
All weather attraction for all the family. Open: 10am–5pm daily Apr to Oct
Ⓟ  ♿  ŤŤŤ <Family Ticket  ☂

## Exmouth Museum

Sheppards Row, EX8 1PW
☎ (01395) 263785
devonmuseums.net/exmouth
The town's history told in local artefacts. Open: Apr to Oct, Mon to Sat 10.30am–12.30pm plus 2.30–4.30pm Tue to Thu.
♿ (Ground Floor)  ŤŤŤ <16yrs FREE  ☂

## Fairlynch Museum

Budleigh Salterton EX9 6NP
☎ (01395) 442666
A decorous museum for the dilettante, housed in a thatched *cottage orné*. Open: 2–4.30pm daily, mid-Apr to late Oct (closed Sat pm).
☂

## Bicton Park Botanical Gardens

East Budleigh EX9 7BJ
☎ (01395) 568465
www.bictongardens.co.uk
Museums, gardens, train rides and playgrounds in a beautiful parkland setting. Open: 10am–6pm in summer, 10am–5pm in winter, 363 days per year.

## Otterton Mill

Otterton, Budleigh Salterton EX9 7H9
☎ (01395) 568521
www.ottertonmill.com
Restored watermill & craft centre. Open: 10am–5pm daily.
Ⓟ  ♿ (Limited)  ŤŤŤ <FREE  ☂

## Sidmouth Museum

Church Street EX10 8LY
☎ (01395) 516139
www.devonmuseums.net
A repository of Victoriana, East Devon lace and Geographical displays. Open: 1–4pm Mon, 10am–4pm Tue to Sat, Easter to Oct.
♿ (Ground Floor)  ŤŤŤ <16 FREE  ☂

## Norman Lockyer Observatory

Sidmouth
☎ (01395) 579941 for details of events and public openings.
www.normanlockyer.org

## Donkey Sanctuary

Slade House Farm, Sidmouth EX10 0NU
☎ (01395) 578222

# Places to Visit

| | |
|---|---|
| Ⓟ | Parking Available |
| ♿ | Disabled Facilities |
| ♔♔ | Family Attraction |
| <№ | Concession for under certain ages |
| ☂ | Suitable in Wet Weather |

www.thedonkeysanctuary.org.uk
A 'nursing home' for hundreds of donkeys. Open: 9am to dusk daily, all year round.

Ⓟ ♿ ♔♔ <FREE

## Branscombe Church

Notable for its Norman tower, three-decker pulpit, box pews and Elizabethan gallery.

# In the Honiton area

## Beer Quarry Caves

Quarry Lane, Beer EX12 3AT
☎ (01297) 680282
www.beerquarrycaves.fsnet.co.uk
2000 years of heritage brought to life. Open: 10am–5pm daily, Mon before Easter to end of Oct; 10am–4pm in Oct.

Ⓟ ♔♔ <Family Ticket ☂

## Pecorama

Underleys Seaton EX12 3NA
☎ (01297) 21542
Railway fun for all the family. Outdoor model railway and Beer Heights Light Railway. Wonderful gardens. Open: Apr/May to Sep. Telephone for times or visit www.peco-uk.com

Ⓟ ♿ (Limited) ♔♔ <15 Child Rate ☂

## Seaton Tramway

Harbour Road EX12 2NQ
☎ (01297) 20375
www.tram.co.uk
Experience the clanking transportation of the tram as it travels along the Axe

marshes. Open: Daily Apr to Oct. Weekends only Mar, Nov and Dec.

Ⓟ ♿ ♔♔ <Family Ticket ☂

## Hooken Landslip

Between Seaton and Lyme Regis
A 6-mile (10km) long strip of natural landscape on the coast. Geological and floral interest intermixed.

## Axminster Museum

Church Street EX13 5AQ
Past and present history including the carpet industry. Open: 10.30am–4pm Mon to Wed; 10am–4pm Thu and Fri; 10.30am–12.30pm Sat, Jun to Sep. Closed 12.30am-2pm (exc Thu) & bank holidays.

☂

## Loughwood Meeting House (N.T.)

Axminster EX13 7DU
☎ (01752) 346585
A tiny, remote, dissenters' meeting house, dating from 1653. Open: all year.

## Colyton Tannery

EX24 6PD
☎ (01297) 552282
www.jf;baker.co.uk
The last tannery in the country to tan leather using oak bark.

## Allhallows Museum

High Street, Honiton EX14 1PG
☎ (01404) 44966
www.honitonmuseum.co.uk
Specialises in Honiton lace, and is

housed in the original Allhallows School building. Open: 9.30am–4.30pm Mon to Fri, Sat 9.30am–1pm, Apr to Sep; 9.30am–3.30pm in Oct.

## St Margaret's Leper Hospital

Honiton
One mile (1.5km) west of Honiton. A medieval leper hospice, now adapted as an almshouse.

## Ottery St Mary Church

A 'miniature Exeter Cathedral', packed with architectural and historic interest.

## Cadhay House

EX11 1QT
☎ (01404) 813511
www.cadhay.org.uk
1 mile (1.6km) NW of Ottery St Mary
A privately-owned Tudor mansion, open to the public at certain times. Open: 2–5.30pm Fri, May to Sep plus bank holiday Sun and Mon during this period.

Ⓟ ♿ ♟ <16 Child Rate ☂ (House)

## Escot Park and Gardens

Ottery St Mary EX11 1LU
☎ (01404) 822188
www.escot-devon.co.uk
250 acres of parkland and gardens. Otters, birds of prey and wildfowl. Open: All year, daily 10am–5pm (except Christmas).

Ⓟ ♿ (Very Limited) ♟ <15 Child Rate

## Yearlstone Vineyard

Bickleigh EX16 8RL
☎ (01884) 855700
www.yearlstone.co.uk
Call or check web for opening times.

## Hembury Neolithic and Iron Age Hillfort

Blackdown Hills
Probably Devon's largest and finest earthwork, occupied in two prehistoric eras.

# North, West and South of Exeter

## Killerton (N.T.)

Broadclyst EX5 3LE
Georgian house with costume collection in a series of period rooms. Extensive gardens and parkland with spectacular displays of azaleas and rhododendrons. Iron Age hillfort on Dolbury.
☎ (01392) 881345
Open: House – 11am–5pm daily except Tue; closed Mon in Oct (except half-term); seven days a week in Aug. Park and garden – 10.30am–7pm daily, all year.
Budlake Old Post Office Room
☎ (01392) 881690
Clyston Mill ☎ (01392) 462425
Marker's Cottage ☎ (01392) 461546
Open: 2–5pm Sun to Tue, Apr to Oct
☂

## Cullompton Church

The perpendicular rood screen and colourful roof are memorable.

## Coldharbour Mill

Uffculme EX15 3EE
☎ (01884) 840960
www.coldharbourmill.org.uk
A working museum of the wool trade, with steam engine and waterwheel.

# Places to Visit

Giant New World Tapestry, gardens and walks. Open: 10am–5pm daily, Easter to Oct. 10am–4pm Nov to Feb. ☂

## Grand Western Canal

Tiverton EX16 4HX
www.tivertoncanal.co.uk
Built as part of an uncompleted larger scheme, now a linear country park with a horse-drawn boat operating at the Tiverton end. Day-boat and rowing boat hire. Park open all year.

## Tiverton Canal Co.

The Wharf, Tiverton EX16 4HX
☎ (01884) 253345
www.tivertoncanal.co.uk
Horsedrawn, canal-boat trip. Refreshments on board.Open: Apr to Oct, ring for times
℗ (Charge) ♿ (by prior arrangement)
♔♔♔ <15 Child Rate on morning visits

## Hemyock Castle

Nr Cullompton. EX15 3RJ
☎ (01884) 253345
www.hemyockcastle.co.uk
Medieval house, scheduled ancient monument. Normally open for public tours on B. H. Mon (2 to 5 pm) between Easter and September or at other times for schools and groups.
℗ ♿ (Mainly) ♔♔♔ <Half Price Child

## Old Blundells School (N.T.)

Tiverton
Serene 1604 buildings where Blundells School began. Not open to the public.

## Tiverton Castle

Park Hill EX16 6RP
☎ (01884) 253200 / 255200
www.tivertoncastle.com
Open: 2:30–5:30pm Easter to Oct–Sun, Thu and Bank Holiday Mon.
℗ ♿ (Ground Floor & Garden Olny)
♔♔♔ <7 Child Rate ☂

## Tiverton Church

A splendid town church, richly endowed in 1517 when the Greenway aisle and porch were added to the south side.

## Tiverton Museum of Mid Devon Life

Beck's Square EX16 6PJ
☎ (01884) 256295
www.tivertonmuseum.org.uk
An award-winning small town museum with displays on agriculture, transport, industry and especially social history. Open: 10.30am–4.30pm Mon to Fri, 10am–1pm Sat, all year except Jan. Closed Christmas to New Year.
℗ ♿ ♔♔♔ <17 Child Rate ☂

## Knightshayes Court (N.T.)

Poolham, Tiverton EX16 7RQ
☎ (01884) 254665
Nineteenth-century house designed by the eccentric architect William Burges, standing in beautiful grounds. Open: 11am–5pm Sat to Thu, mid-Mar to early Nov.
☂

## Fursdon House

Cadbury, Tiverton
☎ (01392) 860860
www.fursdon.co.uk
Walks on estate, tours of the house, teas. Open: 2–5pm, bank holiday weekends (Sun and Mon) Easter to Aug, and Sun and Wed Jun to Aug. House tours at 2.30pm and 3.30pm.

## Bickleigh Mill

☎ (01884) 855419
www.bickleighmill.com
Crafts, shops and restaurants all in a small area. Open: 10am–5pm all year.

## Crediton Church

Stately town church with a fifteenth-century clerestory and some notable monuments.
Haldon Hills Forest Walks
Long and short walks through Forestry Commission plantations.

## Lawrence Castle (Haldon Belvedere)

Penn Hill, Higher Ashton EX6 7QY
www.haldonbelvedere.co.uk
A folly building erected as a memorial to Major General Stringer Lawrence.

## Kenton Church

☎ (01647) 252455
www.haldonbelvedere.co.uk
Splendid rood screen and restored pulpit. Open: 1.30–5.30pm Sun and bank holidays Feb to Oct.
ⓟ  ♔<15 FREE

## Powderham Castle

Starcross, Kenton EX6 8JQ
☎ (01626) 890243
www.powderham.co.uk
An historic structure incorporating many different architectural styles standing in a large deer park. Children's secret garden and gift shop. Open: daily all year for shops and restaurant. Tours of castle every half-hour 11am–3.30pm (4.40pm in Aug) Apr to Oct (except Sat).
ⓟ  ♿ (Ground Floor Only)
♔<Family Ticket

## Dawlish Warren Visitor Centre

☎ (01626) 863980
www.dawlishwarren.co.uk
Information on the area's natural history. Haven for overwintering birds.

## Diggerland

Verbee Manor, Cullompton
EX15 2PE
☎ 0871 22 77007
www.diggerland.com
Try your hand at driving a JCB! An adventure park for the whole family. Open: weekends 10am–4pm Mar to Sep; daily during school holidays.
ⓟ

# 2. South Devon and Torbay

Chapter 1 included the top of the Haldon Hills. Once beyond Haldon, the visitor is definitely in South Devon, or
on Dartmoor, depending on the direction he takes. South
Devon abuts Dartmoor to the north and the hinterland of
Plymouth in the west, and includes within its boundaries
the South Hams. This sub-region serves to distinguish
the fertile countryside between the Rivers Dart and
Yealm, and Kingsbridge may justly claim to be the capital
of the South Hams. The name 'South Hams' is first found
in 1396, but the meaning of 'Hams' is unclear.

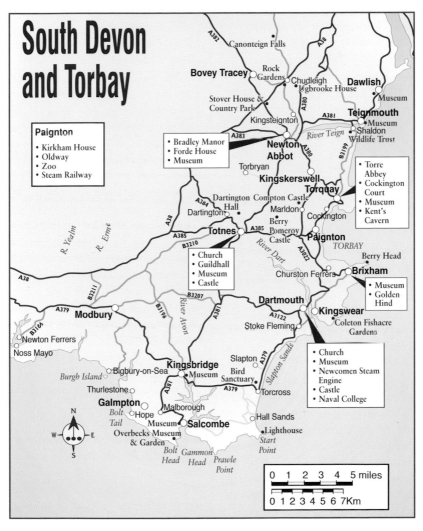

# South Devon and Torbay

**Paignton**
- Kirkham House
- Oldway
- Zoo
- Steam Railway

Canonteign Falls

**Bovey Tracey** · Rock Gardens · Chudleigh · Ugbrooke House **Dawlish**

Stover House & Country Park

Museum

Kingsteignton

A381 **Teignmouth**

Museum

*River Teign* · Shaldon Wildlife Trust

- Bradley Manor
- Forde House
- Museum

**Newton Abbot**

Torbryan

**Kingskerswell**

**Torquay**

- Torre Abbey
- Cockington Court
- Museum
- Kent's Cavern

Dartington Compton Castle
Hall
Dartington

Marldon

Berry Pomeroy Castle

Cockington

**Totnes**

**Paignton**

*TORBAY*

Berry Head

- Church
- Guildhall
- Museum
- Castle

*River Dart*

Churston Ferrers

**Brixham**

- Museum
- Golden Hind

**Dartmouth**

Stoke Fleming

**Kingswear**

Coleton Fishacre Gardens

**Modbury**

Newton Ferrers

Noss Mayo

Slapton

**Kingsbridge**
Bird
· Museum Sanctuary

- Church
- Museum
- Newcomen Steam Engine
- Castle
- Naval College

Burgh Island

Bigbury-on-Sea

Torcross

*Slapton Sands*

Thurlestone

**Galmpton**

*Bolt* ·Hope
*Tail* Museum **Salcombe**

Overbecks Museum
& Garden

Malborough

Hall Sands

Lighthouse
*Start Point*

*Bolt Gammon Prawle
Head Head Point*

| 0 | 1 | 2 | 3 | 4 | 5 miles |

| 0 | 1 | 2 | 3 | 4 | 5 | 6 | 7Km |

As the county's prime holiday area, South Devon owes its success to three factors: the discovery of its beauty and mild climate at the end of the eighteenth century, when the Continent was closed to visitors; the grafting onto these natural characteristics of the social facilities of early watering places such as assembly rooms, accommodation and bathing machines; and the arrival of the Great Western Railway in the late 1840s. The larger resorts, Torquay and Paignton (now, with Brixham, gathered together under the umbrella title Torbay), are still tossing about in the backwash of the developmental surge which came in the second half of the nineteenth century, when they sped headlong into the forefront of British holiday destinations. Most visitors now enter South Devon by road, especially the A380 up Telegraph Hill.

# Ugbrooke House

A few miles further on the motorist will see a sign reading '**Ugbrooke House**', the stately home and estate belonging to Lord Clifford, which sits retiringly in the quiet countryside between the A380 and the A38. The house dates for the most part from about 1750 when Robert Adam rebuilt the earlier Tudor manor house and Capability Brown landscaped the park. He planted trees and formed three lakes by damming the Ug Brook.

However, the house's recent history is equally interesting. In the 1930s the 11th Lord Clifford left Ugbrooke as he could not afford to live there, and during the war it became a school for evacuees and a hostel for Poles. In the 1950s several downstairs rooms, now beautifully restored, were used as grain stores. The parents of the present Lord Clifford returned from Australia in 1957 and began the enormous task of bringing life and beauty back into the house and park, and it was subsequently opened to the public. The interior is noteworthy for the care taken in restoring the fabric, and for the collection of paintings, dolls, furniture and military uniforms.

# Chudleigh

A short distance from Ugbrooke is **Chudleigh**, once on the busy A38, but now bypassed by the dual carriage-way to Plymouth. Much of medieval Chudleigh was destroyed in the great fire of 1807, when two-thirds of the town was burnt down.

As the town is on a ridge of limestone, there were problems with a reliable water supply in the Middle Ages, but in about 1430 Bishop Lacey provided a town leat (similar to the one at Tiverton), which brought water along a circuitous route 7 miles (11km) from a spring on Haldon. Some potwater dipping wells may be seen near the top of New Exeter Street.

At the other end of the town are **Chudleigh Rocks**, a limestone outcrop little visited by strangers. A scramble along its crest is an enjoyable experience, and the view westwards from the top of the cliff is breathtaking. The crags are much used by rock climbers, and, as you would expect on a limestone feature, the rock is penetrated by caves. In the old Palace Quarry are **The Rock Gardens**, a spectacular hidden garden (8 acres/3ha) with plants, ponds and caves.

About 3 miles (5km) up the B3193, just west of Chudleigh, is **Canonteign Falls and Farm Park**. A natural hillside gorge was landscaped by the first Viscountess Exmouth in the mid-nineteenth century. Water was fed to a cascade by a leat. After many years of neglect this beautiful corner of the Teign Valley has been restored and the paths cleared. The site now claims the highest waterfall in England.

Westwards from Chudleigh along the A38 for 3 miles (5km) as far as the Drum Bridge intersection, there is a left turn, signposted 'Newton Abbot', and almost immediately a left turn into

**Stover Country Park.** A large granite lodge of classical design beside the dual carriageway was built on one of the approaches to Stover House, which dates from 1776; it is not open to the public as it is now a private school.

The park has become a Country Park managed by Devon County Council. There is a pleasant walk round the lake. A great deal of work was done a few years ago to make the park, which had become derelict, beautiful once again, and available to the public. Birds and dragonflies are in abundance, and fishing can be tried from special platforms.

Close to the Park is **Burnham Nurseries** the home of **Orchid Paradise**, a superb orchid collection. Also near the Park, **Trago Mills** is a shopping complex with a number of play areas.

In this part of the Bovey Basin, as the low-lying area between the Haldon foothills and Dartmoor is called, are the white workings of the ball clay operations. Ball clay is found at only one other place in Devon, between Okehampton and Great Torrington. (China clay occurs on south-west Dartmoor.) Ball clay differs from china clay in that it is china clay washed down millions of years ago from deposits higher up. China clay is decomposed feldspar, one of the three constituents of granite. Ball clay is used to make pottery and tiles.

# Newton Abbot and District

**Newton Abbot** is at first sight an unprepossessing town. Its attractions have to be searched for, but many decent small buildings are waiting to be discovered. It grew rapidly when the railway arrived, and became a junction for the Torbay and Moretonhampstead branches and a necessary stop for the heavier trains to attach a 'banker' locomotive to assist them over the fierce Dainton and Rattery inclines between Newton Abbot and Plymouth.

As a market town for rural South Devon it retains its usefulness and is highly regarded by country people who find little to attract them to Torquay, where you can buy china animals but not a pair of hard-wearing trousers. For workaday things it is ideal.

The River Lemon passes through the built-up area and is largely culverted, a fact which fails to allow for the occasional flash-flood. The St Leonard's Tower, which stands at the central crossroads, is all that remains of a church built about 1350 and demolished in 1836.

Close to the town centre are the **Hedgehog Hospital** at Prickly Ball Farm on the Denbury road where visitors can learn more about these delightful animals, and **Tucker's Maltings,** the only traditional malthouse in the country which is open to the public.

Two outstanding buildings are within easy reach of Newton Abbot, albeit in opposite directions. **Bradley Manor** (National Trust) stands in its own grounds just off the Totnes road, and is frequently open to the public. It is a small fifteenth-century manor house, and its great hall, emblazoned with Queen Elizabeth's royal arms, is a notable feature. In the woods beyond Bradley Manor is Puritan Pit, a deep natural cavity where early nonconformists held their meetings in secret 300 years ago. At the other end of the town **Forde House**, now used by

Teignbridge District Council, dates from 1610. King Charles I visited in 1625, and William of Orange read his proclamation here in 1688, on his way to London, after landing at Brixham.

'Racing at Newton Abbot' refers to the national hunt racecourse on the Kingsteignton road. During the rest of the year, it is used for regular antique fairs and car boot sales.

A little way out, and beyond the large village of Ipplepen, is the parish of **Torbryan**, which should be visited for the sake of its church and the Old Church House Inn. This remote church – it stands at the end of a cul-de-sac – was never restored, and retains to a remarkable degree the fittings of a medieval church. Large clear perpendicular windows admit much light to illuminate the striking hues of the screen, pulpit and altar. A short walk up a nearby public footpath to Tornewton takes one along a delight-ful valley through limestone country. One of the features of South Devon are these pockets of limestone, and in caves concealed by scrub on either side have been found animal remains from millions of years ago.

# Dawlish

Approaching South Devon down the Exe Estuary, **Dawlish** (not to be con-fused with nearby Dawlish Warren) is the first of the south coast holiday resorts to be reached. The heart of the town is built on both sides of a pleasant open space called the Lawn through which runs the Dawlish Water, or simply the Brook, much frequented by ducks and black swans, who paddle about above some seemingly uncon-cerned trout. The railway cuts off the view to the sea and creates its own attractions, overpowering the coastal end of the town.

Teignmouth Beach

Dawlish developed early in the nineteenth century as a quiet watering-place, although a small settlement half a mile inland had existed for hundreds of years. The long sandy beach, the coves and the proximity of the railway assured the town's success, even if the crowded and hilly site prevented expansion.

The town is well worth exploring; here and there one can feel the atmosphere that Jane Austen and Charles Dickens must have encountered when they visited Dawlish. (Dickens contrived to have Nicholas Nickleby 'born' here.) A visit to **Dawlish Museum** will strengthen this feeling, as local history, trades and Victoriana figure largely in the exhibits. Off Exeter Road is a fine recreation ground, including an 18-hole approach golf course and a heated indoor swimming pool.

At the top of the hill heading towards Teignmouth is the award-winning housing development of Oaklands Park, a successful attempt to group buildings of intimate scale in a pleasurable composition while echoing Devon's heritage of vernacular buildings.

# Teignmouth and Shaldon

The road to **Teignmouth** undulates violently, and descends into the town down a long hill from the thatched house called **Minadab**, a well-known landmark of the kind commonly found in Sidmouth. Teignmouth combines a workaday face with a fun-loving holiday image, and it is too facile to say that the former is based on the estuary while the latter faces the sea. To an extent, this is true, as the boat-building yards and ball clay exporting quays are on the Teign Estuary; but this makes no allowance for the sailing, windsurfing or angling holidaymakers for whom the estuary is their playground.

Teignmouth's buildings reflect its ambivalent outlook. Some splendid nineteenth-century houses look across the seafront open space known as the Den, but at the back of the town are the old, narrower, winding streets. There are two parish churches, and that belonging to West Teignmouth, rebuilt about 1820, has cast-iron pillars airily supporting a roof lantern of unusual delicacy.

Teignmouth was largely destroyed by the French in 1690, and was in the front line too in World War II when seventy-nine people were killed in German air raids. Keats stayed at No. 20 Northumberland Place with his mother in 1818 – a plaque marks his sojourn.

Much of Teignmouth's holiday activity takes place near the Den. The pier, theatre, cinema, model railway, tennis and novelty golf are all here. On Dawlish Road is a heated swimming pool. **Teignmouth & Shaldon Museum** is in French Street, so-called as it was built with money given in a public appeal after the 1690 raid.

Across the estuary from Teignmouth is **Shaldon**, reached by a long road bridge (only freed from tolls in 1948); its old toll house stands at the north end, and Shaldon's late nineteenth-century church (completed 1902) is at the south end. This building has been likened to a tunnel of stone, and from outside it possesses an air of gloom that a visit inside does little to dispel, even if one knows that connoisseurs of Victorian architecture hold it in high regard.

The village of Shaldon, however, has an air of unspoiled period charm. Lines of simple flower-decked terraced cottages look out on the constantly changing scene of the estuary mouth, at the ferry boats with their lines of imitation gun ports, and perhaps a ball clay ship stuck on one of the ever-shifting sand banks.

At the sea end of the village the great tree-topped headland known as the Ness rears up, and here are found the holiday trappings of the village and the **Shaldon Wildlife Trust**. A tunnel through the cliff to the popular Ness beach is often attributed to smugglers, but they would hardly have advertised their trade in this way; more likely, it was cut during the Napoleonic Wars.

On the higher slopes of Shaldon is an approach golf course, and just below the Torquay road is a public park.

That part of the **South Devon Coast Path** between Shaldon and Torquay makes a very good day's walk. As it cuts across the grain of the landscape, it is a strenuous expedition, but may be shortened at several places by turning off the coast path to the A379 for a bus back to Shaldon.

The three towns of Torquay, Paignton and Brixham are now gathered together under the title Torbay for administrative and municipal convenience. But in this book, the individuality of the three constituent towns will be retained using the term Tor Bay in its two-word form to describe the natural feature only.

# Torquay

Torquay has an abundance of interest. The prehistoric and historical scene was set in the introductory chapter with references to Kent's Cavern and the presence of the fleet in Tor Bay during the Napoleonic Wars. The medical officers on duty with the fleet were quick to realise its climatic benefits and recommended a stay in the mild embryo resort to their private consumptive patients. So it was as a haven for invalids that the popularity of Torquay developed, a reputation perpetuated in the present-day Borough motto *Salus et felicitas* – Health and Happiness.

At the same time, of course, when the Continent was out of bounds, a few shrewd entrepreneurs, who owned land or added to their estates, built Mediterranean-type villas with Italian-sounding names like Villa Borghese and Villa Como, and were then in a position to re-sell. Two of these families were the Carys and the Palks, and one is not in Torquay long before these names appear in one form or another. Much of Torquay is therefore nineteenth-century, though the tall apartment blocks and hotels, some with gull-wing fly-away roofs, are clearly post-World War II.

An exception is the interesting complex of buildings centred on **Torre Abbey**. Here there flourished, from 1196 until the dissolution of the monasteries, an abbey for Premonstratensian canons. After 1539 the property passed through several owners before being bought by the Carys in 1665, and it was they who built the present mansion early in the eighteenth century. The gatehouse probably dates from 1320, and the so-called **'Spanish barn'**, the monastic tithe barn, is another relic from pre-dissolution days. It acquired its name after being used as a temporary prison for

397 Spanish captives from the Armada ship *Nuestra Senora del Rosario* in 1588. The property was bought by Torquay Corporation in 1930 and the house is now used as an art gallery. The Pre-Raphaelites are well represented and there is a good collection of English drinking glasses. The gardens are immaculately kept, and floral displays of the highest quality draw admiring visitors year after year.

The **Bygones Museum** in Fore Street, St Marychurch features a life-size Victorian street, together with a World War I trench and model railway. Not far away on Ilsham Road is the award-winning **Kent's Cavern**. Stalagmites and stalactites can be seen, along with finds from the Stone Age, while evening tours are arranged by candlelight for those who enjoy a spooky theatrical experience.

There is one other reminder of olden times within the bounds of Torquay which must be seen – **Cockington**. only a mile from the seafront, it consists of an ancient forge and Cockington Court, a pleasant but not outstanding mansion in 287 acres (115 hectares) of beautiful grounds. Around this core there are other attractive buildings, notably the Drum Inn (1934) designed by Sir Edwin Lutyens. The survival of Cockington within Torquay is a considerable achievement, even if a price in tourist exploitation has been paid. Horse-drawn carriages are on hand to take visitors to and from this village within a town.

**Babbacombe Model Village** is far more than its name implies. It is a triumph of landscape miniaturisation, and stays open with illumina-

## Beaches

Torquay's success as a holiday resort has been achieved despite not having any large beaches. **Torre Abbey Sands** are mostly covered at high tide, and the other opportunities are at **Meadfoot Beach**, **Anstey's Cove** and **Oddicombe**, where a cliff railway assists visitors to reach the shore. **Petitor** is the unofficial naturist beach. It was Paignton which developed as the family resort and remains so to this day, with better sandy beaches, both off the promenade and at **Goodrington**. Torquay's natural advantage of a Riviera image has channelled its growth along more adult lines, and there is no shortage of entertainment to suit all tastes and pockets.

tions to 9.30pm until September. Tiny trains move round the site. **Torquay Museum** in Babbacombe Road contains many of the finds from Kent's Cavern and the unique Agatha Christie exhibition, as well as displays of Devon folk life, pottery, archaeology and Victoriana.

Sporting possibilities abound. Several golf courses, pitch and putt, squash, ten-pin bowling and swimming are all there to be tried. Water sports are as varied. Waterskiing, windsurfing, sea fishing, sailing or simply taking a boat trip across the bay or round the coast are some of the opportunities available. There are also two cinemas, three theatres, night clubs, discos and casinos.

Many people enjoy walking along the promenade and the piers. The public gardens entice visitors and a steep climb through the beautiful **Rock**

**End Gardens** behind and above the Imperial Hotel leads to that curiously-named viewpoint, Daddyhole Plain. (A 'daddy' is thought to be a demon in folklore.) The visitor should also walk or motor along the Ilsham Marine Drive, diverting onto the cliffs to get a close look at Thatcher Rock. This is one of the limestone 'horns' of Tor Bay. Berry Head is the other.

Torquay

## Paignton

**Paignton** developed as the family resort beside Torquay. Children like sand, and there is more of it at Paignton. There are hills in Paignton – very steep ones – but they are further back from the sea than at Torquay, and the town was already established before land hunger pushed Paignton to encroach on its hilly hinterland.

Historically, Paignton was some distance inland – the old streets are unmistakable – but when the railway arrived, the settlement grew towards the station, and soon the rapidly expanding town was filling in the land between the railway and the sea. Fortunately, a pleasant open space was allowed to remain between the front row of buildings and the beach.

Architecturally Paignton is not as distinguished as Torquay, although there are two surprises. **Kirkham House** in Kirkham Street may have been a four-teenth-century priest's house; it is now owned by English Heritage and open on Sunday afternoons in summer.

The other surprise, even more unexpected, is an opulent mansion, **Oldway**, built in 1874 for the Singer family (of sewing machine fame) in the French style. Rows of neoclassical pillars around the exterior prepare one for a

Paignton Pier

*Above: Berry Pomeroy Castle just off the Totnes to Paignton road*
*Below: Brixham*

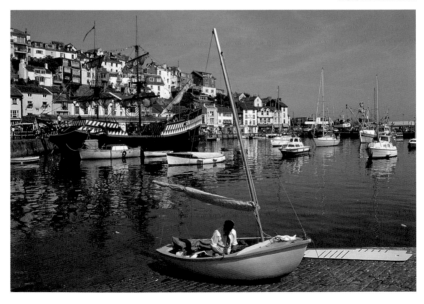

sumptuous interior of marble staircases and painted ceilings. Incongruity is added by the local authority's interior signing, for this ostentatious building is now owned by the council and much of it is used as offices. However, it is open to the public, as are the equally splendid grounds. This ambitious mansion – ambiguously called the Wigwam by Isaac Singer, its builder – copied many features of Versailles, perhaps because his second wife was of French extraction. The family originally came to Paignton for health reasons, and Oldway was built with the money they made from sewing machines.

Facing Oldway's main entrance is a round building with a pointed roof, looking rather like a miniature Royal Albert Hall. This was originally built as a riding and exercising pavilion, and may well have been based on the Albert Hall, which was built three years before Oldway, in 1871.

Before leaving Paignton to explore the countryside nearby, there is a final attraction, the **Paignton and Dartmouth Steam Railway** which uses steam engines to haul trains from the GWR station at Paignton to Kingswear. The railway calls first at Goodrington Sands, skirts Tor Bay behind Saltern Cove and Broad Sands, and then calls at Churston before diving into Greenway tunnel. Emerging, the railway follows the River Dart to Kingswear. A ferry links Kingswear with Dartmouth across the water. At Goodrington Sands, **Splashdown@Quaywest** is Devon's premier waterpark and features a variety of waterslides.

'Behind' Paignton, as it were, are two ancient and historic buildings of the highest interest. **Compton Castle** (National Trust) nestles in a valley in a seemingly indefensible site about a mile (1.6km) north of the Torbay ring road at Marldon. The earliest part of the building, dating back to about 1330, is the great hall, with various associated rooms and cellars. The owners were

## Paignton Zoo

**Paignton Zoo**, on the Totnes road, the largest in Devon, is a constant delight for visitors. A feature of the zoo is the exotic birds which walk and fly around the grounds. On a tree-covered island in the lake, the gibbons whoop their eerie cries and swing from branch to branch, bringing up their young in cosy barrels loftily sited in the trees.

the Gilbert family. Later, in 1450–75, various additions and replacements were effected including a withdrawing room and a chapel.

About 1520 further reconstruction and enlargement took place. The towers and curtain wall with their impressive machicolations (holes through which missiles could be dropped on attackers) were built as well as the portcullis entrances. French raids on Teignmouth, Plymouth and Fowey (in Cornwall) had made the family feel vulnerable, and this protection was adequate against lightly armed raiding parties even in this overlooked site. Civil War activity is unknown, but by 1750 the hall was ruinous. The Gilberts – who had included Sir Humphrey Gilbert (founder of Newfoundland) and his half-brother Sir Walter Raleigh – sold Compton Castle in 1800 and bought it back in 1930. Commander and Mrs Walter Raleigh Gilbert then restored and rebuilt the structure, and gave it to the National Trust in 1951.

The other historic building is **Berry Pomeroy Castle**, not far away, but difficult to find from Compton. It is better to return to the ring road, take the Totnes road at Marldon Five Lanes and look for the sign after a few miles. This is another site where several structures have followed one another, but unlike Compton Castle, the present-day result is a ruin, even if a highly atmospheric one. It stands in dense woods on a spur above a small stream.

Three sides could be easily defended; only the south side needed massive walls, and here is the gatehouse, curtain wall and St Margaret's Tower. This part of the castle, the oldest, was probably built in the fourteenth century, though the records are silent, by the Pomeroy family. Between 1548 and 1613 a large mansion was built inside the castle walls by the Seymours, who acquired it in 1548; the gaping windows of this abandoned house still taunt us with their mystery. Why was it left to fall down? No one knows. A fire may be the answer. The whole scene is very picturesque, and there are walks in the woods that surround the castle, which is open to the public.

# Brixham

The third of the Tor Bay towns is **Brixham**, until not so long ago a quiet fishing backwater, but now caught up in the holiday business, though separated from Paignton's southern satellites of Goodrington and Galmpton by a green belt.

Like Torquay, Brixham sits on limestone. Traces of early man have been found here. In medieval times, the town developed as Higher and Lower Brixham, with the fishing industry concentrated round the creek, which is now largely filled in, but which penetrated nearly half a mile beyond where the inner harbour now ends.

The fishing industry was so suc-cessful that the ships sought to exploit the fishing grounds of the North Sea, following the migratory shoals, and they were largely responsible for the development of Lowestoft, Grimsby and Fleetwood as fishing ports. Markets for their fish near where they were caught were needed.

Many nautical connections are incorporated in the **Brixham Heritage Museum** in New Road.

The quay at Brixham buzzes with industry most of the time. An extensive inshore fishery survives, and there is much coming and going of holidaymakers' pleasure craft, as well as trips to Torquay or round the coast to Dartmouth. A replica of the **Golden Hind** offers visitors a glimpse of life aboard a Tudor ship.

A worthwhile exploration of **Berry Head Country Park** can well take a couple of hours; there is so much here to see, whether one is interested in plants, sea birds, history or technology. Out to sea are the tankers and supertankers performing their loading or lightening logistics before heading off, shallower in draft, to cope with the Dover Strait, or waiting until the world oil price increases.

The vertical cliffs – do watch children and dogs – provide superb nesting sites for kittiwakes, fulmars, guillemots, gulls of various kinds, kestrels, jackdaws and rock doves; a visit here in the spring is the best time to see hectic avian activity. The limestone rocks carry an unusual flora, which includes autumn squill, fellwort, scabious, rock sea lavender and wall pennywort. As several rarities are known here, visitors are asked not to pick specimens.

Across this elevated promontory in Iron Age times the local tribe built a defensive earthwork. This gave Berry Head its name; Berry is a corruption of Byri or Byrig, the Saxon word for fortification. The huge Napoleonic War fort, now such a landmark and an interesting feature to explore, destroyed most of this. A certain irony must have been felt by the garrison of that fort when HMS *Bellerophon* put in to Tor Bay bearing Bonaparte to St Helena.

The coastguard station monitors maritime comings and goings, and nearby is Berry Head Lighthouse, which is sometimes said to be the highest, the smallest, and the lowest lighthouse in Great Britain. At 191ft (67m) above sea level there is none higher; being only a few feet high it is very small. When originally built it was turned by the action of a weight falling down a 150ft (52.5m) shaft; this has been replaced by a motor. Inland is an aircraft navigational device, and by the café is a cloud-determining device; the Royal Observer Corps is also represented. Sometimes on a very clear day Portland is visible 35 miles (56km) away across Lyme Bay.

From Berry Head the **South Devon Coast Path** perambulates St Mary's Bay and Sharkham Point, then runs along National Trust land nearly all the way to Kingswear. Much of this magnificent coast was bought by the Trust in late 1982, and is open for public access. At Inner Froward Point is a World War II gun battery, almost complete except for the guns, and inland a little way, on a high point is the 80ft (24.4m) high, hollow, tapering stone pillar known as the Day Mark,

an unlit navigational beacon dating back to the 1860s. A good walk from Berry Head is to follow the cliff path to Kingswear, returning to Brixham by bus. Four hours are needed for the 10 miles (16km) of strenuous walking.

Tucked in a small valley leading down to the sea near the Day Mark is **Coleton Fishacre Garden** (National Trust), a 15-acre (6 hectares) subtropical paradise only begun by the D'Oyly Carte family (of Gilbert and Sullivan fame) in the 1920s. It is open to the public.

# Dartmouth

Two ways of arriving at **Kingswear** have already been mentioned: by steam train or on foot. **Dartmouth**, the little town across the water, so redolent of our British heritage, must be in the top ten of any Devonian's list of towns. The charm of the place is its cramped site. Steep hills slide straight into high water, or at least they did so before man altered the waterfront. Lacking space on the hillsides, Dartmothians have pushed outwards into the river in the same way as those who live in Brixham.

In about 1600 the muddy creek of Mill Pool was filled in, to become the lowest part of the present town. It met the estuary at the significantly named New Ground and the gardens by the bandstand. The **Market Square** occupies part of this made-up land. Likewise, every building in front of Fairfax Place and Lower Street (in other words, the whole of the South Embankment) is built on land reclaimed from the river. Knowing this, it is easier to understand the pressures for space that must have exercised the local merchants. They

*Above: Washed Up Crab Pot Infront Of Thatcher Rock, Torquay*

*Right: Kingswear*

*Below: Brixham inner harbour*

needed flat land near their ships; there was little point in building high up on the hillsides. Dartmouth was the leading trading port of Devon. It possessed a deep-water, sheltered anchorage, easily and well defended by the twin castles of Kingswear and Dartmouth, between which a chain could be strung in times of war. The Second and Third Crusades left from here – what a chaotic turmoil of people, animals and supplies the port must have witnessed – and trade with Spain, Portugal and later Newfoundland burgeoned.

**Bayard's Cove**, just downstream from the Lower Ferry, is a reminder of these rollicking days of sail. Old buildings line the quay in harmonious disarray. Other attractive buildings are the seventeenth-century **Butterwalk**, a Grade I listed building containing the comprehensive **town museum**, and St Saviour's Church, with its splendid gallery dating from 1633.

The **castle**, already mentioned, should be visited as well as the lesser-known fortifications at Bayard's Cove. Within the precincts of Dartmouth Castle is another church, St Petrock's, rebuilt in the seventeenth century, but containing several memorial brasses.

Much of the coast south-westwards for 1½ miles (2km) belongs to the National Trust, and this includes the wooded hill behind Dartmouth Castle called **Gallants Bower**. On its 400ft (140m) summit is a Civil War earthwork, a relic of the Royalists' determination to hold on to Dartmouth in 1645. However, when the Parliamentarians besieged the town, the Royalists put up little resistance, and it soon fell to General Fairfax in January 1646.

The cliff walk to **Little Dartmouth** (where there is a National Trust car park) is delightfully varied, with views ahead across Start Bay to Start Point.

The smoke from the steam railway across the Dart prompts one to recall that **Thomas Newcomen** was born in Dartmouth. Newcomen recognised the power of steam, and he produced the first industrial steam engine, although James Watt gained most of the credit when he improved the invention 50 years later. In a building near the Butterwalk can be seen an example of a steam engine based on Newcomen's principle, but in this case built in the early nineteenth century.

Dartmouth's position makes it a good place for boat trips. Pleasure cruises come here from **Torbay** in the summer, and leave Dartmouth for holiday trips along the coast. One of the classic English river journeys is up the Dart to Totnes, a winding, ever-changing voyage of delight. Birdwatchers especially will see much to enchant them. There is one waterside tree where

## Royal Naval College

Dartmouth, of course, is synonymous with the training of naval officers, so much a part of our naval tradition that one is almost surprised that the **Royal Naval College** was only built in 1905. Before this, the trainee officers lived in superannuated wooden hulks moored in the Dart, but as these began to rot a permanent building became necessary. The college is officially called *Britannia* after the first of the hulks it succeeded.

It is open to the public at certain times.

cormorants dry their wings, managing to look prehistorically sinister in the process. Kingfishers can often be seen where the channel narrows, and occasionally an osprey. The Scottish birds sometimes rest a while on the Dart and feed themselves up before setting off for the tropics.

# Totnes and District

An exploration of **Totnes** is best begun from the top end by visiting the **Norman castle**. As it dominates the town the visitor can quickly get a baron's eye view of Totnes from its walls. The small but perfect keep stands on its motte beside the inner bailey or court. Alongside the castle on the west you will see a housing development, Castle Court, which fits neatly into the town in scale and texture, proving that modern buildings can after all be good to look at. The line of the town walls can be picked out, and is traceable on the ground in several places.

Down **High Street** are the two covered pavement arcades of the **Butterwalk** and the **Poultry Walk**, similar to other pillared ambulatories at Dartmouth, Kingsbridge and Plympton. Clearly this was a fashionable and sensible South Devon convention in the early seventeenth century, as were the slate-hung elevations.

The red sandstone church is worth a visit. The Beer stone rood screen is notable as a superb example of fifteenth-century stone carving. At the 'back' of the churchyard is the **Guildhall**, built in 1533. The council chamber, court room and mayor's parlour contain a great deal of interest. The Ramparts Walk leads to the East Gate, where High Street gives way to Fore Street.

After passing through East Gate, **Totnes Museum** is on the right in the Elizabethan House. An unusual exhibit relates to early computers. Charles Babbage, the 'father' of British computer science, spent much of his

## Totnes

Totnes is another of Devon's top ten towns. One can go further. In 1965 it was recognised by the Council for British Archaeology as of such quality that it was listed as one of the CBA's forty towns 'so splendid and so precious that the ultimate responsibility for them should be regarded as a national concern'. The reasons for the CBA's assessment can be succinctly listed here:

- Ancient town plan well preserved
- Ancient bridge crossing and approaches
- Georgian bridge
- Waterfront of historical importance
- Town wall, ditch and gates well preserved
- Castle precinct well preserved
- Medieval to seventeenth-century buildings worthy of preservation
- Georgian and Regency buildings worthy of preservation

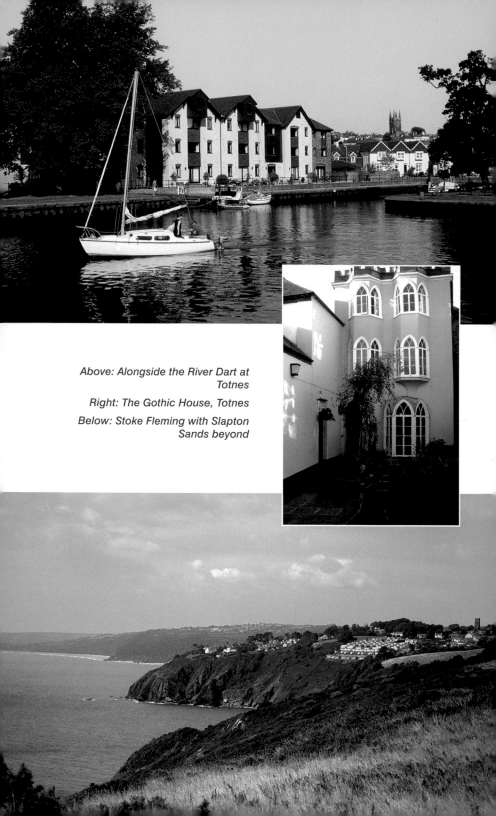

*Above: Alongside the River Dart at Totnes*

*Right: The Gothic House, Totnes*

*Below: Stoke Fleming with Slapton Sands beyond*

early life in Totnes; he virtually invented the punch-card system and a kind of prototype computer, the analytical engine. He was far ahead of his time and like many such men of genius was not appreciated or understood in his lifetime. The house occupied by the museum is only one of many which preserve their original form, but may have false or later façades, belying their age. A notable feature of many of these early town houses is their decorated plaster ceilings. As these are mainly in private houses they are not often seen, although some owners seem to leave the lights on and the curtains open in the upstairs rooms on summer evenings so that the elaborate plasterwork can be appreciated by passers-by.

Across the road, set in the pavement, is the **Brutus Stone**. A legend links this lump of rock with the Trojan who is said to have landed here in 1000 BC. Opposite is Atherton Lane, often festively floral. Indeed, Totnes on summer Tuesdays has local people, mostly shopkeepers, dressed in Elizabethan costume.

Further down still is the distinguished Georgian front of **The Mansion**, now part of the King Edward VI School, and, on the same side, tucked up another lane, is the **Gothic House** which has a public right of way running through it. **Fore Street** opens out at its foot onto the Plains, where an obelisk stands to local boy William Wills (with Burke, the first person to cross Australia). He died in 1861 on the return journey. The river is crossed by an 1828 bridge designed by Charles Fowler, architect of the old Covent Garden market, the lowest bridge on the Dart.

The main street is so crammed with historic buildings that it is worthwhile to walk up and down on opposite pavements. Opposite the Civic Hall is the **Devonshire Collection of Period Costume** in 43 High Street. It is well worth a visit to see beautiful things delightfully displayed.

At the top of the town, not far from the large car park, are the **Leech Wells** in Leechwell Lane. Water gushes into three stone troughs, and the lepers came here in an attempt to cleanse themselves in what they thought were healing waters. There was a leper hospital nearby through the Middle Ages; the water formed the local supply. Leprosy was rife in this country for thousands of years. Even after the Civil War, in 1646, 257 leprosy burials took place in Totnes.

South of Totnes, near Blackawton, is the **Woodlands Leisure Park** with a huge number of rides and slides (wet and dry) and several play areas.

Continuing up the Dart Valley, the next stop is at **Shinner's Bridge**, where the A384 and A385 meet, our first encounter with 'Dartington'. This many-sided concept began in 1925, when Leonard and Dorothy Elmhirst, both idealists, purchased an 820-acre (328 hectares) estate based on **Dartington Hall**, with the intention of reviving life in the countryside. The estate was run down, Dorothy Elmhirst had a considerable fortune, and they saw the property as capable of development.

Since then, the activities at Dartington have blossomed and multiplied. The retail trade is carried on at the Cider Press at Shinner's Bridge, where one can buy furniture, good quality gifts, farm

67

foods, clothes and tweed cloth, and eat at an excellent vegetarian restaurant, Cranks. Other activities over the years have been building, forestry, education (adult courses and a boarding school) and the arts in the broadest sense.

Various walks around the estate begin from the Cider Press car park, some short, some long. Dartington Hall itself ought to be visited; but, as it is about 1 mile (1.5km) from Shinner's Bridge, one can turn off the A384 at Dartington church and park in the hall car park. The courtyard is under the arch, and opposite is the Great Hall, a roofless ruin in 1925, but now beautifully restored with timbers drawn from the estate. A chamber music concert here is a sublime experience. Behind the hall in the gardens is the restored tilting yard, with terraced grassy banks and twelve enormous clipped yews looking like giant skittles. Modern tournaments, outdoor plays, masques and *son et lumière* presentations are held here. The Hall is now a hotel and conference centre.

# From Dartington to Kingsbridge

The rest of this chapter deals with that part of Devon known as the **South Hams**. There is no general agreement about exact boundaries, but the rivers Yealm (pronounced 'Yam') and Dart on the west and east, Dartmoor to the north and the sea to the south are usually reckoned to define this fertile rural area of farms and villages. The name South Hams is first noticed in documents in 1396, but scholars have found the meaning obscure. At local government reorganisation in 1974, it was applied to the southernmost district council in the county, with headquarters at Totnes. Kingsbridge, Salcombe, Modbury and Ivybridge are the only other places that could be classed as towns in the area, and for the purposes of this book Ivybridge is included in the Dartmoor chapter (chapter 4).

The A379 coast road from Dartmouth dips, climbs and winds through the villages of Stoke Fleming and Strete, and past **Blackpool Sands**, an attractive cove overhung with Monterey pines, and bearing no resemblance to its north country namesake. The local people repulsed a Breton invasion force here in 1404.

After several switchback miles, the road drops down to sea level at the north end of **Slapton Sands**, a 2.5-mile (4km) bank of shingle and pebbles, thrown up when the glaciers melted after the last Ice Age. Trapped behind this pebble ridge are the waters of **Slapton Ley**, the largest natural freshwater lake in Devon, and divided into the Higher and Lower Ley by the road leading to the village of Slapton.

The **Higher Ley**, being smaller and shallower, and receiving the largest stream, the River Gara, has silted up in the thousands of years since it was created, and is now largely reed-grown and bordered with willow. **The Lower Ley**, however, is open water, fringed with reed. The lake is shallow and has an average depth of about 6ft (2m). Eels find the muddy bottom attractive, and four-pounders are regularly taken. The eels, roach and perch fall prey to the pike, as do frogs and ducklings.

As a pike fishery the Ley is highly thought of but it is as a bird sanctuary that it is so important. The scarcity of other freshwater ponds and lakes in the south-west makes Slapton Ley a place of avian concentration, particularly in the spring and when birds are migrating in the autumn. This diversity of natural interest was the origin of the **Slapton Ley Field Centre**, set up between the sea and the village. The Field Studies Council run courses here for many categories of study and student. Investigations do not involve only the immediate locality. Groups range far and wide in South Devon, and the Field Centre minibus may often be seen parked in a Dartmoor layby, while students tramp off through the heather to learn about the Dartmoor tors. Two nature trails have been laid down round the Lower Ley, and leaflets describing the routes are available from the Field Centre. Guided walks are advertised in the summer.

The village of **Slapton** should be visited, too; a pleasing hotch-potch of buildings in the South Hams tradition. The church porch contains a sanctuary ring. In medieval times, it was sufficient to touch it to receive sanctuary, but there then followed a complicated ritual of confession and abjuration, which resulted in the felon having to leave the country. Near the church are the ruins of the chantry, of which the tower is all that now remains.

Along the coast road is **Torcross**, an exposed village partly built on the pebble ridge itself. Torcross is periodically battered by gales, but has not so far suffered the fate of Hallsands 3 miles (5km) to the south, almost at Start Point. To reach Hallsands, turn left off the A379 in Stokenham and follow the road signs. At Torcross a World War II Sherman tank, recovered from the sea, is on display in the car park.

**Hallsands** was a row of thirty-seven houses on a rocky ledge beneath the cliff, protected by a shingle foreshore. The men earned a living by fishing, and life was uneventful until the closing years of the nineteenth century, when a contractor engaged in construction work at Devonport dockyard was given permission to dredge shingle offshore. In a very short time 500,000 tons were taken, and by 1902, when dredging stopped, the beach level had dropped

## Slapton Sands

At Slapton Sands, the tall stone memorial obelisk by the roadside – unveiled by the United States General Grunther in 1954 – commemorates the use of the area in late 1943 and early 1944 for beach landing practice prior to the Normandy invasion. Because live ammunition was used, all the inhabitants and their animals from seven parishes in the Slapton hinterland were forced to evacuate. This involved 3,000 people across 30,000 acres (12,000 hectares). The difficulties of the operation may be judged when it is realised that transport and motor fuel were scarce, most able-bodied men were in the Services, the days were short and the weather bad. During that time the village (one of several) was deserted; rats roamed the streets unmolested. Leslie Thomas has written about the event in *The Magic Army* (1982).

13ft (4.5m). Its natural protection dissipated, the village was exposed to the sea, and in a series of storms all the houses were demolished, the last in 1917. The whole affair was a case of official buck-passing, and little was done for the homeless. The line of ruined buildings can be seen beneath the cliff, and it is surprising that houses were built there in the first place.

Since it is so close, one should visit **Start Point Lighthouse**, which dates from 1836. The light has a range of 20.8 miles (33km). The name Start comes from the same Anglo-Saxon root *steort*, meaning a tail, which is found in the name of the bird, the redstart. From Start Point there is a way through the lanes to **East Prawle**; the route is then signposted to **Prawle Point**, 1 mile (1.5km) further on. This is the southern extremity of the county. There is a National Trust car park at the road end, a few hundred yards from the Point itself.

Start Point is just out of sight beyond Peartree Point, but the other direction looks across the mouth of Salcombe Harbour to Bolt Head. Near at hand, a mile away by cliff path, is **Gammon Head**, the most photogenic promontory on the South Devon coast. Its massive hump protects a sheltered beach, Maceley Cove, from the southwest gales, and it is a lovely spot for a swim, even if the climb down and up is rather a scramble.

To continue the exploration of the South Hams, the A379 leads to **Kingsbridge**, the 'capital' of this part of Devon and the natural route focus at the head of the Kingsbridge Estuary. This wide expanse of water, with many shallow creeks poking tidal tentacles among fertile fields, is not fed by any large river, and is really what geographers call a ria, or flooded valley. Although the channel to Salcombe is used by pleasure boats and yachts, a century ago a weekly 'market packet' steamer ran between Kingsbridge and Plymouth, calling at Salcombe on the way. Where children now feed ducks and swans, ships from far-off places used to tie up to discharge exotic cargoes, and export cider, corn, harness and stone. Ships were built nearby, and the recreation ground is on the site of a tidal millpond. Between Kingsbridge and the sea are the remains of twenty-two limekilns; the limestone came by sea from Plymouth.

Kingsbridge is now a busy, cheerful place with good shops, pubs and restaurants. The appearance of the town is attractive, though there are few outstanding buildings. Perhaps **The Shambles** is the most striking structure. Here the old market building is raised on Elizabethan granite pillars. In **Fore Street** there are quaint passages and alleys on either side. At one time, Fore Street had twenty-six alleys, but some are now closed. Kingsbridge passages have curious names like Squeezebelly Passage, Khartoum Place, Baptist Lane and several named after inns.

At the top of the town, on the east side of the road, is **Knowle House**, one of several fine eighteenth- and nineteenth-century houses. This one was the home of Colonel Montagu, who gave his name to the Montagu's harrier. On the opposite side of the road, and lower down, is the very interesting **Cookworthy Museum** in the Old

*Above: Blackpool Sands between Dartmouth and Slapton*

*Right: This Sherman Tank stands at Torcross as a memorial to servicemen*

*Below: Hallsands*

Grammar School. William Cookworthy (1705–80), the English discoverer of china clay, who made the first English porcelain, was born in Kingsbridge. The exhibition is sponsored by English China Clays Ltd. There are also interesting displays of agriculture and domestic life. To the north of the town, near Loddiswell, is the **Sorley Tunnel Adventure Farm**, where children can feed farm animals or enjoy various play areas. The name is from an old railway tunnel which can be explored. There is also a craft centre.

# Salcombe

**Salcombe** is a drive of 7 miles (11km) through West Alvington and Malborough. Look for Malborough's church spire, a prominent landmark for miles around. The problem at Salcombe in high summer may be finding a parking space, but it is worth the effort! Everyone in Salcombe in July and August seems to be in the boat business. Blue jeans, guernseys and yellow boat boots are as common as top hats at Ascot and as de rigueur, for this is a sailing mecca. As a calling place for coastal cruising, it is a convenient one-day's journey from Dartmouth, Plymouth being the next port of call. Salcombe is also a retirement base, the salubrious climate of Devon's southernmost town helping to make it so.

Salcombe's fame in history is concerned with her fleet of yacht-like clipper schooners, which always brought home the first fruits from the pineapple pickings in the West Indies or the orange harvest in the Azores. Local trades are well portrayed in the Salcombe **Museum of Maritime and Local History** at Custom House Quay, where mementos and maps of the Slapton World War II battle training area – described above – are also found.

Another collection of bygones is at the **Overbeck's Museum** at **Overbeck's House** (National Trust) at the southern end (Sharpitor) of the built-up area. To reach here one passes the sandy beaches of North Sands (with the remains of one of Henry VIII's castles on one of its promontories; it withstood a siege in the Civil War) and South Sands, and at low tide other enticing beaches will be seen across the bay.

Overbeck's House also accommodates **Salcombe Youth Hostel**, and looks over the dreaded Salcombe Bar, a sea-covered sand spit waiting to snag deep-keeled ships, especially at low tide in a storm. In 1916, thirteen of the crew of fifteen of the Salcombe lifeboat were lost in turbulent seas on Salcombe Bar. This hazard may have inspired Tennyson's famous poem '*Crossing the Bar*'. The gardens at Overbeck's are another attraction. The mild climate allows plants and shrubs to grow that one would not expect to find in England.

From here round the cliffs via **Bolt Head** to **Bolt Tail** and **Hope Cove** is a walk of 6 miles (9.5km), and there is no public transport for the return.

There is one 2-mile (3km) walk, however, which the visitor should on no account omit. Up the steep lane behind Overbeck's is a pleasant high-level path leading to a viewpoint indicator on the top of **Sharp Tor**, overlooking Starehole Bay, the last resting place of the four-masted Finnish barque the *Herzogin Cecilie*, which was wrecked in 1936. Along this high route, a steep path leads down to the back of the bay. The return to Overbeck's can be made along the lower path, the Courtenay Walk, which cuts through the spiky rocks of Sharp Tor.

# Westwards from Salcombe

Beyond Hope Cove, which nestles behind the protecting arm of Bolt Tail, the coastline changes in character. Tall cliffs give way to a mixture of low cliffs, sand dunes and popular beaches. Inner Hope is a piece of Devon miraculously preserved from a hundred years ago, a square of thatched cottages unspoilt by modern development.

Off **Thurlestone** (the name means 'holed stone') is the famous arched rock that gave the parish its name, and after the small estuary of the Avon, **Bigbury-on-Sea** is reached, with its sands, shops and sea tractor. This strange contraption is employed to maintain the link between **Burgh Island** and the mainland when the tide is in. It can operate in 10ft (3.5m) of water and cope with seas up to a force nine gale. A large hotel dominates the island and the Pilchard Inn provides refreshments.

One further popular beach, **Chal-** **laborough**, will be found along this stretch of coast before access becomes difficult (unless the continuous South Devon Coast Path is used). The next estuary belongs to the Erme, rising, like the Avon, many miles away on southern Dartmoor, and lacking any sort of ferry or bridge near its mouth. Fortunately, at low tide it may be waded from slipway to slipway, but care must be taken especially during stormy weather or when there is a good deal of floodwater coming downriver.

**Modbury** is the chief settlement in this part of the South Hams. Standing astride the busy A379, it has a Georgian elegance that surprises the first-time visitor. The slate-hung front elevations are very typical of South Hams buildings.

The last slice of the South Hams before the outskirts of Plymouth are reached lies between the Erme and Yealm Estuaries. (The many estuaries along this seaboard make the walking of the South Devon Coast Path as much a triumph of planning as of execution. As some of the ferries are 'summer only' the walk is tedious if attempted off-season.)

The Yealm reaches the sea via a delightfully circuitous fjord-like channel,

## Gateposts

One other aspect of the man-made South Hams landscape which remains to be remarked upon is the massive masonry gateposts, or abutments. Instead of using a wooden post, farmers in times past – the date unknown – built up buttresses of stone on which to hang their gates, and went to some trouble to make a feature of them. A National Trust warden, asked if he knew why the practice had developed, replied, 'Have you ever tried to drive a post into shallow soil with rock not far below the surface?' This may not be the whole answer as one sees these structures where one expects the soil to be good and deep.

dressed with hanging oak woods. Up a wide creek stand the twin villages of **Newton Ferrers** and **Noss Mayo**, the latter a jolly name for a picturesque village. From here the coast path may be traced round the headland for a good distance before cutting back across the peninsula to the starting point at Noss. The path follows a planned route – the **Revelstoke Drive** – cut in the nineteenth century by Lord Revelstoke as a horse carriage drive round his property, the Membland estate. Made with horses in mind, it is nowhere steep, and as it constantly changes direction the views are varied. Down the cliff near **Stoke Point**, and somewhat submerged in a permanent caravan site, is the ruined, but partly restored, church of St Peter the Poor Fisherman, or **Revelstoke church**.

Although this part of Devon in the peak season hums with activity, by going only a short distance perfect peace is attainable.

*Above: Overbeck's House, Salcombe Youth Hostel*

*Below: Salcombe*

# Places to Visit

## In and around Newton Abbot

### Ugbrooke House

Chudleigh TQ13 0AD
☎ (01626) 852179
www.ugbrooke.co.uk
Clifford family home in a lovely park, rescued from decay and now a splendid stately home. Open: Grounds 12.30–5.30pm, admission to the house by guided tours only, at 1.25pm and 3.10pm, Tue, Wed, Thu, Sun & Bank Holiday Mon from second Sun in Jul until 2nd Thu in Sep.

### Canonteign Falls & Farm Park

West of Chudleigh EX6 7NT
☎ (01647) 252434
www.canonteignfalls.co.uk
A nineteenth-century landscaped gorge and cascade brought dramatically to life. Open: 10am–5.30pm daily Mar to Oct. Last admission 4pm.

### The Rock Gardens

Station Hill, Chudleigh TQ13 0EE
☎ (01626) 852134
www.therockgardens.co.uk
Open: 9am–5pm daily (tearoom Easter to Sep)

### Bradley Manor (N.T.)

Newton Abbot TQ12 6BN
☎ (01803) 661907
Small fifteenth-century manor house on the edge of the town. Open: 2–5pm Tue, Wed & Thu, Apr to Sep.

### Forde House

Newton Abbot
☎ (01626) 215185
A 1610 house, restored by Teignbridge District Council. Viewing by appointment only

### Tucker's Maltings

Teign Road, Newton Abbott TQ12 4AA
☎ (01626) 334734
www.tuckermaltings.com
Guided tours and speciality bottled beer shop. Open: Good Fri to 31 Oct, 10am–5pm Mon–Sat.
Ⓟ (Nearby)   ♟♟♟ <18   ☂

### Prickly Ball Farm and Hedgehog Hospital

Denby Road TQ12 6BZ
North of Newton Abbot, off A381
☎ (01626) 362319
www.pricklyballfarm.com
Hands on farm and hedgehog sanctuary. Open: 10am–5pm daily, Apr to Oct.
Ⓟ   ♿ (Most Areas)   ♟♟♟ <Family Ticket

### Stover Country Park

Newton Abbot TQ12 6QG
☎ (01626) 835236
A pleasant open space with woods and a lake, conveniently sited beside the A38 and A382.

### Burnham Nurseries

Forches Cross TQ12 6PZ
☎ (01626) 352233
orchids.uk.com
Artificial climate housing large variety

of orchids. Open: 10am–4pm daily except for winter bank holidays.

Ⓟ 🕭 (Most Area) 👫<14 FREE ☂

## Torbryan Church

Colourful medieval church with original fittings.

## Dawlish Museum

The Knowle, Barton Terrace EX7 9QH

☎ (01626) 888557

Local history, trades and Victoriana reflecting the town's interesting past. Open: 10.30am–5pm Wed to Fri, 2–5pm weekends; May to Sep.

## Teignmouth & Shaldon Museum

29 French Street TQ14 8ST

☎ (01626) 777041

www.teignmuseum.org.uk

A small collection of artefacts reflecting the history of this port and holiday town. Closed for redevelopment until 2010.

👫<Children FREE ☂

## Shaldon Wildlife Trust

Ness Drive, Shaldon TQ14 OHP

☎ (01626) 872234

www.shaldonwildlifetrust.co.uk

A small seaside zoo. Open: 10am–6pm daily, Easter to end of Sep. 11am–4pm daily Oct until Easter (not Christmas Day and Boxing Day).

Ⓟ 👫<16, Family Ticket

# Torquay, Paignton and Brixham

## Babbacombe Model Village

Hampton Ave TQ1 3LA

☎ (01803) 315315

www.model-village.co.uk

Internationally-known triumph of landscape miniaturisation. Open: daily except Christmas Day. Evenings as well, Jul and Aug.

Ⓟ 🕭 👫<Family Ticket

## Cockington Country Park and Village

Cockington Court TQ2 6XA

☎ (01803) 606035

A forge, the Drum Inn and Cockington Court, preserved within the town by Torbay Council. Call for details of special events

Ⓟ 🕭 👫<FREE ☂

## Kent's Cavern Prehistoric Caves

Ilsham Road, Torquay TQ1 2JF

☎ (01803) 215136

www.kents-cavern.co.uk

Man's earliest home in the area – 20,000 to 30,000 years BC. Open: from 9am daily, all year.

Ⓟ 🕭 👫<16 Discount ☂

## Oddicombe Cliff Railway

☎ (01803) 391415

www.torbay.gov.uk/cliffrailway

One of Devon's two cliff railways drops steeply down to Oddicombe beach. Open: 9.30–5pm Easter to

Whitsun; 9.30–5.30pm Whitsun to
end Sep.

## Torquay Museum

Babbacombe Road TQ1 1HG

☎ (01803) 293975

www.torquaymuseum.org

Many artefacts from Kent's Cavern
are here as well as folk life displays
and Victoriana. Open: 10am–5pm
Mon to Sat all year. Sun 1.30–5pm
mid-July to Sept.

℗ (On Street)  ♿  ♔ <Child Rate  ☂

## Bygones

Fore Street, Torquay TQ1 4PR

☎ (01803) 326108

www.bygones.co.uk

Look back in time through recreated
street scenes, domestic interiors and
World War I trench.  Model railway
and miniature fantasyland. Open:
10am–6pm, daily Apr to Oct; 10am–
4pm daily, Nov to Jan; 10am–4pm
daily,Feb and Mar.

☂

## Torre Abbey

Kings Drive, Torquay TQ2 5JE

☎ (01803) 293593

www.torre-abbey.org.uk

Interesting complex of buildings
including a tithe barn. Torquay's
art collections are housed in the
eighteenth-century mansion. Open:
Every day, 10am–6pm Mar to Oct;
10am–5pm Nov to Feb.

℗  ♿  ♔ <18 Child Rate  ☂

## Kirkham House (E. H.)

Paignton

Fourteenth-century priest's house.
Open: on selected days from Easter
to end of Aug including every
Sunday in Jul and Aug 2–5pm.

## Oldway

TQ3 2TE

☎ (01803) 201201

An enormous mansion modelled on
Versailles and paid for by the money
made by the Singer sewing machine
family. Open: 8.30am–5.30pm Mon to
Thu,  9.30am–4.15pm, Fri, all year.
☂

## Paignton Zoo

TQ4 7EU

☎ (01803) 697500

www.paigntonzoo.co.uk

Devon's largest collection of exotic
birds and animals. Open: from 10am
daily, all year.

## Paignton and Dartmouth Steam Railway

Torbay Road, Paignton TQ4 6AF

☎ (01803) 555872

www.paignton-steamrailway.co.uk

A scenic, privately-operated steam
railway run on authentic GWR
principles. Also sea-train trip. Open:
Steam trains run Easter bank
holidays, most days in Apr, May and
Oct; daily from Jun to Sep.

♿  ♔ <Child Rate  ☂

## Splashdown@Quaywest

Goodrington Sands TQ4 6LN

# Places to Visit

*Gardens at Coleton Fishacre, National Trust*

☎ (01803) 555550
www.splashdownquaywest.co.uk
Large outdoor waterpark plus other amusements for all the family.
Open: 10am–6pm daily, Late May to Oct. Shorter hours for the water attractions depending on the season.

## Compton Castle (N.T.)

Marldon TQ3 1TA
☎ (01803) 661906
Splendidly restored medieval castle with impressive defensive works.
Open: 11am–5pm Mon, Wed and Thu, Apr to late Oct.
☂

## Berry Pomeroy Castle (E.H.)

Nr Totnes TQ9 6LJ
☎ (01803) 866618
www.english-heritage.org.uk/berrypomeroy
A slightly spooky ruined mansion within the remains of a medieval castle. Open to the public. Open:

10am–5pm daily, Apr to Sep (until 6pm Jul and Aug); 10am–4pm in Oct.
Ⓟ 👪 <Child Rate ☂

## Berry Head Country Park

Brixham TQ5 9AL
Spectacular limestone cliff scenery and birdlife. Wide ranging views, lighthouse and coastguard station. Interesting remains of huge Napoleonic fort.

## Brixham Heritage Museum

Bolton Cross, Brixham
☎ (01803) 856267
www.brixhonheritage.org.uk
Tells the story of Brixham. Open: 10am–4pm Tue to Fri, 10am–1pm on Sat, Easter to Oct.
Ⓟ ♿ (Ground Floor Only)
👪 <Family Ticket ☂

## Golden Hind

Brixham quayside
☎ (01803) 856223

www.goldenhinde.co.uk
Open: normally 10am–4pm Mar to Oct.

## Coleton Fishacre House and Garden (N.T.)

TQ6 0EQ

☎ (01803) 752466

House designed for the D'Oyly Carte family in the Arts and Crafts tradition and a well-wooded coastal garden with a stream. Open: 10.30am–5pm Wed to Sun, Mar to Oct; Sat and Sun only Feb.

## Day Mark

Kingswear
Prominent hollow stone navigational aid from 1860s.

## Inner Froward Point Gun Battery (N.T.)

Kingswear
Well-preserved survivor from World War II in beautiful pine tree and cliff setting.

# Dartmouth and Totnes

## Dartmouth Museum

The Butterwalk TQ6 9PZ

☎ (01803) 832923

www.devonmuseums.net/dartmouth
A small but fascinating collection of memorabilia connected with the town, in the Butterwalk, a listing building. Open: 10am–4pm Mon to Sat, Apr to Oct; noon–3pm Mon to Sat, Nov to Mar. Closed Christmas

Day & New Years Day.
👫 <18 Child Rate ☂

## Newcomen Engine

Dartmouth, Tourist Information Centre TQ6 9YY

☎ (01803) 834224

Thomas Newcomen produced the first industrial steam engine, and was born in Dartmouth. A beam engine based on his principles is preserved here. Open: 9.30am–5.30pm daily (Sun 11.30am–4.30pm) in summer. Of little interest to young children.
👫 <FREE ☂

## St Saviour's Church

Dartmouth
Notable for its splendid 1633 west gallery.

## Dartmouth Castle (E.H.)

Castle Road TQ6 OJN

☎ (01803) 833588

www.englishheritage.org.uk/dartmouth
A stern estuary-mouth castle containing within its walls a church having several memorial brasses. Open: 10am–5pm daily, Apr to Oct (until 6pm Jul and Aug); 10am–4pm Oct; 10am–4pm Sat and Sun, Nov to Mar. Of little interest to under 7s.
℗ 👫 <Child Rate ☂

## Gallants Bower (N.T.)

Dartmouth
A hilltop earthwork, dating from the Civil War.

# Places to Visit

## Royal Naval College Britannia

Dartmouth TQ6 OHJ

☎ (01803) 677787

Royal Navy officers' training college and Museum. Open: from 2pm most Sat, Sun and Wed from Easter to Oct. Of little interest to under 7s.

††† <Family Ticket ☂

## Devonshire Collection of Period Costume

43 High Street, Totnes TQ9 5NP

☎ (01803) 862857

A well-displayed collection of clothing through the ages.
Open: 11am–5pm Mon to Fri, late May to Sep.

Ⓟ (Town Parking) ††† <Child Rate ☂

## Leech Wells

Totnes

Cleaning troughs for local lepers in medieval times.

## Totnes Castle (E.H.)

☎ (01803) 864406

www.english-heritage.org.uk/totnescastle

A small but perfect Norman keep

Dartmouth Castle

stands beside the inner bailey. Open: 10am–5pm daily, Apr to Sep (until 6pm Jul and Aug); 10am–4pm Oct.

Ⓟ ††† <16 Child Rate

## Totnes Guildhall

Castle Street TQ9 5HQ

☎ (01803) 862147

Built 1533. Open to the public. Open: 10.30am–1.30pm and 2–4.30pm Mon to Fri.

☂

## Totnes Museum

70 Fore Street TQ9 5RU

☎ (01803) 863821

devonmuseums.net/totnes

Excellent local history museum in a half-timbered building. Special room devoted to Charles Babbage, the father of British computer science, who lived in Totnes. Open: 10.30am–5pm Mon to Fri, Apr to Oct. Of little interest to children.

††† <Child Rate ☂

## Woodlands Leisure Park

TQ9 7DG

☎ (01803) 712598

www.woodlandspark.com

Indoor and outdoor playzones for all ages. Rides, toboggan run and falconry centre. Open: From 9.30am daily, mid-Mar to Nov.

☂

## Dartington Cider Press Centre

Shinner's Bridge TQ9 6TQ

☎ (01803) 847500

www.dartingtonciderpress.co.uk

The retail side of the Dartington Hall enterprise. Fifteen shops, restaurants & workshops. Open: 9.30am–5.30pm Mon to Sat 10am–5pm Sun all year.

ⓟ ＆ ᴪ <FREE ☂

## Dartington Hall

Dartington Totnes TQ9 6EL
☎ (01803) 847100
www.dartingtonhall.com
A medieval estate rescued by two idealists in an attempt to revive the many-sided activities of country life.

ⓟ ＆ ᴪ <FREE

# Around South Hams

## Slapton Ley Field Centre

TQ7 2QP
The base for natural science and bird research in South Devon. Two nature trails are marked out nearby.

## Slapton Sands American Memorial

Commemorates the use of the area by Americans in World War II for battle practice.

## Hallsands Ruined Village

A row of cottages between the beach and the cliff demolished by a storm in 1917.

## Start Point Lighthouse

☎ (01803) 770606
Significant feature on the South Devon coastline.

## Cookworthy Museum

108 Fore Street, Kingsbridge TQ7 1AW
☎ (01548) 853235
www.kingsbridgemuseum.org
Celebrates the work of W. Cookworthy, discoverer of china clay, born in Kingsbridge. Displays of agricultural and domestic items. Open: 10.30am–5pm Mon to Sat, Apr to Sep; 10.30am–4pm Mon to Sat in Oct.

＆ (Ground Floor Only) ᴪ <Family Ticket ☂

## Sorley Tunnel Adventure Worlds

North of Kingsbridge TQ7 4BP
☎ (01548) 8540708
Open: 10am–6pm, Easter to Oct, weekends in winter.

## Overbecks House & Gardens (N.T.)

Salcombe TQ8 8LW
☎ (01548) 842893
Maritime miscellany and beautiful gardens in memorable surroundings. Open: Museum – times vary. Garden – 10am–5.30pm (dusk if earlier) daily all year.

## Salcombe Maritime and Local History Museum

Market Street TQ8 8DE
☎ (01548) 842522
www.devonmuseums.net
A local history museum with details of the World War II training area at Slapton. Open: 10.30am–12.30pm and 2.30–4.30pm Easter to Oct, daily.

ᴪ <12 FREE ☂

# 3. Plymouth and District

The city of Plymouth has one of the finest natural sites in Britain, and ranks with Edinburgh, Bath, Cambridge and Bristol for position and historic interest. Although tucked away in one corner of Devon, its influence has been felt far and wide. This is exemplified by its having given its name to forty other Plymouths throughout the world. The deep, wide and fast-flowing waters of the River Tamar effectively prevented much westwards expansion of Plymouth into Cornwall, so that it is only in the last 150 years or so since the railway bridges were built across the Tamar and Tavy that Saltash, and to a lesser extent, Bere Alston, Calstock and Gunnislake have come under the influence of Plymouth.

The city pushed north and east, to Crownhill (where the massive fort, built in the 1860s, is the finest of Plymouth's Victorian fortifications) and Roborough, Plympton St Mary and Plympton St Maurice, Plymstock, El- burton and Wembury. More recently, the growth in car ownership has pushed Plymouth's sphere of influence out to Tavistock in the north and Ivybridge in the east, and the Tamar road bridge has made commuting possible from

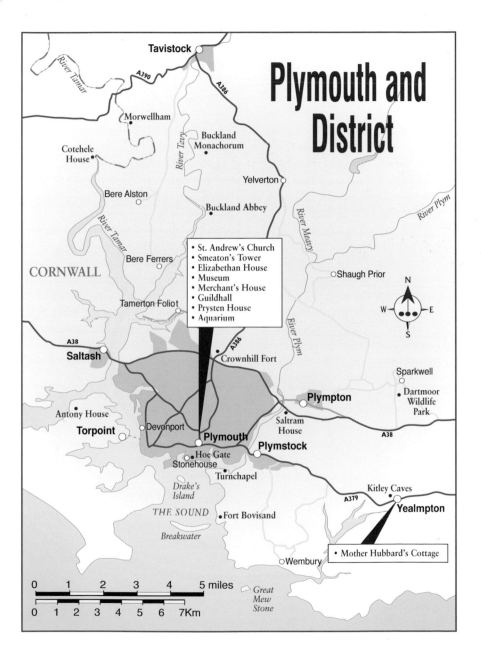

Tavistock

*River Tamar*

A390

A386

Morwellham

Buckland
Monachorum

Cotehele
House

*River Tavy*

Yelverton

Bere Alston

Buckland Abbcy

*River Meavy*

*River Plym*

CORNWALL

*River Tamar*

Bere Ferrers

Shaugh Prior

- St. Andrew's Church
- Smeaton's Tower
- Elizabethan House
- Museum
- Merchant's House
- Guildhall
- Prysten House
- Aquarium

Tamerton Foliot

N

W        E

S

*River Plym*

A38

A386

Saltash

Crownhill Fort

Sparkwell

Plympton

Dartmoor
Wildlife
Park

Antony House

Devonport

Saltram
House

A38

Torpoint

Plymouth

Plymstock

Hoe Gate

Stonehouse

Kitley Caves

Turnchapel

A379

Yealmpton

*Drake's
Island*

*THE SOUND*

Fort Bovisand

- Mother Hubbard's Cottage

*Breakwater*

Wembury

# Plymouth and District

0   1   2   3   4   5 miles

0  1  2  3  4  5  6  7Km

*Great
Mew
Stone*

deep into east Cornwall.

Just across the water, at **Mount Batten**, much evidence was turned up early last century of an Iron Age and Roman settlement, perhaps lasting for a thousand years. The diversity of artefacts discovered indicates another trading settlement. The name Stonehouse for a district west of the present central city area may have first been given to a masonry structure discovered by the wood-building Saxons, who found it sufficiently unusual to accord it the permanence of a place name, and Romans are the most likely builders.

There are other equally hazy descriptions of Roman and Dark Age settlement, but what is undisputed is the development of medieval Plymouth round Sutton Harbour and the area to the north-west. St Andrew's Church on the present Royal Parade is an ancient foundation, and Old Town Street nearby has an early origin; so the Plymouth of the Middle Ages should be sought in the arc encompassed by the mouth of Sutton Harbour, behind New Street to St Andrew's Church, north to Old Town Street and back to the waterfront on the east side of Sutton Harbour.

At **Plympton**, a few miles to the east, a castle was built by the Norman Richard de Redvers, and it was a stannary town in medieval times. (Here the tin from the south-west side of Dartmoor was weighed and stamped – coigned – before being sold. *Stannum* is the Latin word for tin.) Plympton itself was two settlements – Plympton St Maurice and Plympton St Mary – and the difference is markedly discernible still. Plympton also had a priory.

One of the reasons for the growth of Sutton (Plymouth) at the expense of Plympton was the silting up of the Plym Estuary, a change brought about partly by the activities of the tin streamers on Dartmoor. So the material that contributed to Plympton's growth worked against it in another way.

Plymouth, however, being nearer the open sea, was more vulnerable to raids, and in 1403 a large French force attacked the town and burnt 600 houses. The event is remembered in the name Bretonside, at the bus station site. The inhabitants asked for a wall to be built round the town, and this was eventually done; nothing of it remains to be seen today, although the names of the gates remain: Old Town Gate and Hoe Gate, for instance. One end of the wall was built against Plymouth Castle, and that too has all but disappeared. A remnant survives in Castle Street. The name Barbican, now widely applied to the area of New Street and Southside Street, is derived from a part of this castle.

The part of Plymouth known by Drake and his captains, and, later, by the Pilgrim Fathers sailing on the *Mayflower* (1620) was, therefore, Sutton. Plymouth sided with Parliament in the Civil War and suffered a three-year siege. It was King William, who had landed at Brixham in 1688 as William of Orange, who sanctioned the building of the dockyard on virgin land fronting the Tamar Estuary, where it is called the Hamoaze.

This immediately pulled development across the intervening land and Stonehouse grew, as it was situated halfway between the growing town of Dock and Plymouth itself. During the Napoleonic Wars the upstart

Dock (32,000 people) outstripped its neighbour Plymouth (22,000) and Stonehouse (6,000), and in 1824 was granted the dignity of the name **Devonport**. The column in Ker Street (to be noticed later) was erected to mark the event. Nearer our own time, in 1914, the so-called 'Three Towns' were amalgamated into one municipal authority to become Plymouth. The city suffered disastrous air raids in World War II, and much of the middle was destroyed. St Andrew's Church and the Guildhall were both gutted, but have been rebuilt.

# A walk around Plymouth

Instead of wandering aimlessly round Plymouth (or indeed any town!) it is a good plan to get one's bearings, perhaps by visiting a high building or some prominent landmark. In Plymouth's case stand where Armada Way intersects Royal Parade, with your back to the main shopping area.

In front, **Armada Way** rises gently up to the Hoe with the Naval War Memorial prominent in the view. About halfway up is the massive anchor, which once belonged to the *Ark Royal*, and beside where you are standing is the civic flagstaff, a shaft rising from a replica of Drake's Drum. The unveiling of this memorial in 1947 by the king marked the start of the rebuilding of the new Plymouth. On the left is the **Guildhall**, dating from 1873, but gutted in 1941 and rebuilt after the war, somewhat altered.

**St Andrew's Church** is the largest parish church in Devon, and, as it stands, is a post-war restoration. Only the stonework remained, and for several years it was used as a garden church before completion in 1957. It possesses some very striking modern stained glass, which may not be to everyone's taste.

Leaving the church through the south door, the **Prysten House** is opposite. The foundation of this, the oldest building remaining in Plymouth, is unknown, but a record listing a rent in 1490 is extant. The priests from Plympton Priory were probably accommodated here while ministering at the church. Stoutly built of local limestone, it contains a variety of unusual features, as well as sundry relics on show from elsewhere in the city. The carved bishop's throne and the model of Plymouth as it looked in 1620 are items of more than usual interest. Notice the **Plymouth tapestry**, 28ft/8.5m long, which was executed by a team of volunteer workers, depicting the life and times of the Prysten House.

Leaving the Prysten House, turn right and right again to see the **Merchant's House** in St Andrew's Street. This sixteenth-century four-storied town house is the best example in Plymouth of a well-to-do entrepreneur's dwelling. William Parker, an Elizabethan privateer, merchant and mayor of Plymouth, was living in the house in 1608. The house is now a museum of early Plymouth history.

Walk down St Andrew's Street, left into Notte Street and right into Southside Street, where on the right is the **Black Friars Distillery** building, owned by the Coates Gin Co. This seems to have been a friary long before Coates Gin Co came on the

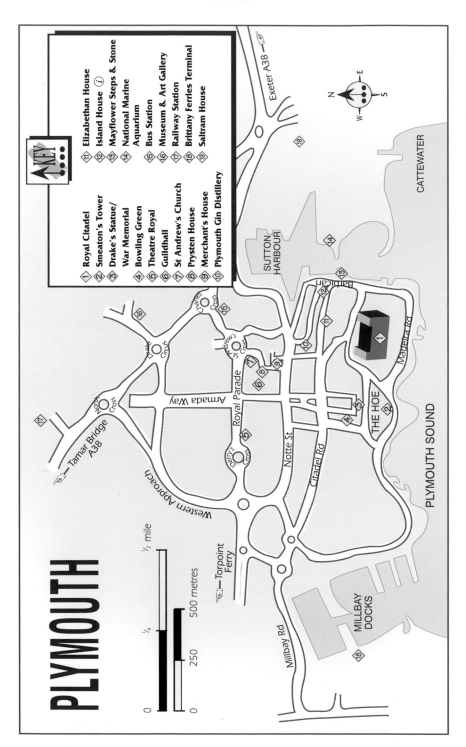

# PLYMOUTH

KEY

1. Royal Citadel
2. Smeaton's Tower
3. Drake's Statue/ War Memorial
4. Bowling Green
5. Theatre Royal
6. Guildhall
7. St Andrew's Church
8. Prysten House
9. Merchant's House
10. Plymouth Gin Distillery
11. Elizabethan House
12. Island House (i)
13. Mayflower Steps & Stone
14. National Marine Aquarium
15. Bus Station
16. Museum & Art Gallery
17. Railway Station
18. Brittany Ferries Terminal
19. Saltram House

Exeter A38

CATTEWATER

SUTTON HARBOUR

Barbican

Madeira Rd

THE HOE

PLYMOUTH SOUND

Armada Way

Royal Parade

Notte St

Citadel Rd

Tamar Bridge A38

Western Approach

Torpoint Ferry

MILLBAY DOCKS

Millbay Rd

½ mile
¼
0

500 metres
250
0

scene in 1793, and the refectory, with a fine arch-braced timber roof, is open to the public.

Southside Street, with its neat lamps bracketed to the shop fronts, is a pleasant busy street with shops selling secondhand books, antique prints, the better type of gifts, and there are several restaurants and public houses. It once looked directly out on Sutton Harbour. The north side of the street, with its 'opes' (an opening onto a waterfront)

breaking it up into small blocks, was built later.

Now follow the quay round the western side of **Sutton Harbour**. The early nineteenth-century **Customs House** faces the old Customs House of the Tudor period, now given over to other uses. A few steps along New Street stands the **Elizabethan House**, a half-timbered house which is now open as part of the Plymouth Museum Service. It once belonged to an Elizabethan sea

Plympton St Maurice church and old grammar school

captain and the rooms are furnished in appropriate period style. Almost opposite and overlooking Sutton Harbour is the **Barbican Visitor Information Centre**, and, in the same building, the **Plymouth Mayflower**. This interactive exhibition tells the history of Plymouth, especially the coming of the Spanish Armada and the voyage of the Pilgrim Fathers to America on board *Mayflower*.

Across the way from here is **Island House**, a building standing on its own, dating from about 1590, where tradition says some of the pilgrims lodged prior to their departure for North America. A board on the outside wall lists those who sailed aboard the *Mayflower*.

A short walk across the mouth of Sutton Harbour leads to the **National Marine Aquarium,** the largest in Gt Britain with deepest tank in Europe. Here the living wonders of the ocean are revealed, with opportunities to talk to experts about the creatures on view, learn about marine conservation, watch divers feeding the fish by hand and see sharks at very close quarters.

---

## Mayflower Stone

Beyond the market building is the **Mayflower Stone**, one of several memorials to great events which have started from this spot. The Union flag and the Stars and Stripes fly over this shrine, marking the departure point of the Pilgrim Fathers in 1620. Other events remembered are the sailing of the *Tory* in 1839 on an early migrant trip to New Zealand, and the return of the Tolpuddle Martyrs a year earlier, who had been transported to Australia for daring to form a trade union.

---

Behind Island House is **New Street**, an attractive narrow cobbled highway, 'new' only because it came after other parts of old Plymouth. New Street is interesting as the actual stone road surface is 'listed', being of historic importance. Its builder was John Sparke, the first Englishman to describe tobacco and the potato. The original carved door frames are on Nos 34, 35, 37 and 38, and No. 32 is an Elizabethan house. This original house of about 1584 was well restored from near dereliction in 1926, New Street having slipped from its former eminence as a residential area of merchants to become a street of warehouses. The house is very sympathetically furnished with pieces of the period. Notice the ship's mast round which the spiral staircase wraps itself. A rope steadies anyone using the stairs, another nautical touch. Through No. 40 is a pleasant little garden behind, where plants known to have been cultivated in Tudor times are grown.

At the foot of New Street, Madeira Road has the last remaining ruin of old Plymouth Castle on the right, beneath the massive walls of the **Royal Citadel** (1666), still used as barracks for the Royal Marines. Guided tours take visitors round the walls at certain times. The baroque gateway is considered the finest in Britain.

In the opposite direction, the **Cattewater**, the actual mouth of the Plym, is where Drake's fleet anchored. Beyond, the radio masts stand on **Staddon Heights** and the wall on the top is the 'safety curtain' of a rifle range. Round the corner, **Plymouth Breakwater** comes into view. This immense civil engineering project made Plymouth a much safer port, especially in the days of sail, though paradoxically, when it was completed in 1847, having been 35 years in the making, powered ships were beginning to be built. It is almost a mile long and contains 3,620,440 tons of local limestone.

Until it was destroyed in the Plymouth blitz, the 1884 promenade pier jutted out from the Hoe and provided a venue for concerts and dancing. On the Hoe itself, an elevated promenade gives views one way to the sea, and the other along the 3/4 mile (1km) Armada Way. **The Hoe** gives the finest view of Plymouth Sound, which, with the Thames at London and the Dover Strait, is the most evocative maritime landscape in Great Britain. from here, have begun and ended countless epic voyages, from the naval task force against the Armada to the more recent task force to the Falklands.

Many visitors over the years were saddened to see the lido on the Hoe fall derelict. Originally built in 1935 but falling into disuse in the 1980s, it acquired listed status in 1998. Now a £3.4 million refurbishment has taken place and the Art Deco **Tinside Lido** is open for swimmers once more. Even if you are not brave enough to swim outdoors in the British climate it is well worth a visit to admire the restoration of one of the few lidos left in Britain.

An even better view can be enjoyed from the top of **Smeaton's Tower**, the Eddystone Lighthouse of 1759, which was superseded in 1882 by Douglass's present lighthouse. On a clear day the tower can be seen on its rock 14 miles (22km) out at sea. The cramped living quarters will perhaps surprise the visitor.

Also on the Hoe is the enormous **Naval War Memorial**, surmounted by a dented globe. The damage was caused by a barrage balloon in World War II. Around its base are the names of 22,443 men who lost their lives in both wars There are other monuments; the **National Armada Memorial**, one to the Boer War, while the jaunty figure of Sir Francis Drake looks out to sea, a copy statue of one at Tavistock, his birthplace. Not far away, probably where the Royal Citadel was later built, he is supposed to have been playing bowls when the Armada was spotted. 'Time enough to finish our game, and beat the Spaniards', he is supposed to have replied, knowing that wind and tide didn't allow his fleet to leave port in any case!

To return to the starting point on Royal Parade, walk north to Citadel Road. Turn left here, and follow Citadel Road to Millbay Road. On the corner is a Victorian Gothic extravaganza, the **Duke of Cornwall Hotel**, dating from 1865. Though hardly beautiful,

## Drake's Island

**Drake's Island**, a kind of English Alcatraz, narrows the navigable channel up to the Dockyard. From being St Nicholas' Island in medieval times, it became known as Drake's Island when he was appointed island governor and began to fortify it. The island remained in military occupation until 1956, and was used as a prison for a few years after 1669. Some truly enormous muzzle-loading guns of late nineteenth-century vintage were recently discovered, buried under rubble at the top.

# Devon

*The Merchant's House, Plymouth*

*The Drake and Navy War Memorials, The Hoe, Plymouth*

*Plymouth Barbican*

*Plymouth Guildhall*

it is enormously impressive and has managed to survive German bombs and developers' bulldozers: its roof is crowned by a château turret.

Opposite is the site of the old Millbay Station (opened 1849, closed 1941). In the great days of transatlantic sea travel, ships from the USA would put in to Plymouth Sound, to land those passengers in a hurry to reach London, before resuming their journey up Channel. A few years ago the area was given a new lease of life when Britanny Ferries developed their roll-on roll-off car ferry terminal on the western side of Millbay Dock by the enormous disused grain silo. Ships leave for Roscoff (France) and Santander (Spain). Millbay Road leads one back to Royal Parade.

Nearby is the distinctive architecture

## The Plymouth Coastline

The best way to get to know Plymouth's dissected coastline is to take a boat trip as far as possible up the Tamar. The point where the boat turns back will depend on the tide, but if it reaches as far as Weir Head or Morwellham, the trip will take 5 or 6 hours. Other cruises go outside Plymouth Sound past the Breakwater and the Great Mew Stone to the Yealm Estuary. (Boats leave from the Phoenix Wharf just outside Sutton Harbour.)

of **Plymouth Pavilions**, an all-purpose recreational complex for all the family. An ice rink, pool, several restaurants and a huge auditorium make it a versatile resource in bad weather.

The **Plymouth City Museum and Art Gallery,** by Drake Circus, occupies one of the few buildings in the city to survive the bombing. Its collections are strong on Plymouth porcelain, Plymouth silver, paintings by local artists including Sir Joshua Reynolds, and local archaeological finds are well represented.

# Touring Plymouth by car

There are other parts of the city visitors should see, with a car or by using the local bus service. A good street map of the area, including Plympton to the east, will help.

The first of the mini-tours should be to Western King Point through Stonehouse. At the end of Union Street (built in 1815 to unite the Three Towns, and the destination for thirsty sailors

when they come ashore, though its disjointed and disfigured building line betrays the damage inflicted during the war), at a roundabout, turn left into Durnford Street, a road of elegant early nineteenth-century houses whose rear elevations are in many cases as attractive as the fronts. Some of these houses were occupied by retired sea captains who had balconies and large windows built at the back to give views over the Hamoaze.

On the left are the **Royal Marine Barracks** and the 1830 church of St George and St Paul, designed by John Foulston. Follow the road to its termination at a car park overlooking Firestone Bay. To the right, on a disused gun emplacement is **Western King Point**, with superb views across to Mount Edgcumbe Country Park (in Cornwall), and left to the Hoe and right towards the Dockyard. At the back of Firestone Bay is an artillery tower dating from Henry VIII's reign and now a restaurant. At low tide the shallow stretch of water between Drake's Island and the slopes of Mount Edgcumbe can be seen. This is known as the Bridge, and was made even shallower during World War II to prevent enemy penetration to the Dockyard by that route.

The channel is narrowest opposite Devil's Point, and the largest ships have to choose the right moment – high slack tide and quiet airs – before passing through the Narrows. This is complicated by tight turns before and after negotiating the constricting passage.

The **Royal William Victualling Yard** (named after King William IV, whose 13½ft (5m) statue surmounts the main entrance) is a complex of 14 acres

(5.5 hectares), designed by Sir John Rennie, who was also responsible for Plymouth Breakwater. Along Cremyll Street the rear of Durnford Street is visible, passing the **Cremyll foot ferry** on the way. A day roaming the slopes of Mount Edgcumbe (Cornwall) is well spent.

Back at the roundabout, one should turn left, heading for Devonport, and left again by the Old Chapel into **Ker Street**. The bottom end is ordinary enough, with post-war flats on either side, but at the top is an odd collection of buildings. The classical **Doric Guildhall** of 1825, even more massive than most Doric buildings, faces down the street with the strange **Egyptian Oddfellows Hall** (1823) to one side. Behind is the 125ft (44m) column marking the change of name from Plymouth Dock to Devonport (1824). These eclectic buildings were all designed by John Foulston, the architect who had such an influence on early nineteenth-century Plymouth. A Calvinist chapel employing eastern motifs formerly stood between the Column and the Egyptian building, but has disappeared. They look forlorn now, surrounded by late twentieth-century run-of-the-mill local authority housing, but at least we have a hint of the civic pride responsible for their construction 180 years ago.

These forays into selected parts of Plymouth do not by any means exhaust the interest of this fine city. Because so much is owned by HM Government, such places as the Dockyard, Stonehouse Hospital, the King William Yard and the Citadel are not usually open to the public, but the Dockyard, for instance, may be open one day a year for what used to be called Plymouth Navy Day: some ships may be visited.

# Around Plymouth

Further afield, about 4 miles (6km) east of the heart of Plymouth, is the delightful small town of **Plympton St Maurice**, older than the city, but now a sleepy backwater. A castle was built here not long after the Norman Conquest, and a settlement grew up nearby. Plympton Grammar School, built in 1664 and restored in 1870, is remarkable for the painters it has produced. England's finest portrait painter, Sir Joshua Reynolds, was educated here, as well as James Northcote, Benjamin Haydon and Charles Eastlake.

The town, particularly Fore Street, is unspoilt. The Guildhall juts out over the pavement, not unlike the Guildhall at Exeter, and there is a covered Butterwalk, like those at Totnes and Dartmouth. None of the buildings is in the top bracket, but together they make a very pleasing harmonious group.

Not far away is **Saltram House** (National Trust), the largest house in Devon: other superlatives apply equally. Because of Sir Joshua Reynolds' lifelong association with the owners, the Parkers, it contains many paintings by him and is the only complete example in south-west England of Robert Adam's interior design.

The house was begun in the late sixteenth century, but has been considerably changed over the years, the last alteration being in 1820, when John Foulston – whose name we have come across already – added the Doric porch and other exterior refinements.

*Buckland Abbey (National Trust),*
*founded in 1278*

*Saltram House (National Trust), the largest house in Devon*

## What's in a Name?

The origin of the name Saltram is obscure, but it must have a connection with the making of salt, for which purpose its situation beside the Plym Estuary was admirably convenient.

Inside, the rooms that startle and sparkle with eighteenth-century freshness are the saloon and the dining room. The former is a double cube; the latter occupies a corner position. Neither is lit by electricity; both have Axminster carpets reflecting, but not imitating, the delicate design of the ceilings. To stand in these rooms is an unusual experience, for one is literally surrounded by beauty; beneath the feet, above your head, and of course on the walls. All so delicately done as not to be overpowering. Reached from outside is the Great Kitchen, with a variety of old utensils on show.

The gardens are of the informal kind, with trees and shrubs predominating. Near the house is the restored orangery (1775), the chapel (1776) (now an art gallery), and, scattered round the grounds, the castle (1772) and the folly-type structures of Fanny's Bower and the Amphitheatre overlooking the Plym.

Between Saltram and the sea, and occupying the broad peninsula from the Yealm to Plymouth Sound are the suburbs of **Plymstock** and **Elburton** and the sweeping pastures of **Wembury** parish. The best way to explore it is to walk the 6 or 7 miles (9–11km) of the South Devon Coast Path from Turnchapel round to the Yealm Estuary. This can be done by taking one bus to Turnchapel and returning on another from Wembury. (It is best not to rely on the ferry across the Yealm.)

The first major landmark on the circuit is **Stamford Fort**, now used recreationally, but originally built as one of a ring of forts and batteries round Plymouth in response to the threat posed by an increase in French sea power. Dover, Chatham and Portsmouth were similarly defended. They are sometimes referred to as Palmerston Follies, after Lord Palmerston, who set up the Royal Commission in 1859 'to consider the Defences of the United Kingdom'. As he died in 1865, and many of them were built after his death, he can hardly be blamed for the enormous expense of public money. The ring of forts was continued around Plymouth's northern (landward) approaches, and they represent the climax of British castellar architecture. Never again were fortifications on such a heroic scale constructed in Great Britain.

The road above **Jennycliff Bay** is a pleasant scenic drive, but where the road turns inland the coast path continues along the cliff. Soon **Fort Bovisand** is seen below, another of the Palmerston forts and one of the best preserved. From 1970 to 2000 it was used as a training base for underwater activities, and oil rig divers came here to learn their trade. The port at Fort Bovisand was built between 1816 and 1824 to enable ships to take on fresh water without having to go right into the dockyard. A reservoir was built nearby.

The coast path descends to the back of **Bovisand Bay** and stays low for the next mile or so, where the cliffs are virtually non-existent. After Heybrook Bay, a bit of suburbia-by-the-sea, the path passes near where the guns of HMS *Cambridge* used to be. **Wembury** is soon reached.

The village is set back from the coast and largely enveloped in modern development. The church, however, stands boldly on the cliffs and should be visited, as it has some notable monuments and good woodwork. John Galsworthy's ancestors came from Wembury, and he made a pilgrimage here in 1912 – later transferring his own kinship to the fictional Forsyte family. In his *Swan Song*, Soames Forsyte visited a similarly-sited fictional church stated to be in Dorset.

Below the church is the old mill building (National Trust), used as a café in the summer. The Trust land starts here and runs for 1½ miles (2km) to the Yealm, before leap-frogging the estuary to encompass the cliffs beyond, where the Revelstoke Drive acts as a pedestrian marine drive. (This was described towards the end of the previous chapter.)

Inland from Wembury, at **Yealmpton** (pronounced Yampton), is the building known as **Mother Hubbard's Cottage**. This improvident lady is thought to have been the housekeeper at nearby Kitley.

Before leaving the environs of Plymouth an interesting visit can be made to **Crownhill Fort,** just off the Tavistock Road to the north of the city. It is the largest and best preserved of Plymouth's Victorian fortifications. Built in the 1860s it is hidden from outside view but inside there is a complete re-creation of life as it was for the soldiers of that time.

Continuing round the north-eastern outskirts of Plymouth and getting up into the foothills of Dartmoor the visitor will find the **Dartmoor Zoological Park** at Sparkwell. The illusion of animals in their natural setting is obtained by allowing them space and encouraging trees to grow, with a minimum of wire fencing and iron bars, though (obviously) the tigers and wolves are securely enclosed! Visitors are allowed to mix with the more friendly birds and animals.

Just out of Plymouth, up the Plym Valley, are **Plym Bridge Woods** (National Trust). A remarkable survival of woodland, only 3½ miles (5.5km) from the heart of Plymouth, this strip of beautiful varied country is not quite

2 miles (3.2km) long, by half a mile wide, but it contains a truly incredible collection of industrial archaeological interest. The tracks of three old railways – all defunct – may be followed. The Plymouth and Dartmoor Railway was the first, built in 1823 to link the two places by taking lime, sand, timber and coal up to the moor and bringing stone and peat down; horse-drawn trucks were employed. Another horse-drawn tramway passed through the woods as far as Cann quarry, where slate was quarried for the roofs of Plymouth. The railway to Tavistock was the last to be built, and the last to go out of use: it lasted from 1859 to 1962 and crossed the valley by Cann viaduct.

One further relic deserves a mention: **Cann Quarry Canal**, which carried the stone from the quarry before the tramway was built later on its towpath. Deer are often seen in the woods, and adders enjoy the habitat provided by the discarded slabs of slate in the enormous spoil heaps. Devon County Council has negotiated a continuous recreational footpath up the Plym Valley beyond Plym Bridge Woods to link up with the Dartmoor National Park at Shaugh Bridge.

Not far from the village of **Shaugh Prior** and overlapping the National Park boundary are the white heaps belonging to the china clay workings of Lee Moor and Shaugh Moor. This open-cast industry has expanded enormously from small beginnings early last century to the present mammoth undertaking covering several square miles. The tips of waste are the most obvious manifestations of the industry and can be seen from well out at sea on a clear day.

# The Tamar and the Tavy

Once across the north striking A386, an ancient ridgeway, the land dips to the valleys of the Tavy and Tamar, the former a private and wooded river, the latter more open, larger, and carrying on its tidal waters considerable

---

## Granite & China Clay

Granite consists of three main components: feldspar, quartz and mica, and china clay is the product of rotted (kaolinised) feldspar. First the overburden of peat, soil and rock is removed, then high-pressure water jets, called monitors, disintegrate the matrix, and the slurry finds its way to the pit bottom where the sand settles out. The china clay is then carried in suspension to a series of refining and drying plants. Apart from its obvious use in the ceramic industry – china, porcelain, tiles, sanitary ware – china clay is also used in the manufacture of paper; the paper of this book contains a proportion of china clay. Cosmetics, paint, rubber, crayons and many other commodities requiring a filler free from impurities and possessing chemical inertness all use this rare mineral, and Devon and Cornwall have the total United Kingdom reserves. Much is exported. Unfortunately the unsightly waste cannot be backfilled into the gaping pits as none of them have yet been 'bottomed', and this would inhibit future operations.

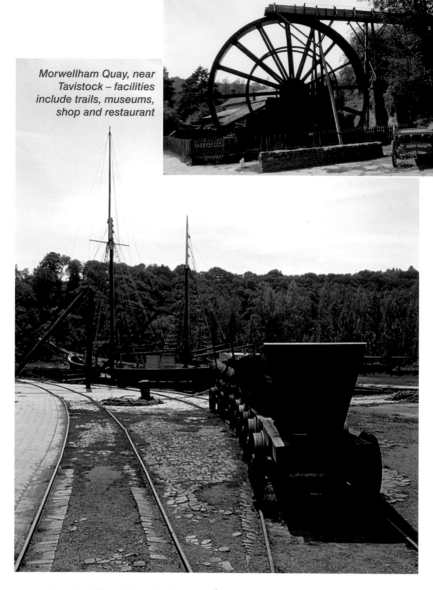

recreational traffic. A hundred years ago much commercial transport used the Tamar also. Both rivers meander sinuously.

The undulating peninsula between the two rivers is occupied by the small town of **Bere Alston** on the top and the ancient parish of **Bere Ferrers** by the estuary edge of the Tavy. The area is still served by a branch railway line from Plymouth, which crosses both rivers by large viaducts and stops at Bere Ferrers and Bere Alston, before terminating in Cornwall at Gunnislake. The line is a delight to use. Communications were always difficult in this hilly landscape, and the rivers were used extensively until the railways arrived. The old quays are peaceful now and pleasant places to while away an hour or two. On the south and west-facing slopes, quantities of strawberries are grown. Bere Ferrers church is one of the most interesting in Devon, with much fourteenth-century work, and a canopied tomb to Sir William de Ferrers and his wife.

# Buckland Abbey

Overlooking the Tavy Valley near Yelverton is Sir Francis Drake's old home, **Buckland Abbey** (National Trust), like the rest of this corner of Devon, a peaceful retreat. Amicia, Countess of Devon, founded the abbey in 1278, and white-robed Cistercian brothers came to Buckland from the Isle of Wight to establish their estate.

At the dissolution the property was initially leased to George Pollard, but in 1541 the king sold the abbey to Sir Richard Grenville. His son, Roger, was the commander of the *Mary Rose* which sank with all hands in the Solent in 1545. The hulk of the ship has now been raised and can be seen during restoration in the Ship Hall in Portsmouth dockyard.

The next two tenants of Buckland Abbey were also to die at sea, notably Sir Richard Grenville (the son of Roger) of the *Revenge*. The buildings in the meantime had been converted into a country house, though their monastic ancestry is obvious. At this point Francis Drake comes on the scene. Born not far away, outside Tavistock, he was looking for a property to match his new-found fame, not far from Plymouth. Grenville was living more at Stowe, just over the North Devon border in Cornwall. There is little doubt that the aristocrat Grenville regarded Drake as an upstart, and would

not have sold the abbey to him direct. Drake knew this and persuaded two intermediaries to purchase the estate and, as Sir Francis, he moved in, aged thirty-six, in 1581; he had already achieved the circumnavigation of the world, but his victory over the Spanish Armada was still seven years away. He died of dysentery on the Spanish Main in 1596, childless. Fortunately his brother Thomas was with him when he died and must have brought home Francis' drum, Drake's Drum, such a treasure from those stirring days, and it is still on view at Buckland Abbey.

Life went on, with the Drake heirs, through Thomas, occupying the abbey. A skirmish occurred there during the Civil War in 1643, and a serious fire, which broke out in 1938, was put out before it did irreparable damage. In 1942 Captain Meyrick put the property on the market. He was the last Drake to live there, his great-grandfather's mother's mother's great-great-great-grandfather being Thomas Drake, brother of the original Sir Francis Drake. The property was bought by Captain Rodd, who gave the estate to the National Trust; after repairs it was opened to the public by Lord Mountbatten in 1951. In 1987/8 it was given a facelift to mark the 400th anniversary of Drake's defeat of the Armada in 1588. At **Buckland Monachorum**, a little way north of the Abbey, the **Garden House** has a magnificent 8-acre (3.5 hectare) garden, one of the best in the county.

# Tavistock

Keeping to the valley of the Tavy, the next place of substance is **Tavistock**, the most attractive, after Totnes, of

Devon's inland towns, its character wrought by the mixture of a good natural site, the presence of certain minerals in commercial quantities, a good building stone, and enterprising landowners.

Tavistock made little impression on history until a Benedictine abbey was established on the banks of the fast-flowing River Tavy near a Saxon *stoc* (a stockade or enclosure) about 974, and this part of the present-day name is the lasting memorial to the early settlement. The abbey became enormously wealthy, and a nearby borough developed, with its own market and fair, and with the discovery of workable quantities of tin on Dartmoor in the twelfth century, Tavistock became one of the three stannary towns on the edge of Dartmoor. (The other two were Ashburton and Chagford; Plympton, a fourth, is off the moor.)

To these towns the tinners brought the metal to be 'coigned' by the assay master. A small piece was struck off the corner of each ingot to test its quality, and the metal was then sold. Tin, however, made but a small impact compared with what was to come later.

When the monasteries were dissolved in 1539, the town and much land nearby was bought by the Russell family, from whom sprang the dukes of Bedford.

The Dartmoor tin was worked out in the early years of the seventeenth century, and Tavistock turned briefly to producing cloth; but this in turn failed. However, copper was fortunately discovered nearby at Mary Tavy in large quantities in the 1790s, and this caused a kind of West Devon 'copper rush'.

More advanced mining techniques now enabled mining to be carried on at a greater depth, where the copper lodes were found.

The Russells, curiously, were no more anxious to exploit this underground wealth than the abbots had been to develop tin; but eventually they submitted to local pressure, and the appearance of Tavistock today is largely derived from the rebuilding they carried out. Tavistock is virtually a nineteenth-century new town.

At first sight, the abbey ruins are disappointingly incomplete, built over and around by later construction. But there are several significant parts visible within 150 yards (136.5m) of Bedford Square. (The name 'Bedford' appears, too, in the name of the hotel, and Woburn Terrace is also a reminder of the Russell era.) **Betsy Grimball's Tower** beside the Bedford Hotel, and the Still **Tower** and abbey wall on the river bank, are the most substantial and unaltered remains. Who Betsy Grimball was, nobody knows. Next to the Post Office is a dining hall, preserved intact though with one end altered, and now a nonconformist place of worship, and the large Gothic gate across the way was the main entrance to the abbey. In the churchyard is a section of late thirteenth-century cloister wall.

Bedford Square is a product of the Victorian age, an expression of civic pride shared by the Duke of Bedford and the citizens. This duke, Francis, now looks straight down his boulevard, Plymouth Road, from his plinthed statue at another more famous Francis, Drake, who stands at the western entrance to the town. Francis Drake is believed to have been born at Crowndale, just outside Tavistock, but while there are no other claimants, proof is lacking.

Beside the Drake statue is the rebuilt gatehouse of the Fitzford estate. Hard by the gatehouse is the Tavistock Canal, on either side of which are many mid-nineteenth century industrial cottages erected by the Duke of Bedford for the miners who flocked into the area with the copper boom. There are others at the north end of Tavistock, and they are a good example of a socially enlightened housing policy.

Dominating the south end of the town is the massive church, given to the town by the duke in 1865, and designed by Henry Clutton, using the pleasantly distinctive green Hurdwick stone in the neo-transitional Romanesque style. Built for Anglican worship, since 1951 it has been the church of the local Roman Catholic congregation. The internal height is loftier than Exeter Cathedral.

# Morwellham

Mention has been made of the Tavistock Canal and the nineteenth-century copper boom. This brings the West Devon story neatly to **Morwellham** (the accent is on the last syllable), a place with a story. There had been a port of sorts at Morwellham for hundreds of years prior to the copper boom of the 1790s. This was the nearest point on the river to Tavistock which seagoing ships could reach, but trade was desultory. Although, as the proverbial crow flies, Morwellham is only 3 miles (5km) from Tavistock, by road the distance is nearer 5 miles (8km), and the 600ft (210m) obstacle of Morwell

Down lies between, as well as the valley of the River Lumburn, no small impediments in the days of horse transport and poor roads. So, when copper was discovered at Wheal Friendship, a mine at Mary Tavy north of Tavistock, in the 1790s, an efficient way of exporting it to the South Wales smelting works had to be devised.

For twenty-seven years Morwellham was moderately prosperous, and then in 1844 much larger quantities of copper were found 5 miles (8km) north at Blanchdown. This became the Devon Great Consols mine, and it was the richest copper mine in Europe for more than ten years. The canal passed nowhere near it, and the roads were still unsuitable for the carriage of quantities of ore, so a standard gauge railway was constructed in 1858 to the top of the hill above the port and a second, larger, inclined plane built alongside the one servicing the canal.

After twenty years of continuous working, the copper lodes began to

## Tavistock Parish Church

The parish church stood on its present site when the abbey was a going concern and served the common people of the neighbourhood. There is an especially good monument to Sir John Glanvill in the Lady Chapel, and the modern William Morris glass in the north-east window is worth a detailed study. Morris' father had made enormous sums of money from investments in copper mines.

# Tavistock–Morwellham Canal

The moving spirit behind the idea of a canal to link Tavistock with Morwellham was John Taylor, a mining engineer in his early twenties and the manager of Wheal Friendship, the mine that so sorely needed relief. He calculated that by taking water off the River Tavy just below the Abbey Bridge at Tavistock, the canal could follow the contours round as far as Morwell Down, through which a tunnel, well over a mile long, could be driven. Then, from a basin at the far end, an inclined plane would take the copper ore down to the busy quays beside the Tamar.

The canal was started in 1803, and simultaneously work began at each end of the tunnel and, to achieve quicker progress, a series of shafts was sunk so that several faces could be worked at once. Even so, the tunnel took 14 years to complete. In the meantime, the canal had been finished from Tavistock to Creber, where the tunnel began, and was in use to that point by 1809.

be exhausted, but a secondary product from the mines came into its own. Arsenic is found in association with copper ores, and had hitherto been little regarded. Now it was suddenly in demand for various commercial and agricultural uses, especially as an insecticide against a cotton pest, the boll weevil. So, arsenic roasting furnaces and flues were built, and thousands of tons exported, in barrels made at Morwellham. By 1901 the mines were abandoned; 236,000 tons of copper had been produced, valued at £3 million. The canal was closed in 1872, never having been able to compete with the railway, which had reached Tavistock in 1859.

Morwellham quietly mouldered away. The docks silted up and became choked with weeds. The tiled quays were stolen, and the inn closed. However, the canal was revived in 1933 to bring water to the Morwellham hydro-electric station.

Then in 1970 Morwellham had life breathed into it again, when work began to restore its buildings, equipment and docks. It became an open-air museum with trails, museums, a shop, restaurant and most exciting of all, a trip underground after a riverside train ride to see what conditions were really like. Morwellham is currently in administration and closed until spring 2010. Please check with local T.I.Cs or the website.

*The New Perseverance Iron Works, Tavistock*

# Places to Visit

## Around Plymouth

### Plympton Castle

Plympton St Maurice
Small well-preserved castle, of the early Norman period.

### Saltram House (N.T.)

Plympton PL7 1UH
☎ (01752) 333500
Devon's stateliest home, containing splendid treasures and beautiful rooms. Open: House – 12-4.30pm Sun to Thu late Mar to end of Oct. Park – all year dawn to dusk.

### Wembury Mill (N.T.)

PL9 0HP
☎ (01752) 862314
Small mill building above Wembury beach, now a summer-only café. Times Vary.
Ⓟ

### Dartmoor Zoological Park

Sparkwell PL7 5DG
☎ (01752) 837645
www.dartmoorzoologicalpark.co.uk
Animals are allowed to roam free in large open paddocks. Open: 10am-6pm summer, 10am-4pm winter.

### Bere Ferrers Church

On the tidal stretch of the River Tavy, one of the most interesting churches in Devon.

### Buckland Abbey (N.T.)

Yelverton PL20 6EY
☎ (01822) 853607
A monastic building, converted to domestic use and once the home of Sir Francis Drake.
Open: House and estate – 10.30am-5.30pm Fri to Wed, late Mar to Oct; daily in Jul & Aug.
☂

### The Garden House

Buckland Monachorum, Yelverton PL20 7LQ
☎ (01822) 854769
www.the gardenhouse.org.uk
Superb walled garden, tea room. Open: 10.30am-5pm daily, Mar to Oct; 11am-3.30pm weekends in Feb.

### Tavistock Canal

A narrow watercourse built to carry copper to Morwellham.

### Morwellham Quay

Tavistock PL19 8JL
☎ (01822) 832766
www.morwellham-quay.co.uk
Nineteenth-century port on the Tamar revived as a recreational and educational attraction. Quays, museum, nature trail with bird hides, shops, and a real mine railway which takes one into a mine. Open: currently in administration, check website or T.I.C.s

### Plym Valley Railway

Plympton PL7 4NW
www.plymrail.co.uk
Open: 1-4pm Sun, Easter to Sep. Trains run on selected days only.

# Places to Visit

## The New Perseverance Iron Works

Pixon Lane, Tavistock
☎ (01822) 615960/854108
Open: 11am-5pm, Sat and other times by appointment.
Steam Fair, normally 1st Sunday in June; Heritage Open Days over 2 days in September.

# Plymouth

## Plymouth City Museum & Art Gallery

PL4 4AG
☎ (01752) 304774
Porcelain, silver, paintings by Reynolds, archaeological finds. Open: 10am-5.30pm Tue to Fri, 10am-5pm Sat and bank holiday Mon. Closed 2008 for refurbishment.

## Plymouth Mayflower

3, The Barbican PL1 2LS
☎ (01752) 306330
www.plymouth.gov.uk
Open: 9am-5pm Mon to Sat, 10am-4pm Sun, Apr to Oct; 9am-5pm, Mon to Fri, 10am-4pm Sat, Nov to Mar.
& ﬁ﬙﬙<Family Ticket 🔆

## Plymouth Pavilions

Millbay Road PL1 3LF
☎ 0845 146 1460
www.plymouthpavilions.com
An all-the-family recreation complex, with ice rink, pool and huge auditorium.
Ⓟ & ﬁ﬙﬙<Family Ticket 🔆

## Elizabethan House

Barbican PL1 2NA
☎ (01752) 304774
A well-preserved 1584 house in New Street, suitably furnished. Open: 10am-5pm Tue to Sat and B.H. Mons, Apr to Sep.
🔆

## National Marine Aquarium

Rope Walk, PL4 OLF
☎ (01752) 600301
www.national-aquarium.co.uk
Opened in 1998, state-of-the-art display of life in the marine environments of the world. Open: daily all year, 10am-5pm in winter; 10am-6pm in summer.
& ﬁ﬙﬙<Family Ticket 🔆

## Merchant's House

33 St Andrew Street PL4 4AJ
☎ (01752) 304774
Well-restored house, now a museum of old Plymouth. Open: 10am-5pm Tue to Sat, from Apr to end of Sep.
🔆

## Black Friars Distillery

Southside Street PL1 2LQ
☎ (01752) 665292
The remains of a friary incorporated into the premises, tours available. Open: 10am-5.30pm Mon to Fri; 10am-5.30pm Sat; 11am-4pm Sun.
🔆

## Plymouth Guildhall

Interestingly restored hub of Plymouth's public life.

## Tinside Lido

The Hoe, Plymouth
☎ (01752) 261915
Art Deco lido, fully restored with fountains. Open: 12noon-6pm weekdays, 10am-6pm weekends, late May to early July; 10am-6pm daily, early July to mid Sep. Late swims 6-7.30pm Wed.

## Smeaton's Tower

The Hoe PL1 2NZ
☎ (01752) 304774
An earlier Eddystone Lighthouse re-erected on Plymouth Hoe. Good views from the top. Open: 10am-4.30pm, Tue to Fri, 10am-4pm Sat and B.H. Mons, Apr to Sep; 3pm Tue-Sat and B.H. Mons Oct to Mar (closed for lunch 12-1pm)

## Prysten House

Finewell Street PL1 2AD
☎ (01752) 661414
Plymouth's oldest building, containing many interesting relics. Open: 10am-4pm Mon to Sat, Apr to Oct.
☂

Royal Citadel
Madeira Road
☎ (01752) 775841
Still garrisoned, but guided tours round battlements at certain times. Open: for guided tours only. 2.30pm Tue and Thu, May to September.

## St Andrew's Church

Devon's largest parish church, gutted in the war, now restored.

## Theatre Royal

Royal Parade PL1 2TR
☎ (01752) 267222 (Box Office)
www.theatreroyal.com
Opened in 1982, it provides splendid entertainment in comfortable surroundings.

## Ker Street

Devonport
Interesting buildings relating to Devonport's past.

## Crownhill Fort (Landmark Trusl)

Off Tavistock Road PL6 5BX
☎ (01752) 793754
www.crownhillfort.co.uk
Nineteenth-century cannons, barrack rooms, parade ground. Regular events depicting Victorian military life. Open on events days only, telephone or check website for details.

# 4. Dartmoor

Dartmoor is not only the last great wilderness in southern England. For some it is the place for an afternoon car ride or coach trip. The more energetic walk many miles across its open solitudes. Criminals have a special understanding of 'the moor'. Soldiers train on it, foresters plant it with trees, and water engineers regard its high rainfall as a valuable natural resource waiting to be impounded. Farmers try to increase its productivity.

These different objectives reflect the variety of interest within Dartmoor. From vast tracts of moorland, where one is further from a road than anywhere else in Great Britain south of Northumbria, to deep-cut tree-clothed valleys, here is a mysterious, often mist-shrouded upland which at first sight may seem forbidding, empty and bleak, but which has a treasury of natural features and prehistoric and historic remains, bewildering in their diversity. Here, too, is the highest land in England south of the Peak District.

The Dartmoor tors (the word is derived from the same root which gives us 'tower') probably stick most in the mind, although they tend to occur only locally, in clusters as it were – there are about 200 on the moor. They are mostly of granite, though a few of metamorphic or altered rock can be found on the moorland fringe. They represent the obstinately harder cores of solidified igneous material that pushed up beneath an overlay of other rock, all of which has eroded away in the 300 million years since the molten matter hardened into granite. The erosion of ages has produced rock piles of curious appearance. **Bowerman's Nose**, near Manaton, is a totally natural feature, which looks rather like an Easter Island figure. As other tors have weathered, their constituent boulders rock or 'log', thus acquiring the names of logan or nutcracker stones. Sometimes the hill slope below a tor is littered with shattered and broken rocks – the ruin of a tor – called on Dartmoor a 'clitter'.

## Flora and Fauna

Many rivers have their sources on the two elevated plateaux north and south of Princetown. Tiny trickles ooze from the peat bogs that blanket the area. The streams gather strength and amalgamate, leaving the moor through beautiful valleys, often densely wooded. Some of these woods give a home to deer; fallow, roe and sika. Red deer were killed off on Dartmoor by 1780, and have not been re-introduced. There seems no reason, apart from a lack of acceptance, why they should not thrive

## Flora

On the higher hills are deep areas of peat, once cut for commercial and domestic purposes. Acidic and mineral-deficient, the peat supports a limited range of plants. One of the most interesting is the sundew, an insect-eating plant which seeks to extract from flies alighting on its sticky tendrils the nutrients necessary to sustain itself. A similarly carnivorous, but less common, plant is the butterwort, whose tacky leaves perform the same deadly function. Another plant of the wet areas is the cotton grass, each stalk bearing a white tuft of silken fluff. This has been used for stuffing cushions and mattresses.

which the grass should be passing on to the grazing animals.

Perhaps the commonest bird of the open moor is the skylark, and in the early summer the air seems to be full of its song. The raven and crow flap across the sky, stopping to feed on dead lambs or frogs. On the edge of the moor, the buzzard circles and soars, sharp eyes scanning the ground for small rodents, birds and adders. Snakes are not uncommon, but need not deter the visitor. They are sensitive to the walker's approach long before he sees them, and they slide away to hide under a rock, and so an actual encounter is infrequent.

on Dartmoor as they do on Exmoor. The occasional stray comes in from the Forestry Commission plantations to the north-west of Dartmoor, but a herd has not become established.

Many square miles of moorland, and some farmland, were planted with conifers between the wars, smothering the open country and altering the landscape. The archaeological remains suffered too, until the forestry interests undertook to safeguard this heritage from damage by forest machinery.

Dartmoor is not particularly well endowed with heather, the best areas being on the eastern moor around the Warren House Inn/Grimspound area. When it is in bloom here, the subtle smell and delicate hues entrance the senses.

Bracken, an unloved plant, seems to be encroaching. Farmers say it shelters ticks, and its deep roots grow on the best land ('plough bracken and find gold'), sucking out the goodness from the soil

# Ancient tracks

Stone walls switchback over the hills, many of them hundreds of years old, assisting the farmers in stock control, for this is a hill-farming region. The whole of Dartmoor is grazed with sturdy sheep, cattle and ponies. The Dartmoor ponies, as well as the sheep and cattle, all belong to someone, but they stay on the moor the year through until rounded up at the end of the summer. Much of central Dartmoor is owned by the Duke of Cornwall, Prince Charles, and he takes an active role in the management of his Devon estate.

Crossing the wilder parts of the moor are ancient tracks and disused railways, which the visitor can follow on foot. Perhaps the oldest of these, the **Lich Way** (named after the Saxon word for corpse) linked the Bellever/Postbridge area with Lydford in whose vast parish they are. (In 1260, the inhabitants were granted a dispensation to use the nearer church of Widecombe for funerals to save them the harrowing journey across miles of open moor carrying a deceased relative.) Other tracks, which may enter the realm of folklore in some cases, are the **King Way**, the **Abbots' Way**, the **Mariners' Way**, the **Jobbers' Path** and the **Blackwood Path**. They are well described in a splendid book, William Crossing's *Guide to Dartmoor*, which was originally published in 1909 and reprinted in 1965 and 1991.

# Archaeology

The Dartmoor tin worker is less remembered than his Cornish counterpart, though in places the disturbance caused by his tin streaming activities is on a major scale. Scenes very reminiscent of the Klondike occurred, but happily the healing quality of time has returned the landscape to something approaching the natural scene. Tin streaming, which pre-dated tin mining, was very similar to panning for gold, and involved working over the valley gravels. To crush and smelt the ore, the tinner built small water-powered smelting houses – often called blowing houses on the map – which are interesting relics of this medieval industry.

Dartmoor's old buildings make it a fruitful locality for the study of vernacular architecture. Because the buildings were constructed of the long-lasting local stone many of the farmhouses still lived in today date back to the 15th and 16th centuries, and remains exist of houses in a similar form – **'longhouses'** they are termed – going back to the 12th century.

The visitor will notice subtle changes in the appearance of buildings between east and west Dartmoor. On western Dartmoor the older farmhouses and cottages owe more to Cornish traditions and influence than Devon's. There is more slate, and less thatch.

# Folklore

It is hardly surprising that a region so overlaid with hundreds of years of history should have a rich folklore. Stories of spectral hounds and black dogs, and people turned into stones, are commonplace, though children with access to tv and the internet are less likely to believe them than the youngsters of a hundred years ago. Of course it was to Dartmoor that Sir Arthur Conan Doyle came to gather material and atmosphere for a book about the moor that he called *The Hound of the Baskervilles*. A young coachman, Harry Baskerville, drove him round the moor, and Conan Doyle asked him if he could use his name in the book. The Dartmoor ethos is truthfully, if melodramatically, portrayed, but the places are topographically inexact. Grimpen Mire is probably **Fox Tor Mire**, one of the few valley bogs whose unpleasantness matches its reputation.

The twentieth-century story of the hairy hand defies logical explanation. In the early 1920s there were several accidents on the road west of Postbridge, and surviving drivers spoke of muscular hairy hands closing over theirs and forcing the car or motorcycle off the road.

# National Park status

In 1951, Dartmoor was declared a national park. This designation did not alter the status of the land: the moor remains in private ownership. It means that all developments are looked at very carefully by the planning authority, the Dartmoor National Park Committee. This committee also has a duty to help the public enjoy the park. This is achieved through information and interpretative services, guided walks, the erection of signposts, stiles and foot bridges, subsidised bus services and a team of rangers out on the moor making contact with residents and visitors.

## Ancient history

Much has been written in the introductory chapter of this book about the chronology of early man and something about the stone remains that one can see on Dartmoor in great abundance. Dartmoor is probably the best place in Britain to study the homes and graves of prehistoric man. There are several reasons for this. Firstly, his settlements, burials and ritual sites were numerous to start with; secondly, they were built of the enduring local stone, granite, and lastly, they have suffered relatively little disturbance since man abandoned them.

The question is often asked, why did men live on what we regard as a fairly inhospitable, infertile upland? The answer is probably (and many of our statements about prehistoric man are qualified by the word 'probably') that the climate was less rigorous; the soil was less acid, meaning the grazing was better; man's economy demanded open pastures; the lowlands were still largely covered with trees; and if people did live in these lower areas their houses have been obliterated by later activities.

The **Bronze Age** on Dartmoor – say from 2,500BC to 750BC – has left an exceptional number of sites. The term Bronze Age indicates that man had learned to make and use metal (bronze is an alloy of 90 per cent copper and 10 per cent tin): it does not mean that the use of stone and flint implements

### The Longhouse

The word 'longhouse' aptly describes their shape. Built on a slope to the similar proportions of a shoebox, with a door in the middle of each of the longer sides, the shippon for the animals was in the lower half, while the family occupied the higher end. A screened passage with doors to the living quarters and shippon linked the two outside doors which were shared by people and animals. In an area where it is tiresome to have to go out on a cold night to tend stock, this arrangement had much to commend it. The family end was divided into two sections with a hearth on the floor. Only later were chimneys built, roofs raised and first floors inserted, and there are still houses with smoke-blackened roof timbers and thatch, indicating an open hearth when they were first built. Few longhouses with unaltered shippons exist today; most have been altered to increase the living accommodation, but the Dartmoor National Park Authority owns one at Higher Uppacott, near Poundsgate, opened occasionally.

# Dartmoor

0  1  2  3  4  5 miles

0 1 2 3 4 5 6 7Km

was entirely discontinued.

The settlements are of the greatest interest; it is highly evocative to stand in the ruins of a prehistoric house and imagine life going on in this very spot 3,000 or more years ago. There are about 2,000 such sites on the moor, but some were destroyed by wall and road builders; as many were probably occupied simultaneously, only a guess at population figures is possible.

The circular stone footings we now see – called 'hut circles' by the Ordnance Survey – represent what is left of the

---

## Childe's Tomb

One of the best-known Dartmoor stories concerns a spot beside the Mire known as **Childe's Tomb**. A fairly modern cross surmounts a circle of stones, but what one sees today is a nineteenth-century reconstruction of an older monument, possibly a prehistoric burial chamber. The tale relates that Childe, while out hunting, became detached from his friends, was benighted and beset by a blizzard. To save himself he killed his horse, disembowelled the animal and crawled into its skin, dying nevertheless. Before he expired he wrote his will on some convenient parchment (!) in the horse's blood:

> *They fyrste that fyndes and bringes mee to my grave*
> *The priorie of Plimstoke they shall have.*

Professor Finberg has analysed this folk memory using contemporary records in a fascinating historical detective story (*Devonshire Studies*, 1951) and concludes that the tale had its origin in Saxon times.

---

walls which supported a conical roof of thatch propped up on a central pole or poles. A complete prehistoric Dartmoor house must have looked very like a native hut in the wilder parts of Africa. The door was usually on the south side to catch the sun and keep out the cold north wind. Some have been excavated which had internal plank walls. The houses were usually found in groups, and may be inside a stone wall. Such a village settlement is **Grimspound**, 300yd (274m) east of the minor road 1½ miles (2km) south of the B3212 at **Challacombe Cross**. Although some of the ruined huts at Grimspound have been 'restored' or built up, and as most of the huts on the moor are not so recognisable, it is a good introduction to similar antiquities.

At Grimspound a ruined stone wall encloses an area of nearly 4 acres (1.5hectares) in which archaeologists found the remains of twenty-four huts, as well as what may have been cattle pens built against the wall. A stream, the Grims Lake, passes through the side of the enclosure, and was an obvious source of water, though unreliable, as it dries up in drought conditions. The paved entrance is on the higher side and gave access to the pastures on Hameldon, the high ground to the south. Its position, overlooked as it is on both sides, indicates that the inhabitants must have lived peaceably with nearby people, for the village was not defensible in an age of slingstones, arrows and spears. The wall was probably not less than 5ft 6in (2m) high and was built to keep domestic animals in and wild animals out.

The inhabitants were certainly not ignorant savages, although their skills were used for different occupations from ours. They could weave and spin, and make pottery, but their pots could not withstand direct heat. Water was heated by placing hot stones in a pot. Meat was cooked by packing it round with hot cooking stones.

In recent years, much attention has been given to extensive systems of fairly straight, parallel land boundaries or field banks, called 'reaves' on Dartmoor. These are made of stone or soil, and extend for many miles, leap-frogging considerable natural obstacles like the Dart Valley near Dartmeet. Here and there, the ruins of circular houses are found among the strips. Their vastness and complexity are only beginning to be understood, and the theories on Dartmoor prehistory are being revised from year to year.

To these wide-ranging remains of domestic activity, we must add the barrows, cairns and cists where prehistoric man buried his dead, the enigmatic stone rows, and the stone circles where he probably worshipped.

When one puts together all that is known about Dartmoor's prehistory it is interesting how little is really understood. The moor dwellers of 3,000 years ago lived and died without written record, and their culture is so different from ours that it requires an enormous mental effort to subvert our own values and perceptions in order to contemplate their lifestyle.

If the main holiday area in Devon is based on Torquay, and visitors tend to come to Dartmoor while on holiday, then the approach through Newton Abbot and **Bovey Tracey** (pronounced 'Buvvy') is a natural one, and will be the starting point for a figure-of-eight journey across and around the moor. It helps to have a basic understanding of Dartmoor's shape; two upland plateaux, separated by two roads bisecting each other like a pair of scissors at Two Bridges. Within the eastern angle of these roads, and especially on the eastern side of the moor, are a tangle of minor roads for which the visitor certainly needs either the 1:25,000 Ordnance Survey Explorer map or the sheets in the 1:50,000 Land-ranger series. (The visitor should not attempt to do everything described here in one day!).

# Bovey Tracey

The name Bovey refers to the river, which passes through the parish, and the second element connects it with the de Tracey family, one of whose members, Sir William de Tracey, was in the party which murdered Thomas à Becket in Canterbury Cathedral in 1170. The de Traceys owned land in the area, but the rededication of the church to include the name of St Thomas of Canterbury six years after his assassination may not prove that the church was rebuilt by Sir William in expiation of his crime, as is sometimes suggested. The church is very beautiful, with a fine rood screen and carved stone pulpit, while the **Riverside Mill** is now home to a number of craftsmen of the Devon Guild of Craftsmen. The site includes a shop and café. To the south of the town, near the **Drum Bridges** roundabout on the A38, the **House of Marbles** and **Teign Valley Glassworks** give visitors the opportunity of watching glassmaking, as well as visiting the marbles and games museum (with probably the biggest collection in the world) and potteries museum.

At the other end of the town is **Parke**, the headquarters of the Dartmoor National Park Authority. The house and estate were left to the National Trust by Major Hole, on his death in 1974. The house was built on the site of an older building by the major's grandfather in the 1820s. The Trust leases the house to the National Park Authority. There are other **Dartmoor National Park information centres** at **Postbridge**, **Newbridge, Haytor**, **Tavistock**, **Okehampton** and **Widecombe** (shared with the National Trust, and using Trust premises).

# Haytor

Beyond Parke, the road divides at a stone direction post at Five Wyches Cross, where you should fork to the left and climb steadily for 3½ miles (5.5km) to the car park near **Haytor**. Haytor is without doubt the most noticed, most recognised and most visited tor on Dartmoor. The superlatives arise from its position on the edge of the moor. On one side the land falls away; on the other the open moor rolls

into the distance – there is no better viewpoint from which to get one's Dartmoor bearings.

The two main rock piles show it to be an 'avenue' tor (for reasons not fully understood, even by geologists), and both humps can be climbed. The right-hand tor had steps cut in the nineteenth century but this did not please a local parson who wrote of the 'unsightly stair step to enable the enervated and pinguitudinous scions of humanity of this wonderful nineteenth century to gain its summit'. The other rock is slightly higher and has iron rings as climbing aids and, by a quirk of landform, looks far superior from the north.

A few hundred yards to the northeast is a large quarry boasting a pool where goldfish lurk, saved from predatory herons by the depth of the water. A cutting leads from the lower quarry, and if this is followed, a double line of grooved stone blocks will be seen bearing round to the left beside a tip of

*Deserted medieval village at Hound Tor, Dartmoor*

Haytor, Dartmoor

waste rock. This is the **Haytor granite tramway.**

Between 1825 and 1858 stone was transported from this quarry and others nearby, on flat-top horse-drawn, wooden-wheeled trucks for 8 miles (13km), down a tramway built of continuous lines of these grooved sets. The material was available for the cost of extraction and dressing, but eventually it became uneconomic, as two trans-shipments were necessary at the end of the 'line'. The stone was loaded into boats for a journey along the Stover Canal and down the Teign Estuary to Teignmouth, where it was loaded into seagoing ships. Nevertheless the enterprise supplied stone for many London buildings, including parts of London Bridge and the British Museum Library.

The stone tramway is visible for much of its course on the moor, and to follow it makes an easy and fascinating walk of discovery. The 'points' in particular are of the greatest interest. Of course, the system reverses the usual railway practice of having the flange on the wheels. Here the flange was on the 'rails', and the trucks' wheels were plain wood with iron hoops.

If the walk is extended past **Great Tor** to **Hound Tor** the interesting remains of a deserted medieval village can be explored. Enclosures, houses, including what was probably a small manor house, and corn-drying kilns can be recognised. By the fourteenth century the climate had deteriorated, so that farming on these bleak moors was not practical, and the settlement was abandoned. Alternatively by parking at the Hound Tor car park and walking

the short distance past the tor, the site can be clearly seen.

# Widecombe-in-the-Moor

After looking round the area, carry on towards **Widecombe-in-the-Moor**, 4 miles (6km) or so further on. Over the top of Widecombe Hill, an enormous panorama is spread out in front. Southern Dartmoor and northern Dartmoor are recognisable, joined by the high saddle of North Hessary Tor beyond Princetown, this summit surmounted by a 650ft (200m) BBC television mast. The long whale-back hill 'behind' Widecombe is **Hameldown**, and Grimspound, mentioned earlier, is on the far slope at the north end of Hameldown.

Although **Widecombe** appears to be low down, the village is nevertheless 800ft (280m) above sea level, and the containing hills are as high again. The altitude brings its own weather, which has given rise to the saying off the moor to the south when it is snowing that 'Widecombe folks are picking their geese'.

Widecombe's rise to fame as a result of the popularity of the famous song 'Widecombe Fair' is probably due to the shrewd commercial sense of those who would profit from it. The song was first written down and popularised in the 1880s, when Widecombe Fair was in its infancy, and of course the individuals mentioned in the chorus – Bill Brewer, Jan Stewer, Peter Gurney, Peter Davy, Dan'l Whiddon, Harry Hawke, Old Uncle Tom Cobley and all – were all going to the fair from somewhere else. Their home territory is understood to be north of Dartmoor in the general area of Sticklepath and Spreyton.

When the fair began, it was what we would now call a market, with some revelling for good measure. Now, it is more of a gymkhana, with a sheep, cattle and pony show, demonstrations, competitions, sideshows, races and refreshments. It is held on the second Tuesday in September, and thousands of people head in the direction of the village.

**The church** is the finest on the moor, with a tall tower of noble proportions. During a severe thunderstorm in 1638 one of the pinnacles was struck by lightning and fell through the roof, killing four people and injuring over sixty others. The local schoolmaster's verse about the tragedy is recorded on boards on the church wall.

Outside is the **Church House**, now owned by the National Trust, and used as an information centre and shop. Church houses were originally built to serve as rest houses for the parishioners from far-flung parts of the parish – Widecombe extends to 11,000 acres (4,400hectares) – when they journeyed to the village on Sundays. This one may have been where the lord of the manor brewed ale for the village, and later it became the poorhouse and, later still, the school. Part of it is used for village meetings – after 450 years it still serves the local community.

The village green was formerly called Butt Park, as this was the field ('park' means field) where the young men practised archery. Under an Act of 1466 every Englishman…should have a bow of his own height… and that butts should be made in every township which the inhabitants are to shoot at every feast day under the penalty of a halfpenny when they should omit that exercise.'

A mile up the Natsworthy road from the village is a bucolic milestone in the hedge. The distance is carved on a natural boulder and reads '1 moil', and thus the word is still pronounced in these parts. Driving down the valley to Dartmeet, one travels through the attractive village of **Ponsworthy**, with its watersplash and thatched cottages.

# The Central Area

**Dartmeet** is a famous beauty spot where the East and West Dart Rivers come together among magnificent scenery. Just upstream from the road bridge are the flood-damaged remains of an ancient clapper bridge. ('Clapper' is an old name for a heap of stones.) The age of these primitive bridges is impossible to determine, but they are probably 700 or 800 years old.

Towards Two Bridges, and 2 miles (3km) beyond Dartmeet is **Dunnabridge Pound** on the right, near some farm buildings. This is a medieval enclosure recorded as long ago as 1342, and probably built on a prehistoric site. Until recent times it was used as a corral for strays. Just inside the gate is a massive stone seat with uprights supporting a coverstone, perhaps the pound-keeper's shelter.

For many people, **Two Bridges** is the hub of Dartmoor, though a glance at a map of the National Park will show that Bellever Forest has more precise claims to that distinction. The Rivers Cowsic and West Dart come together

*Widecombe-in-the-Moor*

here, and a five-span clapper bridge on the Cowsic may be one of the original 'Two Bridges', the one over the West Dart having disappeared.

This is a good place to begin a walk up the **West Dart Valley** to Wistman's Wood: at its shortest the return journey is 3 miles (5km). Leave your car in the quarry, noting the embryo tor in the quarry face – geologists find this a fascinating site. Walk up the track towards Crockern Farm, then follow the yellow waymarked track beyond. Do not attempt to stay close to the river; stone walls and boggy patches will impede your progress. By following the yellow blobs on boulders and gateposts an easier and drier route will make the walk more enjoyable.

Soon **Wistman's Wood** comes into sight, a long grove of gnarled and twisted trees, mostly oaks, growing out of a hillside clitter. These same rocks have safeguarded the trees from browsing animals. The wood is of interest to naturalists, as it is growing on the tree line and may represent a relic of more general tree cover in the distant past. Along its higher side are what appear to be long barrows up and down the slope, but they were thrown up by the warrener to encourage rabbits to breed. For hundreds of years, rabbits were 'farmed' on Dartmoor for their flesh and fur. The last warren survived in the Plym Valley until the 1950s. The warrener's hut at Wistman's Warren was near the north end of the wood on a small flat platform, and was only a wooden shed.

On the opposite side of the valley is an early nineteenth-century leat (artificial watercourse), which takes West Dart water many miles round the contours and through a tunnel, to help top up Plymouth's water supply.

Perhaps before returning to the road you may like to walk up to the pyramid of earth and stone on the ridge above the wood, **Longaford Tor**. It is an easy but rewarding climb to the top. One of Dartmoor's greatest assets is its sense of freedom – the feeling that you can go where you like. This is only partly true, however, as much of the moor is farmed in a conventional way, and this imposes restrictions on the walker as much in the National Park as elsewhere. However, since the passing of the Dartmoor Commons Act in 1985, the public has a right of access to most common land in the national park. The Act also imposes certain standards of conduct on those using the moor, whether as walkers, riders or graziers, and regulates the number of animals which may be pastured. Further access land was made available when the Countryside and Rights of Way Act 2000 came into force on Dartmoor in 2005. Full details of all access land in the area can be found on up-to-date OS Explorer maps and at tourist information centres. Dartmoor's bogs are not dangerous to healthy humans taking reasonable care; they are usually obvious for what they are, and the walker can circumvent them.

So if you want to go further up the valley you are free to do so, but do take proper precautions before setting off on a walk, howevershort, over the moor. Boots are the best footwear, and a waterproof coat is advisable. A map and compass should go into a small rucksack with a spare jumper and some food and drink. Those who are heading into the high land of northern Dartmoor should first ascertain whether the Services are using any of their live firing ranges. The firing programme is distributed widely to Dartmoor National Park information centres, post offices, police stations and hotels in the area and at www.dartmoor-ranges.co.uk.

Back at the road, continue towards Tavistock, taking the right fork after crossing the West Dart. The road climbs, soon crossing the leat, which has been contouring the slope opposite Wistman's Wood. **Dartmoor Prison** comes into view (left) and the road passes through prison farmland. The prison is virtually self-supporting so far as meat and vegetables are concerned. On **North Hessary Tor** is a BBC

## Coffin Stone

On the hillside to the east of Dartmeet, and rather hard to find among the gorse and bracken, is the **Coffin Stone**, a natural earthfast boulder on which it was the custom to rest the body in the days of 'carrying funerals' when the deceased was being borne to the parish church at Widecombe. A cross and the deceased's initials were incised on the stone while the bearers paused to take liquid refreshment and to get their breath. Samuel Caunter and Aaron Cleave are represented by SC and AC.

television mast, erected in 1954–5.

Over the rise at **Rundlestone Cross** an extensive view into Cornwall opens up. About $1^1/_2$ miles (2km) from this spot, just after a left-hand bend, cars may be parked in a quarry on the left, for a 1-mile (1.5km) walk over the moor to see the best and most accessible collection of Bronze Age antiquities on Dartmoor. Within a small area every type of relic is represented. Near **Merrivale** a large stone quarry may be seen on the opposite hillside, at which the stones of the old London Bridge were refinished before being shipped to the USA in 1971. It ceased working some years ago.

Walk up the hill on a line with the television mast. After about 250yd (229m) will be seen a large worked stone propped on small stones. This was meant to be an edge-runner or crushing stone, but for some reason it was abandoned in the working about 150 years ago. It stands within a prehistoric stone enclosure – the walls are broken and scattered, and 15yd (14m) beyond are the ruined circular walls of a Bronze Age house. Turn right towards King Tor and you will see others ahead. In fact there must have been a considerable settlement here, as there are more above the road.

Walk towards a line of upright stones. As you reach them, you will find there are two double rows, each with a large stone at the uphill end. If you walk along the more southerly line, a burial chamber (a cist), with a partly destroyed coverstone, will be noticed, offset a few yards, and at the halfway point another burial chest within a cairn of stones. A little distance to the south is a large standing stone (a menhir) and a low circle of stones. Return to the car, and down the hill from the quarry you will see what appears to be a gatepost standing by itself. This bears a T on one side and an A on the other, and was one of a line of guidestones hereabouts marking the route from Tavistock to Ashburton. These mute memorials give an idea of what cross-moor travel was like 200 years ago. A journey we can now accomplish in half an hour would not have taken an ordinary person less than a day.

# The Western Side, Lydford

Back in the car, pass through Merrivale, look on the left for a very large lump of rock, **Vixen Tor**, and carry on down into Tavistock (described in the previous chapter). Turn right and follow the A386 north to Mary Tavy where you should take the turning left, signposted **Brentor**. Drive to the car park below the church-crowned tor, which gives its name to the village, and walk up the path to the summit. A direct assault is not recommended; take the longer, but less steep, way.

The tiny church was built in 1130 and stands 1,130ft (345m) above sea level, a useful conjunction of numerals. Burials have taken place up to the present time, and one marvels that a sufficient depth of soil exists for the purpose. Now take the road signposted to Lydford, a small village, but a vast parish, about 4 miles (6.5km) northeast. **Lydford** is superficially a very unprepossessing village, cast in a Cornish mould, with none of the thatched-roof cosiness of eastern Dartmoor. The small castle dominates one end of the single street, it is true, but the fascinating story of Lydford has to be sought out, and the casual, uninformed, visitor could miss a great deal.

The village's situation was its *raison d'être*. The deep gorge of the River Lyd blocks the approach on one side, with a secondary valley forming the other. King Alfred adapted these natural advantages by raising an earth bank across the third side, to create Lydford, one of his four strategically-placed *burghs* or fortified positions in Devon against the Danes. (A possibility that Lydford was built on an earlier Celtic site cannot be ruled out.) A mint was established, and it became an important local meeting place, and, as a by-product, the administrative headquarters for Dartmoor. But it never developed to any extent, and was overtaken by Okehampton and Launceston, which lay on the main route through the south-west peninsula, and by Tavistock, with its abbey. For this reason, Lydford's ancient road pattern has not been overlaid by later building. Some of the original Saxon plots and lanes laid out on a grid model can be seen, as well as Alfred's earth bank.

Soon after the Norman Conquest, the invaders refortified the site by building a fort on a corner overlooking one of the steep slopes, but this had a short life, as **Lydford Castle** dates from about 1195. Although it has the appearance of a keep, the castle was constructed for the custody of those who broke the strict forest (hunting) and stannary (tin working) laws. The castle is not built on the mound, as it would appear, for the earth was drawn

> ## Brent Tor
>
> The view from the top is one of the finest in England. A clear day will enable you to see right into the inner recesses of northern Dartmoor, where Fur Tor and Cut Hill stand out. Even Exmoor appears as a blue blur to the north. The dark rounded slopes of **Gibbet Hill** a mile or so away once carried a hanging tree, as the name suggests.

up round the base of the walls at a later date, for an unknown purpose. The courts were held in the second-floor room, and the prisoners confined in the two lower levels. The cellar must have been a noxious dungeon.

Early in the nineteenth century the castle fell into disuse, and has only given up many of its secrets as the result of excavations in more recent years. Beside the castle is Lydford church, dedicated to a Celtic saint, St Petrock, which gives credence to the suggestion that there may have been a Celtic community here before Alfred established it as one of his *burghs*. The font is the oldest feature in the church, and the screen is a splendid example of more modern (1904) craftsmanship.

At the bottom of the hill below the church is **Lydford Gorge** (National Trust), down which rushes the River Lyd. In places 200ft (70m) deep with 60ft (21m) vertical walls at the bottom, the gorge has been formed by the urgent passage of the river carrying rocks which have scoured out potholes along its course. The best is called the **Devil's Cauldron**, and it can be reached by an exciting path cut along

*The ancient clapper bridge at Dartmeet*

the side of the gorge. Much of its course is truly awe-inspiring and a little frightening, and other parts are very beautiful. At the far end of the gorge, which is over a mile (2km) long, a 100ft (30m) waterfall, called the **White Lady** and the highest on Dartmoor, adds her veil of spray to the Lyd. If you visit Lydford in the winter, when for safety's sake the Gorge is closed, the flavour of the place can be felt by looking over Lydford Bridge into the deepest section.

Pass through Lydford and rejoin the A386 at the Dartmoor Inn, turning left, and heading for Okehampton. The high moor is very near the road along here, and by glancing right you will see the prominent stone cross on Brat Tor erected in 1887 to mark Queen Victoria's silver jubilee. A few miles on, turn right towards **Okehampton**, getting a glimpse of Dartmoor's highest tor, Yes Tor, at 2,030ft (710.5m), if it is not obscured by cloud.

# Okehampton

The dramatic ruin of Baron Baldwin's Norman **castle** on the right down a winding tree-lined road into the town

## The Gubbins Tribe

**Charles Kingsley**, in his *Westward Ho!*, mentions the Gubbins tribe, a kind of Dartmoor Doone family, as lawless and predatory as the Exmoor clan. He based his description on an account written down by Thomas Fuller in about 1650. They seem to have been long-lived, fleet of foot, above the law, revengeful and totally pagan, although he wrote that '... they begin to be civilised, and tender their children to baptism ...'. Lydford Gorge is sometimes thought to have been their home, but as the river occasionally rises to fill the defile, it affords no permanent security.

is the great attraction of Okehampton. It is reached by a side road beside the post office. The castle was built along a narrow ridge, with ancillary buildings leading up the slope from the barbican to the keep, past the great hall, guard room, chapel, kitchen and other quarters. Garderobes – medieval lavatories – are built into the outside walls to take advantage of the slope. On a fine spring day when the bluebells are blooming in bud-bursting time, with the chorale of the nearby West Okement River as background music, fairyland seems to have come to mid-Devon.

The town suffered for many years from the lack of a bypass but one was opened in 1988. On a quiet day, the distinguished **town hall** in Fore Street can be appreciated. This three-storied building was built in 1685, as a private

*Below: Lydford Castle*
*Right: Lydford Gorge*

house for John Northmore, and converted to its present use in 1821.

The **Museum of Dartmoor Life**, on the opposite side of the road, reveals how people lived and worked in the area for hundreds of years.

Above the town looms the high

ground of Dartmoor; from the cowering town it has an oppressive presence, a feeling which evaporates when you drive up on to the moor. Here the military are active, for soldiers have trained on Dartmoor for about a hundred years. The public are excluded from the range during advertised firing times, but on other days they may walk the high open moor without concern, except that metal objects should not be touched.

# The North-East

About 4 miles (6km) east of Okehampton is **Sticklepath**, a village frequently visited by John Wesley during the eighteenth-century preacher's journeys to and from one of his most frequented evangelistic areas, Cornwall. Here Wesley found kindred Christian spirits in a community of Quakers, and he preached from the White Rock on the Mount at the Okehampton end of the village. This is whitewashed regularly, and is marked by a flagstaff. The Quaker Burying (sic) Ground by the River Taw is a beautifully peaceful spot.

In the centre of Sticklepath is the **Finch Foundry Museum of Waterpower**. From 1814 to 1960 agricultural equipment was made here by Heath Robinson-type machinery, powered by water from the Taw. After closure, a band of interested people preserved the machinery which is now shown to the public. The giant trip hammer and shears seem unbelievably primitive to have been operating commercially as recently as 1960. It was given to the National Trust in 1994.

Head eastwards from Sticklepath, and fork right at Whiddon Down, along the A382 as far as Easton Cross. Take the right turn here to **Chagford**. The name means gorse ford, although the town stands well above the beautiful River Teign, here crossed by a lengthy line of stepping stones known as Rushford Steps, over which sacks of grain were carried to Rushford Mill.

The church of St Michael is stoutly built of granite, and contains some fine monuments to local gentry. Facing it is the sixteenth-century Three Crowns Inn, with jutting porch, where a young cavalier, Sidney Godolphin, was killed in a Civil War skirmish. The middle of the town is remarkable for its sense of focus. All roads lead to the Square, with its 1862 market house and comprehensive range of shops. Chagford exudes self-confidence.

Chagford was one of Devon's four stannary towns, but nothing survives of that era, except the remains of mining activity for those who search diligently in the surrounding countryside. If the tortuous network of lanes can be unravelled, the open moor at **Kestor** is worth discovering for the tor, the view, and the wealth of prehistoric antiquities – stone rows, burial chambers, huts, field systems and standing stones – which are scattered over Chagford Common.

Chagford is a good spot for exploring this corner of Dartmoor. To the north of Kestor is the elusive village of **Gidleigh**; elusive, as there are those who say that Gidleigh does not exist. Although signs point in its direction from Chagford, the serpentine lanes defeat many who set out. There is no village in the usual sense, merely a church, a tiny late Norman castle and one or two houses tucked away in the folds of the

Dartmoor foothills, between Chagford and Okehampton.

On the open moor nearby is **Scorhill Circle**, a Bronze Age ritual monument, and, where the North Teign River and Walla Brook come together, a strange naturally-holed stone called the **Tolmen** sits in the bed of the stream above normal river levels. It is said that to crawl through will cure rheumatism, but sufferers would probably find the effort too difficult to accomplish. A single-span clapper bridge, made of one piece of granite, crosses the Walla Brook just upstream.

To reach these monuments, park your car in the small pull-in outside the gate of Scorhill House, which is on the moor edge above Gidleigh, and walk up to the moor between a funnel of stone walls. A path goes over the top of Scorhill and presently Scorhill Circle, perhaps the finest on the moor, is visible on the right. The Tolmen and the clapper bridge are as described. This is a gentle walk of 2 miles (3km), but should not be attempted in mist, as nothing is visible and it is easy to become lost.

# Castle Drogo

Another expedition from Chagford must be to **Castle Drogo** at Drewsteignton, which is often described as the last great country house that will ever be built in England. Drogo can be seen from some parts of Chagford, its granite glistening in the sun, or, chameleon-like, glowering in the gloom, depending on the weather. A coalition of the genius of architect Sir Edwin Lutyens and the money of Julius Drewe in the Dartmoor landscape was bound to produce a building of exceptional impact. Castle Drogo was built just in time. The taxing away of family fortunes and the repressive effect of planning laws would nowadays prevent the building of such an expensive showpiece.

The foundation stone was laid in 1911 and the early plans included a great hall standing on walls 6ft (2m) thick. However, possibly on the grounds of expense, or maybe because Drewe had second thoughts about living in a building so monolithic, the plans were reduced in size, and the undercroft of the hall, which was never built, became a highly atmospheric family chapel.

Perhaps feeling that the paring away of a principal feature had emasculated his grand design, Lutyens tried in 1916 to persuade Drewe to build a gatehouse at the northern approach to the forecourt, and had a full-scale timber mock-up built to impress his client. This was never built, and one may conjecture that it was the death of Drewe's eldest son Adrian in 1917 in France that sapped his enthusiasm. Work continued exceedingly slowly, and the two original masons of 1911 eventually finished the castle in 1930. Sadly, Julius Drewe died a year later. The origin of Drewe's fortune was not forgotten and local people disrespectfully christened his house 'Margarine Castle'. Even in its reduced size, Castle Drogo is massive in scale, and inconvenient for modern living. In 1974 it was given to the National Trust with 600 acres (240 hectares) of land, and it has been open to the public since 1975.

The approach is along a wide drive which Drewe and Lutyens deliberately kept free of the usual lodge, and cars

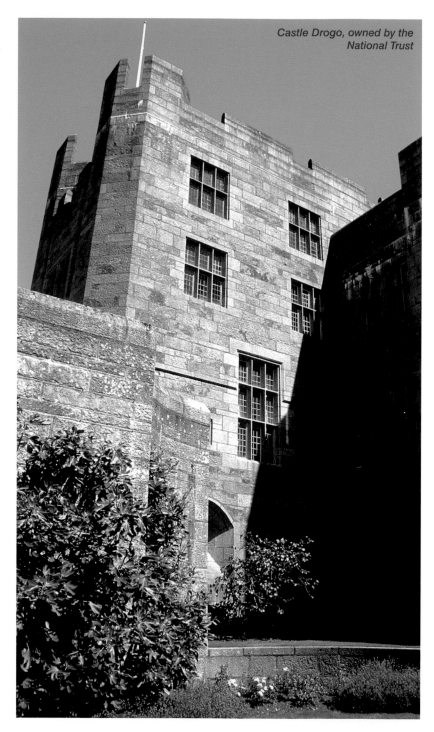

Castle Drogo, owned by the
National Trust

are sensibly kept a little way from the house. The award-winning National Trust reception area and shop is itself an interesting design.

As the visitor enters the house (beneath a Lutyens joke: a working portcullis designed to air the hall while keeping the dog in) the first things that are noticeable are the bare granite walls. The furniture is secondary to the structure. Lutyens' treatment of the corridors and the stairs reveals his understanding of spatial relationships and the texture of that most intractable of stones, granite. The impressive main staircase, lit by a window of cathedral proportions, leads down to a less successful feature, the dining room. The heavy ceiling and mahogany panelling have an overpowering effect, which the single broad window does nothing to mitigate.

The kitchen is 50yd (46m) from the dining room, along a stone corridor, and many visitors will find the domestic quarters the most interesting part of the castle. Both the pantry and the kitchen are equipped with cupboards, dressers and tables designed by Lutyens, and the kitchen is discreetly lit by a roof lantern. The slate slabs of the pre-refrigerator era larder contrast with the service lift in the scullery that took food to the servants' hall one floor up and to the nurseries two further floors higher.

Off the bedroom corridor, the elaborate bathroom apparatus will cause amusement, but the memorial room, arranged by his mother in memory of the eldest soldier son Adrian, is a touching survival of a sad time in British history, and must have been something of a shrine for the grieving parents. In the gun room, the National Trust has arranged a comprehensive display of plans and photographs showing the construction and growth of Castle Drogo. Across the drive are the formal gardens, which rise to a circular lawn used by the Drewes for tennis and now adapted for croquet. A charming Wendy house

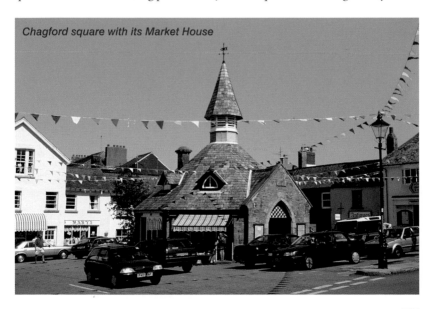

*Chagford square with its Market House*

## Julius Drewe

Julius Drewe made his money from the Home and Colonial Stores. Believing there to be a link between his family and the Norman Drogo (or Dru) de Teigne who gave his name to Drewsteignton, he bought land in the parish, and set his heart on a castle. Mr (later Sir) Edwin Lutyens was recommended to him and, to a budget of £50,000 for the house and £10,000 for the grounds, he began work on Drewe's romantic dream of reproducing on an exciting site, overlooking the Teign Gorge and the eastern slopes of Dartmoor, a twentieth-century version of an all-granite medieval castle.

nearby captivates younger visitors.

# Moreton-hampstead

Before driving across the moor to Princetown, the small town of **Moreton-hampstead** should be visited. Standing where the A382 and B3212 intersect, it is an important road junction. The town is notable for the fine, arcaded stone almshouses dated 1637 in Cross Street. Above the nearby cross which gives the street its name, there was, until it was blown down in 1891, a pollarded elm – the dancing tree – which had a large platform built in its branches for musical performances. In 1801 a local diarist recorded that there was room for thirty people to sit around, for a small orchestra to play, and for six couples to dance. In the Napoleonic Wars, when French officer prisoners were billeted on parole in the town they performed in the dancing tree. Memorial stones to two French officers can be seen in the church porch.

The year after Trafalgar, 1806, the 'calculating boy', George Parker Bidder, was born in Moretonhampstead, the son of a stonemason. He possessed extraordinary mental powers and from an early age could work out complicated sums in his head. Before he was sixteen he could calculate the cube root of 304,821,217 instantly, and the cube root of an eighteen-digit number in $2^1/_2$ minutes. He became an engineer and built the Victoria Docks in London.

The B3212 in the Princetown direction soon passes the **Miniature Pony Centre,** which has a wildfowl lake, adventure play area and pets' corner as well as the ponies of the name. Beyond, the road leads, after a further 2 miles (3km), to a steep climb onto the open moor at Moorgate Hill. The name is a reminder that not so long ago all roads giving access to the moor had gates across them, to prevent the grazing animals from straying. Cattle grids have now replaced these except on one or two minor roads. (The first turning left after reaching the moor leads to Grimspound, mentioned earlier this chapter.)

After the second switchback, the road levels out; beside the road on the south side is the leaning and mis-shapen **Bennett's Cross**. As a monument to medieval piety it served to mark a track over the moor before the road was formalised. WB carved on the shaft stands for Warren Bounds, for it was adapted as a boundary stone for Headland Warren, the rabbit warren in this area.

The next building to the west is

Almshouses, Moretonhampstead

the **Warren House Inn**, which once served the miners from the tin mines below the road. The deep gashes show where they followed the east–west striking tin lodes. Work went on here until earlier last century.

Carrying on towards Princetown, about 1 mile (1.5km) west of Post-bridge, on the north side of the road, are the remains of a nineteenth-century gunpowder factory, known as the **Powder Mills**. Here the three constituents of that compound were brought together – the charcoal at least was provided by locally-grown timber – and the various processes powered by water from the East Dart River. The safety factor of space was available in abundance, and batches of powder were tested by firing a proving mortar, which still stands near the cottages. The old factory buildings house a pottery,

## Fingle Bridge

It would be wrong to leave the neighbourhood without visiting **Fingle Bridge**, a well-known, but unspoilt, beauty spot, 2 miles (3km) away, on the other side of Drewsteignton. Here the River Teign sparkles beneath the 400-year-old stone bridge, among beautiful wooded hills. A licensed restaurant, the Anglers' Rest, stands at the foot of Prestonbury, which has an Iron Age hillfort on its summit. Public footpaths lead up and downstream, and the most beguiling, the **Hunters' Path**, climbs up through the oak woods to come out above the tree line, with the spectacle of expansive views ahead to northern Dartmoor. As Castle Drogo can be reached by turning off the Hunters' Path, this route provides a most pleasant link between the two places.

shop and tearoom.

Another mile further on, a low tor, just north of the road, is **Crockern Tor**, the meeting place from 1474 to 1703 of the Stannary Court, the administrative body of the Dartmoor tinners. The moor was divided into four quarters (stannaries), which came together at Crockern Tor, and each stannary sent twenty-four representatives. Thus Two Bridges is reached by a different route. Continue on the B3212 beyond the West Dart.

# Princetown

**Princetown** came into being through the prison, which was started in 1806 on land owned by the Prince of Wales. The prison was built by French prisoners of war, who had hitherto been incarcerated in overcrowded hulks at Plymouth, and later Americans joined the French within the walls: at one time

## Postbridge

**Postbridge** is like an oasis in the middle of the moor, with beech trees instead of palms. The finest clapper bridge on the moor is easily seen a few yards downstream from the road bridge. This is a good place for a walk up the East Dart River, starting from the stile at the top of the car park. The walker can follow the river up the west bank, cross at some convenient place, and return on the east bank. But after heavy rain, the river may not be crossable, and at the end of Drift Lane, after a gate, following the river slavishly here will produce wet feet early in the walk. It is better to veer away from the river along a track, and pick up the line of the disused Powder Mills leat, which swings back to the river valley. A convenient crossing point may be the waterfall about 3 miles (5km) up the East Dart, making a walk of 6 miles (9.5km) there and back.

*Above: Gunpowder Mills near Postbridge*

*Below: Crockern Tor*

there were 7,000 men held captive, with 500 soldiers guarding them. Initially it was referred to as the War Prison or Depot.

A weekly market was held in the yard to which farmers brought poultry, eggs, butter and vegetables, passing beneath the massive stone gateway bearing the Latin inscription *Parcere Subjectis* – 'Spare the Vanquished'. Prisoners skilled with their hands used the chicken bones to make intricate models of ships and working models of guillotines, which nowadays fetch high prices at auction. Examples may be seen at Plymouth Museum and Buckland Abbey. The prisoners sorted themselves out into a class-dominated hierarchy with 'Les Lords' at the top and 'Les Romans' at the bottom.

At the end of the wars, the prison was closed, and as a result the prosperity of its satellite, Princetown, waned. So Sir Thomas Tyrwhitt, who had initiated the prison scheme, suggested a fresh project to tap what he felt was the agricultural and mineral potential of the moor.

A horse-drawn tramway (the route was later partly converted to a standard-gauge branch line) was constructed from Plymouth to bring up coal and lime, and to export stone, and he intended that the crops grown on the moorland wastes should be farmed. But there is an old saying on Dartmoor, 'You scratch my back, and I'll pick your pocket', and his scheme never achieved the success he desired. The prison opened as a civil institution in 1850, after a short spell as a naphtha factory (the naphtha was extracted from peat), for transportation to the colonies was becoming increasingly unpopular in the empire. And so it has remained to the present time.

Today one can pay a visit to the **Dartmoor Prison Museum**, without first having to commit a terrible crime. Located in the old prison dairy, the centre details the history of arguably England's most famous prison and visitors can purchase items made by prisoners.

Modern Princetown is the home of the **High Moorland Visitor Centre**, housed in what was the Old Duchy Hotel. It provides an excellent starting point to a visit to Dartmoor with its interpretive exhibitions and wealth of information. Beyond Princetown the road once again crosses open moor, and the track of the Princetown branch railway (closed 1956) can be seen on the right. The road also passes close to several hut circles.

# The Southern Fringe

The first turning on the left after leaving the open moor leads (by either road at a fork) to **Burrator Reservoir**, by far the most beautiful reservoir on Dartmoor. It was built in 1898 to solve Plymouth's water problems and increased in size in 1928.

From the dam the foothill lanes bring one, via Meavy and Cadover Bridge, to Shaugh Bridge, below the village of **Shaugh Prior**. From the car park beside the bridge, a delightful 2-mile (3km) walk on National Trust land to the top of the **Dewerstone** leads through woods, along a quarry tramway and up to the breezy summit. This is the Trust's Goodameavy estate; it also owns a stretch of Wigford Down, a landscape peppered with prehistoric remains. The Dewerstone is the highest inland cliff in Devon. In fact it comprises several separate crags of which the highest is the Devil's Rock.

From Shaugh Bridge, head south-eastwards through Cornwood past the china clay workings (see previous chapter) to Ivybridge. Just to the north here, at Harford, the **Lukesland Gardens** are 24 acres (10 hectares) of woodland and garden, with landscaped pools and waterfalls. The rhododendron and azaleas are the highlight of this magnificent site. From Ivybridge the A38 dual carriageway can be followed north-east as far as **South Brent**. This little town has a number of pleasant buildings, especially the Toll House with its list of charges, and the church. Originally a cruciform Norman building with a central tower, at some stage the west end was demolished. Lydia Bridge on the Avon once carried the road between Plympton and Buckfast. On the A38, to the north-east is **Dean Prior**. Robert Herrick, the poet, was vicar here in the seventeenth century, and is buried in an unmarked grave in the churchyard. Sadly, the dual carriageway has isolated it from those who would worship in the church or visit it for the Herrick connection.

# Buckfastleigh & Ashburton

Buckfastleigh was formerly a wool town that derived its power from the River Mardle. Round the edge of the built-up area are the large houses of the mill owners. Diversification has come to Buckfastleigh, however, and many different ventures now thrive in the little town where the moor meets the South Hams. The spired Holy Trinity church, rare on Dartmoor but burnt out in the early 1990s, stands aloof from the town on a nearby hill. In the churchyard is a curious mausoleum-like structure erected over Richard Cabell's tomb following his death in 1677, to make sure his unquiet spirit could not escape to haunt the area, since he was thought to be in league with the devil. Tales of fire-breathing black dogs howling round his tomb were adapted by Conan Doyle when he was researching for *The Hound of the Baskervilles*. Newcomers to Devon will visit the area chiefly to see Buckfast Abbey and the South Devon (the old Dart Valley) Railway, and the two are conveniently sited only about half a mile apart. Just across the A38 from the town is **Pennywell Farm**, where children can meet not only farm animals, but small mammals, falcons and owls.

The **South Devon Railway** runs along the old Ashburton line on Great Western Railway principles, from Buckfastleigh to Staverton, and on to

## The Plume of Feathers

The oldest building in the area is the **Plume of Feathers**, a slate-hung hostelry dating from before the prison. In 1993 Prince Charles opened the splendid **High Moorland Visitor Centre** in the one-time Duchy Hotel, and this is the best place to find out about the national park under one roof.

133

*Scorhill Circle, Dartmoor*

Totnes. Here the locomotives have to change ends and pull trains back to Buckfastleigh. Many films and television serials have used the railway to achieve period atmosphere. There is much to see at Buckfastleigh Station – it has a shop, museum and model railway.

A pocket of limestone occurs in the area, and several caves are known. Scientific research continues at the William Pengelly Cave Studies Centre in Higher Kiln Quarry, which is not normally open to the public. However, the Museum and Bone Cave may be open for certain days in August (☎ (01752) 700293 or www.pengellytrust.org). Near Buckfast Abbey is the **Buckfast Butterflies and Dartmoor**

**Otter Sanctuary** where you can see butterflies from all over the world and watch otters being fed. Pause in the town centre to visit the **Valiant Soldier Museum**, a time capsule of the 1950s. This pub was abandoned in the 1960s after two centuries of use and everything remains as it was when the last customer left.

**Ashburton**, Buckfastleigh's twin, lies 2½ miles (4km) away up the A38, and the way passes a well-restored pigeon cote on the right. It is a pleasant little town with many attractive houses, shops and interesting corners; it repays a leisurely visit. The slate–hung front elevations are locally distinctive. In the middle of the town is a Gothic arch on the site of the Mermaid Inn, now

## Buckfast Abbey

A monastic community lived at Buckfast from before the Norman Conquest to 1539 when, with the dissolution of the monasteries, the buildings were abandoned and fell into decay. In 1882 a band of French monks acquired the site, and in 1907 the abbot decided to rebuild. The only resources available at that time were £1, a horse and cart, and much faith; none of the monks had any knowledge of building techniques. The decision made, one of the monks left Buckfast to learn the basic skills of masonry, and on his return the work went ahead, but with never more than six brothers working at the same time. The abbey we see today was finished exactly thirty years later.

The abbey church and monastic buildings are built throughout of West Country stone, in the transitional Norman fashion. While this style has a certain austerity not inappropriate to a monastic way of life, the fittings are lavish. The altar, centre of Catholic worship, is a sumptuous creation of the modern goldsmith's art; above hangs the richly decorated corona; the font is a magnificent conception in cast bronze. On every side is evidence that there are still craftsmen capable of producing articles as beautiful as those created by their predecessors.

To make the monastery financially self-supporting, many activities are carried on by the monks. Dartmoor heather provides the raw material for the honey which has taken the name of Buckfast to many parts of the world. Another product that finds an overseas market is a tonic wine of secret formula. Cider is also made, cattle and poultry are kept, and the kitchen gardens are carefully cultivated. Other monks, more skilful with their hands, produce works of art in pottery, stained glass, painting, illumination and carving. All of them do what they can for the good of the community. The abbey is open to the public daily.

an ironmonger's shop, where General Fairfax stayed in 1646 during the Civil War.

Ashburton had its quota of French officer prisoners during the Napoleonic Wars, and the grave of one of them, Sous-Lieutenant Francois Guidon, can be seen near the church porch. The nearby willow was grown from a cutting taken from a larger tree on St Helena, where Napoleon was exiled and died. The milestones, which marked their exercise limits, can still be seen on some of the roads leading out of the town. The church is a good example of a Devon town church, with a handsome tower. Ashburton was one of the four Devon stannary towns, but the trade died out there in about 1700.

Near the church is an award-winning new development, St Andrew's Close, and in the middle of the town, in the Bull Ring, is a well-arranged **museum**.

# North of Ashburton

**Buckland-in-the-Moor** is a tiny village high up above the Dart, and reached by a signposted turning right, beyond the country park. The moor-stone church of St Peter is beautifully situated on a hillside, overlooking the deep and wooded valley. The rood screen has some interesting panel paintings, but the church is chiefly visited to see the tower clock, which has letters reading MY DEAR MOTHER instead of numerals.

The memorial was provided by a local landowner who was also responsible for the famous tablets on **Buckland Beacon**, a nearby hilltop. To mark the rejection of a proposed new prayer book in the late 1920s, Mr William Whitley engaged an Exeter monumental mason, Mr W. Clement, to dress certain rocks on the summit, and to carve the Ten Commandments on them. The work was done in the summer of 1928, adding a twentieth-century folly to the Dartmoor landscape. Buckland Beacon is one of the best viewpoints on Dartmoor. Between the church and the Beacon is a well-kept group of thatched stone cottages, which seem to have come to life from a chocolate box. This is probably the single most photographed scene on the moor.

Drive on to a T-junction, turn right and 1½ miles (2km) further on, cross the bleak crossroads known as Cold East Cross. Carry straight on at Hemsworthy Gate and make for Manaton, past **Hound Tor** (on the right), one of Dartmoor's finest tors.

**Manaton** is two places; the part round the church is delightful, with a tree-shaded green, and not a jarring note in the symphony of the senses. But half a mile down the road, a rash of modern buildings has disturbed the serenity of the scene. Another half a mile towards Bovey Tracey are **Becky Falls**, well worth a visit after heavy rain as the falls then have something to show. In dry weather the boulders, which form the cataract, conceal the stream. There is a café at Becky Falls, and the oak woodland is particularly beautiful in spring and autumn.

The road towards Bovey Tracey winds vertiginously over **Trendlebere Down**, a moor-edge eminence giving expansive views eastwards. Leaving the moor, and just after the cattle grid, a turning right leads into **Yarner Wood**, where the Nature Conservancy Council has laid out two nature trails, one short, one longer. Excellent descriptive booklets guide the visitor round this varied woodland. From Yarner, a drive of $1^1/_2$ miles (2km) brings the visitor back to Bovey Tracey, and the start of this wide-ranging tour.

During this tour, which would need about five days to achieve completely, a number of walks have been suggested to take the visitor away from the roads. There are two main wilderness areas which are so inviting to lovers of solitude, where one can wander at will (the Services' live firing programme permitting) all day, and maybe not see another person. The strong walker will not take too kindly to detailed advice as to where to go, preferring to look at an Ordnance Survey map and work out his own route, but a few words of advice may not be amiss. By starting high up you will save yourself a good deal of climbing, so leave your transport well up the contours. Have some goal to reach; a remote tor, antiquity or river head, and work out a circular route there and back. Do not attempt more than you can reasonably accomplish in the time available. Above all, when the days are short, start early in the day.

The custom has developed on Dartmoor of 'signing in' or 'letterboxing' at visitors' books placed in waterproof tins at various remote (and not so remote) places. You can also leave a self-addressed card there for the next arrival to post, and in this way you will discover how soon after your departure someone else visited the spot. The most famous of these letterboxes is at **Cranmere Pool** on northern Dartmoor; there are others at Fur Tor and Duck's Pool (southern Dartmoor). The custom has proliferated in the past few years, with individuals establishing their own letterboxes all over the moor, often with elaborate rubber stamps of imaginative design. Dartmoor does not need these artificial foci. It has plenty of tors to find and antiquities to discover. There are few more difficult objects to locate than a Bronze Age cist, sunk in the heather; and there is a particular satisfaction in navigating across a bleak bit of moor in a thick mist and hitting your destination right on the nose.

Both high plateaux are flat and relatively featureless. When visibility is poor, there are few reassuring 'signposts' like rock piles or trig points. On northern Dartmoor, the red and white range boundary poles and a number of lookout huts and splinterproof shelters help as navigational beacons, though Services' paraphernalia is something most walkers can do without. Southern Dartmoor's high ground may be rather smaller in extent and of a lesser altitude, but it is more menacing when the mist is down. And it has two of the more

> ## Weather
>
> A tor can be a lifesaver in bad weather. The wet and weary walker can nearly always find shelter in a rocky crevice or beneath an overhang. But if the only protection is in the mud under a dripping peat hag, spirits drop and the risk of exposure is very real. Inclement weather is sometimes said to be the norm on Dartmoor. The assertion that the moor attracts 'nine months' winter and three months' bad weather' has a grain of truth. Dartmoor is not to be trifled with; it is to be enjoyed, and this means being prepared.

troublesome mires, **Aune Head Mire** and **Fox Tor Mire**, though the latter is off-centre.

Threading their way through and over the watersheds of the northern blanket bog are some useful '**peat passes**', cut at the turn of the twentieth century by Frank Phillpotts and his friends, to enable them to follow hounds on horseback over this difficult terrain. They are as useful today to walkers and riders, and now appear on Ordnance Survey maps as broken lines. The one on the southern slopes of Cut Hill has acquired the name North-West Passage and winds up this broken slope, taking the easiest line through a succession of open clearings in the peat. By linking up a series of natural erosion areas continuous routes were made. After Phillpotts' death the peat passes were marked by small dressed stones, each bearing a memorial plaque.

# Places to Visit

## On and around Dartmoor

### Ashburton Museum

The Bull Ring TQ13 7AB
☎ (01364) 652698
A well laid out small town museum overlooking the Bull Ring. Open: 2–4.30pm Tue & Fri; 10.30am–12pm Thu and Sat, May to Sep.
♿ 👫<18 FREE ☂

### Becky Falls

Manaton TQ13 9UG
☎ (01647) 221259
www.beckyfalls.com
A heap of enormous boulders down which the Becky Brook tumbles. Spectacular after heavy rain. Lovely woods. Open: 10am–5pm (dusk if earlier) daily, mid-Feb to end of Oct. Wet weather gear essential.
Ⓟ 👫<Family Ticket

### Buckfast Abbey

Buckfastleigh TQ11 0EE
☎ (01364) 645500
www.buckfast.org.uk
A modern building constructed by the monks in the early part of the twentieth century. Physic Garden and Pleasure Garden. Monastic Produce shop. Open: 9.30am–6pm daily, all year (from noon Sun). Services are held daily and are open to the public. Visitor facilities open daily from 9am–6pm Apr to Oct; 9.30am–5pm Nov to Mar. Shops open at 12 noon on Sun. Closed Good Friday and Christmas. oOf limited interest to children.
Ⓟ ♿ 👫<FREE ☂

### Buckfast Butterflies and Otter Sanctuary

Buckfastleigh TQ11 0DZ
☎ (01364) 642916
www.ottersandbutterflies.co.uk
Wander among the exotic insects from many parts of the world and view otters at close quarters. Open: 10am–5pm (dusk if earlier) daily, Apr to Oct.

### Buckland Beacon

Buckland-in-the Moor
A splendid viewpoint overlooking the Dart. The Ten Commandments are carved on the summit rocks.

### Castle Drogo (N.T.)

☎ (01647) 433306
near Drewsteignton EX6 6PB
A granite *tour de force* by Lutyens, less than a century old.
Open: Castle – 11am–5pm Wed to Mon, mid-Mar to early Nov (closes 4pm in Feb).
☂

### Dartmoor Prison Museum

Tor View, Princeton PL20 6RR
☎ (01822) 322130
www.dartmoor-prison.co.uk

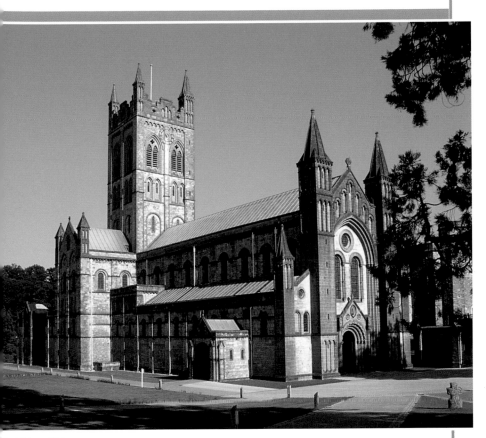

*Buckfast Abbey*

Open: 9.30am–12.30pm & 1.30–4.30 daily (4pm on Fri & Sun). Last admission 30 mins earlier. May be subject to staff/operational requirements, call to check.

Ⓟ ♿ (Mostly) 👪 <Family Ticket ☂

## Finch Foundry (N.T.)

Sticklepath EX20 2NW
☎ (01837) 840046
www.nationaltrust.org.uk
Primitive industrial machinery powered by water. Open: 11am–5pm Wed to Mon, late Mar to Oct.

Ⓟ 👪 <Child Rate

## High Moorland Visitor Centre

Princetown PL20 6QF
Comprehensive high-tech interpretive exhibition with national park shop.
☎ (01822) 890414
Open: 10am–5pm daily Easter to Oct, 10am–4pm daily the rest of the year.
☂

## House of Marbles and Teign Valley Glass

The Old Pottery TQ13 9DS
Bovey Tracey
☎ (01626) 835358
www.houseofmarbles.com

Museum of Bovey Pottery, board games and glass marbles. Glass blowing, restaurant. Open: 9am–5pm daily, all year (10am Sun).

🏨 <FREE ☂

## Lukesland Gardens

Ivybridge PL21 OJF

☎ (01752) 691749/893390

www.lukesland.co.uk

Woodland garden, treasure trail for children, teas available. Open: 2–6pm, Sun, Wed and bank holidays, late Mar to mid-Jun and mid-Oct to mid-Nov (11–4pm).

♿ (Limited) 🏨 <Family Ticket

## Lydford Castle (E.H.)

Built as a prison for those who offended against the forest laws. Open: all reasonable times, free entry.

## Lydford Gorge (N.T.)

EX20 4BH

☎ (01822) 820320

Awesomely deep natural defile closed for safety's sake in winter. NB arduous walk, needs stout footwear. Unsuitable for those with walking difficulties or heart complaints. Open: 10am–5pm April to Sep; 10am–4pm October; 1–3.30pm Nov to March (limited access only).

## Merrivale Antiquities

Near Princetown

The finest collection of Bronze Age remains on Dartmoor.

## Miniature Pony Centre

TQ13 8RG

☎ (01647) 432400

www.miniatureponycentre.com

2 miles west of Moretonhampstead

Hands-on animal sanctuary. Nature trails, adventure play areas. Open: 10.30am–4.30pm (5pm Jul & Aug) daily, Easter to end of Oct.

## Museum of Dartmoor Life

West Street, Okehampton EX20 1HQ

☎ (01837) 52295

www.museumofdartmoorlife.eclipse. co.uk

A comprehensive and constantly growing range of local artifacts. Open: 10.15am–4.30pm daily  Mar to mid Dec.

☂

## Okehampton Castle (E.H.)

EX20 1JA

☎ (01837) 52844

www.english-heritage.org.uk/ okehampton

Norman fortification guarding the road to Cornwall. Open: 10am–5pm, daily, Apr–Sep (close 6pm in Jul and Aug).

Ⓟ 🏨 <16 Child Rate

## Parke Estate (N.T.)

Bovey Tracey

☎ (01626) 834748

Country estate with lovely riverside walks.

## Pennywell Farm

Buckfastleigh TQ11 0LT
☎ (01364) 642023
www.pennywellfarm.co.uk
Range of country activities for all the
family. Adventure play, crafts, animals.
Open: 10am–5pm daily, Feb to Oct.
Ⓟ ♿ ♚ <Family Ticket ☂

## Powdermills Pottery

Near Postbridge  PL20 6SP
☎ (01822) 880263
www.powdermillspottery.com
Pottery,  shop & cream teas in
summer. Open: 10am–5pm daily, all
year (closed Wed Oct to Easter).
Ⓟ ♿ ☂

## Devon Guild of Craftsmen

Riverside Mill
Bovey Tracey TQ13 9AF
☎ (01626) 832223
www.crafts.org.uk
Contemporary crafts centre. Open:
10am–5.30pm daily, Jun–Sept.
Ⓟ ♿ ♚ <FREE ☂

## South Devon Railway

Buckfastleigh TQ11 0DZ
☎ (01364) 642338
or 0845 345 1466
www.southdevonrailway.co.uk
Independent steam railway run on
GWR principles. Services operate
daily from Apr to Oct.  Reduced
services at other times, telephone/
check website for details.
☂

## Valiant Soldier Museum

Fore Street,  Buckfastleigh TQ11 0BS
☎ (01364) 644522
A village inn for two centuries, now
a 1940s/50s time capsule. Open:
12.30pm–4.30pm Wed to Sat,
12.30pm–4.30pm B.H. Sun & Mon,
Easter to Oct.
☂

## Widecombe Church House (N.T.)

TQ13 7TA
☎ (01364) 621321
www.thechurchhouse@nationaltrust.
org.uk
The ancient parish hall, partly used
as a shop by the National Trust.
Open: from 10.30am daily, mid-Feb
to Dec, when not in use as the village
hall, telephone for details.
Ⓟ (Nearby)  ♿ (Ground Floor Only)

## Widecombe Church

Its lofty tower stands high above the
village.

# 5. North Devon

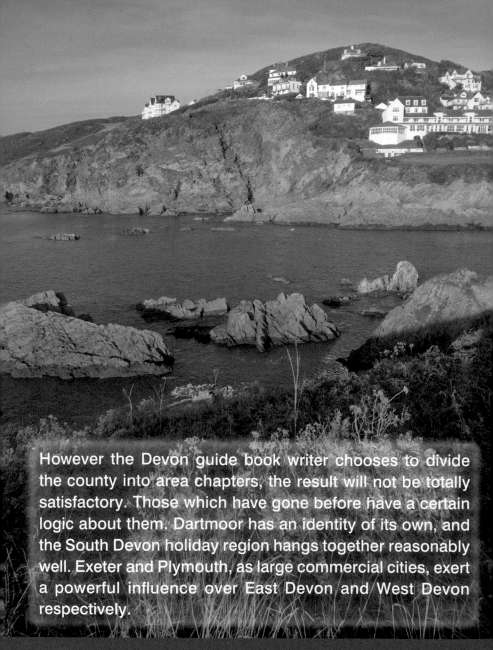

However the Devon guide book writer chooses to divide the county into area chapters, the result will not be totally satisfactory. Those which have gone before have a certain logic about them. Dartmoor has an identity of its own, and the South Devon holiday region hangs together reasonably well. Exeter and Plymouth, as large commercial cities, exert a powerful influence over East Devon and West Devon respectively.

The vast tract of land north of the A30 lacks a focus until Great Torrington, Bideford and Barnstaple are reached. In fact, there is a wide east-to-west swathe of thinly populated land across Devon which is no respecter of county boundaries and runs from the coast, north of Bodmin Moor in Cornwall, to the Vale of Taunton Deane in Somerset. Launceston, Okehampton, Crediton, Tiverton and Wellington form the approximate southern limits of this corridor, and Bude, Great Torrington and South Molton the northern boundary. Within the whole of this 15-mile (24km) wide and 70-mile (112km) long band, there are no towns larger than Holsworthy, Bampton and Wiveliscombe, and the scene is one of scattered farms and villages in a rural landscape.

Agriculture and, to a lesser extent, forestry are the main employers, and other industries like the cheese factory at North Tawton and farm-related ventures on the old airfield at Winkleigh feed off the basic land-based economy. The reasons for this lack of population are complex, and need not be discussed here in detail, but they include geology, soil quality, communications, and quirks of history like the wars against Spain and France which made the south coast important, and North Devon less so.

The effect of this wide strip of small settlements has been to make two counties out of one, North Devon and South Devon, though the actual boundary is somewhat blurred. Those who live within this belt can go south or north for furniture and fridges, school uniforms and entertainment, and all the other once-in-a while purchases.

The interest of the area lies in village churches, old farmhouses and manors, bridges over slow-flowing rivers and distant views of Exmoor and Dartmoor. This is undramatic Devon, where the fun is discovery and finding out for oneself.

North Devon may be split into two roughly equal halves by a line along the watershed – the Taw to the east and the Torridge/Okement river basin to the west. It is an arbitrary boundary.

# North-West of Barnstaple

When visiting North Devon, especially for the first time, many make for the ever-popular coastal resorts between Croyde Bay to the west and the twin villages of Lynton and Lynmouth to the east, often leaving the delights of places like Braunton, Barnstaple and rural villages to occasional rainy days.

The B3231 from Braunton (passing Saunton Court, a 1932 farm rebuilt

# Tourism

Tourism in this area is necessarily thinly spread, and visitors tend to pass through without stopping for long. However, more and more people are enjoying farm holidays, and in the peak weeks of the summer, accommodation is often available inland when the North Devon coastal resorts are full to overflowing. Of course, this area, being less visited than anywhere else in the county, presents a picture of unspoilt, unsophisticated charm, which has long departed from the tourist fleshpots of the coasts and National Parks. This is a place of quiet pastoral enjoyment, of forest walks, and of drinks in real country pubs with the locals. The atmosphere is calm and unhurried, there are few dual carriageways, and resident and visitor alike make their own entertainment.

by Sir Edwin Lutyens; not open to the public) heads straight for the sea and forms the basis of the coastal route from Croyde to Ilfracombe, one of the most popular stretches of North Devon 'seaside'.

At the sea, just beyond Saunton Sands Hotel – a 1937 modernistic building – it is worth pulling into the convenient layby to take in the view. To the left are **Saunton Sands**, with the Atlantic breakers rolling in endlessly, providing the sort of conditions surfers drive hundreds of miles to enjoy. About 3 miles (5km) along the beach, and sometimes rather difficult to see, is the estuary channel with Northam Burrows and Westward Ho! beach beyond. This is Devon's Golden Coast, and these are two of its four great beaches. Out to sea on a clear day the island of Lundy is visible. The saying goes: 'If you can see Lundy it's going to rain; if you can't see it, it's raining already'! Hartland Point is the farthest mainland promontory, but, like Lundy, it may be invisible.

Round Down End, Croyde, the smallest of the four beaches, comes into view. **Baggy Point**, a National Trust headland, is the next feature to the north, and highly recommended as a destination for a 2.5-mile (4km) coastal walk, if one drives round **Croyde Bay** to the Trust car park on the Baggy Point approach, and walks out to the end.

Beside the road are some of the bones of a large whale washed up in 1915, and tucked in under the low cliff but only visible from the rocks is the **Baggy erratic**, a 50-ton boulder of granulite gneiss which found its way here in the Ice Age, perhaps from Northern Scotland. On the cliffs is the plant known as the Hottentot fig whose bright flowers bloom between May and August. (The cultivated species of the plant is the mesembryanthemum.)

Beyond a small stream, the path divides, but the two routes come together at the point. At the point, vertical cliffs fall away, a prime site for nesting birds and rock climbers. Climbers are asked not to climb between the small white posts from 15 March to 15 June. Round the cliff top, and along the north side of Baggy Point, **Woolacombe Sands** come into view with Morte Point the next headland to the north. A signposted path directs the walker across the neck of the point via Middleborough Hill back to Croyde Bay – the stiled path may be followed across farmland back to the car park.

From the car park there is a way through **Croyde**, passing Georgeham (the long-time home of Henry Williamson, the author), to **Woolacombe**. This exposed resort grew up early last century, and is now the focus of a busy camping and caravanning holiday area.

There is a road out to **Mortehoe**, an isolated village with a special church; very dark, with much old work, some of it Norman. Parking can be difficult here, but **Morte Point** (National Trust) is worth exploring. Unlike Baggy Point, as it is all gorse and rough grazing land, the walker can wander where he likes with no pressure to keep to a path: or he can head north along the Bull Point lighthouse road (open to walkers) as far as the lighthouse (built in 1974, to replace the original one of 1879 which had become unsafe due to rock falls), returning to the village past Rockham Beach – about 2 miles (3km) in all. From the north coast of Devon, there are often views across the Bristol Channel to Wales.

**Lee** is the next place to the east, but the first turning left after Mortehoe past Higher Warcombe is not recommended; the lane is exceedingly narrow and steep at the bottom. Better to take the route the buses follow. Lee is sometimes called 'Fuchsia Valley' and the **Old Maids' Cottage** attracts many photographers. The beach is delightful at low tide, with a myriad of rock pools awaiting exploration, and a sandy strath giving good bathing. At high tide all this is covered, and Lee beach is then uninviting.

# Ilfracombe

**Ilfracombe** is North Devon's leading holiday resort, though in the face of increasing competition from self-catering resorts, its hotel trade has fallen away. Old photographs of the quayside show several paddle steamers moored alongside each other, and until quite recently a summer service operated across the Bristol Channel. Pleasure trips to Bristol, Minehead, Lundy and Clovelly used to be part of an Ilfracombe holiday. The restored steamers *Waverley* and *Balmoral* still offer occasional cruises

## Baggy Point

Baggy Point is made of Devonian rock, a rock named for the county in which it was first identified. The headland is composed of Old Red Sandstone, the rock below Exmoor, and is popular with nesting seabirds and rock climbers. From the headland Baggy Leap runs north-westwards, a rocky ridge on which HMS *Weazle* foundered in 1799 with the loss of her entire crew of 106 during one of Devon's most violent storms.

To the north of Baggy Point is Willer's Stone (sometimes, but wrongly, written as Wheeler's Stone), not one but two rocks which are still a hazard to shipping. The name is from William Luscombe, a sailor on the fishing boat *Bessie Gould* . One very calm day, as the *Bessie Gould* neared the rocks, Willer jumped overboard and swam to one of the rocks. He climbed on to it and claimed the pair for Queen Victoria. Sadly, history does not record Her Majesty's response to Willer's increase in the size of her realm. Equally sadly, history makes no further mention of Willer.

during the summer months. Smaller boats ply pleasure trips along the coast to Lynmouth and Combe Martin.

Hillsborough, the 447ft (156m) hill overlooking the quay from the east has an Iron Age hillfort on its summit. **St Nicholas' Chapel** stands on Lantern Hill, adjoining the pier, and is probably the oldest building in the town. As early as 1522 it served as a lighthouse, later suffering many vicissitudes – including being a laundry, dwelling house (two parents and fourteen children) and band practice room. It was finally restored in 1962.

At the western end of the town is the **Torrs Walk** (National Trust) an engineered path up the cliff, starting near the **Tunnels**, a similarly artificial way through a cliff to the bathing pool. Ilfracombe enjoyed its heyday in Victorian times after the railway arrived.

**Ilfracombe Museum** is a cherished collection of artefacts and old photographs. A mile out of Ilfracombe, up a side road, is **Chambercombe Manor**, a huddle of sixteenth- and seventeenth-century buildings round a cobbled courtyard. A number of rooms are open to visitors and there is some good seventeenth-century furniture. At **Hele Bay**, just east of Ilfracombe, on the A399, is the completely restored **Hele Corn Mill**, with an 18ft (6m) overshot waterwheel.

The coast road between Ilfracombe and Combe Martin is 3 miles (5km) of winding switchback, and whether you enjoy the journey will depend on the number of other drivers on the road at the same time. Tempting, fleeting views of the sea will occupy the passengers. After 1½ miles (2km), **Water Mouth** is reached, a rocky boat-bobbing inlet not unlike Boscastle in Cornwall, or a small Scottish loch.

**Watermouth Castle** is an 1825 castellated mansion, now a full-blooded tourist attraction crammed with attractions of every kind, such as antique self-playing musical instruments, a model railway, magic lantern slides, fountain

*Woolacombe*

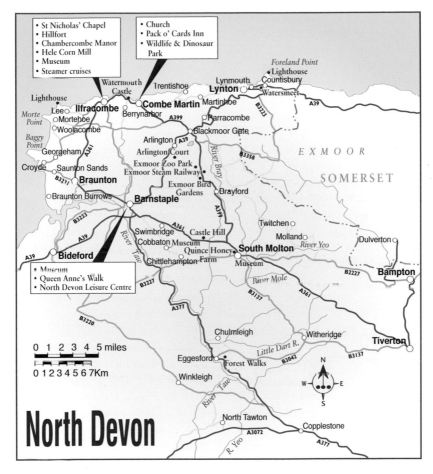

- St Nicholas' Chapel
- Hillfort
- Chambercombe Manor
- Hele Corn Mill
- Museum
- Steamer cruises

- Church
- Pack o' Cards Inn
- Wildlife & Dinosaur Park

- Museum
- Queen Anne's Walk
- North Devon Leisure Centre

**North Devon**

show, water clock and rides. Outside are tropical gardens and a pets' corner.

To underline that Devon is a county of contrasts, after absorbing Watermouth Castle, a visit to the nearby village of **Berrynarbor** is strongly recommended. Here is a true Devonshire village, sufficiently far from the A399 to be relatively unaffected by tourism. The church has a fine eye-catching tower and a Beer stone arcade; surprising material to find so far from the quarry of origin.

# Combe Martin

Back on the main road **Combe Martin** is soon reached, but not so quickly passed through. It must share with Branscombe (East Devon) the distinction of being the largest village in the county, though Combe Martin is continuously built-up, whereas Branscombe is a series of hamlets. Combe Martin must certainly bow to Branscombe's superior beauty, for the North Devon village has little to commend it except the church, the Pack o' Cards

Inn, interesting historic associations and nearby environmental attributes. The church is one of the finest in North Devon, with a splendid tower, rood screen and parclose screen.

The **Pack o' Cards** Inn is sometimes called a folly; it is more accurate to refer to it as an eccentric building (a folly implies worthless impracticality). The story is related that the inn was built in the eighteenth century to celebrate a win at cards. Fifty-two windows, four floors, each with thirteen doors, represent the numerical multiples found in a pack of cards, and the whole heaped-up structure looks like a house of cards.

Combe Martin's silver and lead mines were worked from the thirteenth century to 1875, iron ore was mined from the beach below the Little Hangman, and manganese not far away. All these enterprises have ceased, but a few ruins remain for the diligent searcher. As a sheltered fertile valley, Combe Martin is the market gardening focus of this part of North Devon. Family entertainment with an animal theme is found nearby at the **Wildlife and Dinosaur Park.** This houses the only Wolf Research and Education centre in the UK and is also home of the **Exmoor Brass Rubbing Centre**, formerly based in Lynmouth.

The **Exmoor National Park**'s western boundary marches with the outskirts of Combe Martin, and much of this part of North Devon is in the Park. Unlike the Dartmoor National Park, which is contained within one county, Exmoor is split between Devon (about a quarter) and Somerset (three-quarters). But Devon claims rather more than half the National Park coast-line. This is one of the smallest National Parks: at 265sq miles (686km²) it is exactly 100sq miles (259km²) smaller than Dartmoor. Its special qualities are the coast, the red deer and the deep-wooded valleys. The Park is administered from headquarters at Dulverton in Somerset and there are seasonal National Park information centres in the Devon sector at Combe Martin and Lynmouth, and on the county boundary at County Gate.

The walk up to the summit of the Little Hangman from the beach at Combe Martin is over 700ft (245m) of climbing, about 1 mile (1.5km) each way. But the view and sense of achievement is out of all proportion to the effort. Another mile further on brings you to the Great Hangman, 1,043ft (365m), a mini-mountain where Exmoor meets the sea.

A day-long walk is easily devised along the **North Devon Coast Path** from Combe Martin, and takes in the Little Hangman and Great Hangman, Holdstone Down, Trentishoe Down, Heddon's Mouth, Woody Bay, the Valley of Rocks and Lynton. A bus can bring the walker back to the starting point. It is a strenuous walk, with several descents into deep valleys, and is about 11 or 12 miles (17–19km) long.

Holdstone Down, 1,145ft (401m), is the highest point of a coastal outlier of Exmoor, and, regardless of weather, always seems to possess a sinister aspect, especially when seen from the A39 near Parracombe. The Aetherius Society rate it a holy mountain and hold meetings on its lofty summit. Heddon's Mouth is a deep-cut gash in the North Devon coast, with scree-scarred sides, and a

## The Lynmouth Flood Disaster

**Lynmouth** has recovered from the devastation suffered, when, after a storm of unusual intensity, water, trees and rocks torrented down the East and West Lyn Rivers, sweeping aside bridges, riverside buildings and the harbour, in a catastrophic flood. Several inches of rain fell on an already saturated Exmoor hinterland on the night of 15 August 1952, and the steep hills did the rest. The whole area suffered; thirty-four people lost their lives, and of these, four were never found.

A wonderful job of restoration was achieved, and the harbour was re-designed. Even the **Rhenish Tower**, a folly building on the pier, was rebuilt. The visitor ignorant of the tragedy could be pardoned for thinking that nothing has ever happened to disturb Lynmouth's beauty. But most of the many thousands who flock to the village have heard of that terrible night and maybe perhaps knew it before the destruction and reconstruction.

convenient pub, the Hunters Inn, 1 mile (2km) back from the pebbly beach. High up on either side of this valley are the remote parishes of **Trentishoe** and **Martinhoe**. Both have churches with delightful exteriors, but with over-restored interiors. Woody Bay and points east are best discussed under Lynton.

The road leading east from Combe Martin meets two other main roads at **Blackmoor Gate**, a significant landmark in this part of North Devon. A country livestock market is held here, and the Lynton and Barnstaple Railway, a narrow-gauge branch line, once steamed over this high saddle of land; the station house is now a pub and restaurant. Along the A39 eastwards, past the Parracombe bends, there is, on the left, a sign pointing down a rough lane to Parracombe church.

This is **Parracombe** old church, only occasionally used for services, as another church was built nearer the village in the 1870s. The old church was very nearly demolished, as fears were uttered about its safety. Fortunately, the public outcry was so vocal, and was joined by no less a person than John Ruskin, that the building was saved and is now in the care of the Churches Conservation Trust. The church is a complete survivor from the late eighteenth century. Nothing has been altered since; to enter the building is to go back 200 years. The hat pegs on the wall, the rough benches and the musicians' gallery are all evocative of days when life revolved round the parish church. Now carry on along the A39 and take the B3234 to Lynton, the higher and larger of the Siamese-twin villages of North Devon, the other being Lynmouth.

These two places share the beautiful scenery of the Exmoor coast, but are very different in character. They are linked, and paradoxically separated, by one of the steepest hills in England, Lynmouth Hill. Pedestrians may use the water-operated 1890 cliff railway (see p.151).

# Lynton & Lynmouth

By no stretch of the imagination can **Lynton** be called a beautiful village – it is really a small town. Pleasant corners

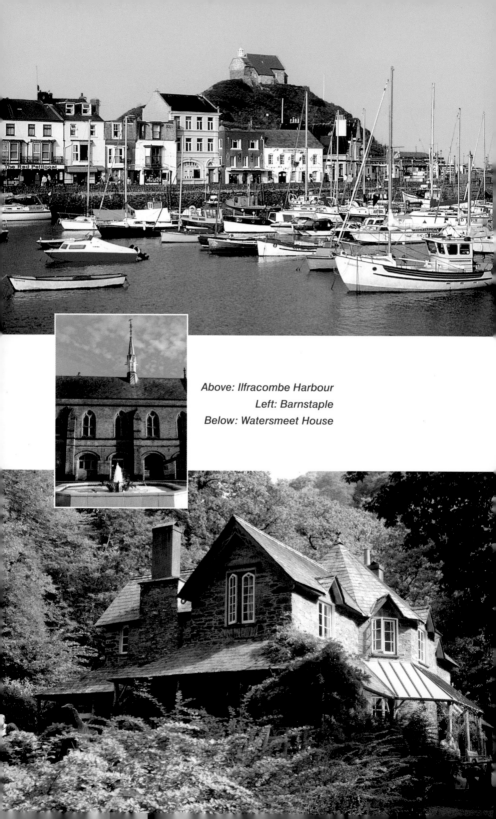

*Above: Ilfracombe Harbour*
*Left: Barnstaple*
*Below: Watersmeet House*

## The Lynton–Lynmouth Cliff Railway

In the mid-nineteenth century the huge, steep cliff between Lynton and Lynmouth was affecting the tourist trade and Bob Jones, a local engineer, decided to build a cliff railway to overcome the problem. After several years of raising finance from local companies and individuals, Jones started work. After the surprisingly short time of three years the railway opened on Easter Monday 1890. The railway is very steep, rising 450 feet in 900 feet (to use Imperial measures for something so clearly Imperial) and is water-powered. At the top a 700-gallon water tank below the carriage is filled, the weight of water dragging the lower carriage (and its empty tank) up the cliff. At the bottom the water tank is emptied, the upper carriage's tank being filled to repeat the process. The trip takes 90 seconds and on the first day cost 3d (three old pennies) for the uphill ride and 2d to go downhill. Bob Jones' design for the railway's hydraulic and emergency brakes were so good that there has been no change since 1890. In all the journeys since that first day, millions of passengers have been transported without one injury occurring, though a dog once lost part of its tail when it wandered on to the track.

here and there and some idiosyncratic buildings like the Town Hall and the Valley of Rocks Hotel rescue it from mediocrity. The hotel is named after a craggy amphitheatre within easy walking distance – half a mile (1km) – of Lynton. Even in an area where hills dominate the scenery, one can walk to the **Valley of Rocks** and back along the North Walk, a well-surfaced cliffside footpath, without having to toil up steep slopes.

The **Lyn and Exmoor Museum** is in the charming St Vincent's Cottage. This is the place to discover more about old Exmoor life, the Lynton and Barnstaple Railway and the Lynmouth lifeboat. Beyond the Valley of Rocks is the aptly-named Woody Bay, once coveted for holiday development, but the plan came to nothing.

At the foot of Lynmouth Hill is the entrance to the **Glen Lyn Gorge**, a privately owned estate where the public may walk on payment of a small charge. A mile-and-a-half (2km) up the A39 valley road at **Watersmeet** the Hoar Oak Water joins the East Lyn River in valley woodland of great beauty (National Trust) beside Watersmeet House (1830). There are so many walks radiating from here, up and down the rivers, or climbing up both sides, that to suggest one in preference to another is invidious. Far better to visit the Trust's information centre and shop in Watersmeet House (it also has a small café), and buy the excellent leaflet map for the Watersmeet area, and the map of the paths around neighbouring **Countisbury**.

This is part of the same Trust property and is best reached by the A39

up Countisbury Hill. This severe ascent – 1:4 at the bottom – is more remarkable for its length, as in 2 miles (3km) it climbs to over 1,000ft (350m). **Countisbury** is a tiny huddle of stone-built buildings around the Blue Ball Inn and the church. This inn is a sturdy, unspoilt hostelry that used to be a stop on the Lynmouth to Minehead horse-drawn coach service which ran until 1913. Yes, horses used to draw coaches up Countisbury Hill.

**Countisbury church**, like others in the district, is more interesting for its situation and exterior appearance than for its interior furnishings. From here there is a view back towards Lynmouth and a great man-made earthwork draped over the slope of Wind Hill in the middle distance like a monstrous caterpillar. This was originally built as a promontory fort in the Iron Age, say 2,000 years ago, but there is good reason to believe it was the battleground in 878 between the men of Devon and Hubba, a Danish invader.

From behind the church there is a walk a quarter of a mile up to Butter Hill, 993ft (348m), crowned by a small television booster mast and a hut which gives shelter for walkers as well as protecting the instruments. This is the high open land (except for a few fields not in Trust ownership) of **Foreland Point**, and paths and a Trinity House road lead down to the lighthouse, now automatic, on the Point itself. The road zig-zags steeply down through Caddow Combe, a curious stony valley with much scree.

Eastwards from Countisbury the A39 undulates pleasantly, giving distant views of the Welsh coast and of ships using the Bristol Channel. Inland, the land falls away to the East Lyn River, then rises again to the high ground of central Exmoor. The Somerset boundary is reached at County Gate.

This is a good place for starting a walk, particularly down the **Glenthorne Valley** to the beach 1,000ft (350m) below, but beware of the distance and climbing involved. Near the beach is the nineteenth-century house, built by the Halliday family and lived in by them until recently, which should not be approached, but there are many other goals, like the **Pinetum,** the **Sisters' Fountain** and the **Seven Thorns,** which can be found. Signposts help the searcher.

At County Gate, the visitor is near 'Doone Land', that strange *mélange* of fact and fiction, folklore and legend which has so overtaken the area that even the Ordnance Survey labels part of the Badgworthy Valley 'Doone Country' on its maps. Authorities are now agreed that the Doones existed as an Exmoor 'mafia' in the seventeenth century, and say that they lived their lawless lives near where the Hoccombe Combe meets Badgworthy Water. Overgrown remains of buildings can be seen in the Combe; grass-covered foundations going back

to the moor.

**Badgworthy Water** is the county boundary here; other places in R.D. Blackmore's book *Lorna Doone* (1869) such as Plovers' Barrows farm, probably Oare Ford farm, and Oare itself, are in Somerset, and do not come within our purview. The Water Slide is on Lank Combe, which joins the Badgworthy Water at the southern end of Badgworthy Wood. Legends of the Doones, perhaps exiles from Scottish justice, circulated by word of mouth and in print before Blackmore wove them into his famous romance, and they continue to delight the tourist to this day.

# Along the County Boundary

The county boundary seems carefully to exclude most of Exmoor's upland from Devon, as if to say 'you've got Dartmoor, at least let Somerset have most of Exmoor!' Even so, Chapman Barrows, 1,574ft, (551m), Shoulsbarrow Common, 1,564ft (547m) and Five Barrows, 1,617ft (566m) are high for Exmoor and are in Devon's share. Dunkery Beacon, the highest point, near Minehead, is 1,704ft (596m). The

## Saving the *Forest Hall*

Before the A39 is left, it is worth pondering on the night in January 1899 when the Lynmouth lifeboat was dragged up Countisbury Hill and along this road before being launched at Porlock. A full-rigged ship, the *Forest Hall*, was in difficulties off Porlock, but the seas at Lynmouth did not allow the lifeboat to be launched there. So the whole village helped with their horses, and pulled, dragged and pushed the 3½-ton lifeboat on its 7ft 6in (2.6m) wide carriage the 13 miles (21km) to Porlock, a party going ahead to widen the road. The effort took 10½ hours, but the ship's crew was saved. There can never have been a more unusual lifeboat launch in the history of the service.

names of these hills with the common element 'barrow' is a pointer to Exmoor's chief antiquity, the barrow. The high-level roads are a feature of the moor. Using the Ordnance Survey map, it is possible to devise a drive of about 12 miles (19km) along the southern ridge of Exmoor, from East Anstey Common in the east to **Five Cross Way** above Brayford in the west, without dropping below 1,000ft (350m).

Occasionally one may see red deer, Britain's largest wild animal, particularly in the open, although they spend most time in the wooded combes. Walkers sometimes find cast antlers. Stags grow antlers afresh each year, and Exmoor 'heads' are usually better than those from the Scottish Highlands, but less good than those from park deer.

Whoever in the past named Exmoor and Dartmoor, though obviously lacking maps, nevertheless knew which river was dominant. The Exe, with the Barle, drains nearly all central Exmoor, leaving its birthplace swollen by its tributary, the Haddeo, to run past **Bampton**, a small market town which only comes to life during the Charter Fair in late October, when the annual Exmoor Pony Sale is held. West of Bampton, and nestling in the southern foothills of Exmoor is **Molland**, a tucked away village with a lovely parish church. A three-decker pulpit, box pews and interesting monuments make it well worth a special visit.

# South Molton

**South Molton** is the only place of any size in these parts, and the kind of Devon market town where one can find old-fashioned courtesy and values. Happily the North Devon link road now takes traffic past the town to the north, making South Molton a much more pleasant place. The main street is lorded over by the Guildhall (1743), which contains the town **museum**. At the Barnstaple end of the town is the **Quince Honey Farm** that advertises itself as England's largest honey farm. The mysterious process of honey-making from flower to table is explained in galleries, demonstrations and observation hides.

The rural route from here to the Barnstaple area first visits **Chittlehampton**, a large village between the A377 and the A361, with a church possessing the finest tower in Devon, 114ft (40m) tall. Inside is a medieval stone pulpit and seventeenth-century monuments. The tower may have been paid for by the offerings of pilgrims to the shrine of St Urith, the patron saint, martyred nearby in Saxon times by savage scythe-carrying villagers.

Not far from Chittlehampton, at **Cobbaton**, 2 miles (3km) north-west, is the **Cobbaton Combat Vehicles Museum**. Strange perhaps to find a collection of World War II vehicles, armoured cars and tanks in deepest Devon, but the collection began as a private one, and has just grown. A children's assault course is a bonus.

To the north the A361 leads to **Swimbridge**, where the church is splendid and should be seen. Under its fourteenth-century broach spire, the fifteenth-century church is rich and fascinating, with a stone pulpit (dating from about 1490), rood screen, bench ends and wagon roofs. The Rev Jack

Russell, the original breeder of the famous terrier strain, and a notable hunting parson, was vicar here in the nineteenth century and is buried in the churchyard.

Some 3 miles (5.5km) east of Swimbridge, at **Filleigh**, is the very grand domed house known as **Castle Hill**. It stands to the north of the road and faces a triumphal arch, an eighteenth-century folly on the hill opposite at the end of a long avenue. The gardens are open to visitors during the summer months. The House was originally built in the seventeenth century, and subsequently enlarged; the middle portion was destroyed by fire in 1934, though since rebuilt. As a stately mansion, it is probably second only to Saltram House in Devon, a county not renowned for sophisticated rural residences.

# Barnstaple

The A361 also leads, of course, to **Barnstaple**, the unrivalled capital of North Devon, a fact acknowledged by health and education authorities, local government, civil servants and industrialists. It is the only place in North Devon to which a railway, the romantically named 'Tarka Line', still penetrates, though one hardly dares to ask for how long. The town, busy and well served with shops and a wonderful market, has the ethos of a county town, and it is surprising that its population falls below that of Exmouth and Newton Abbot to make it the sixth largest town in the county. But Plymouth, Torbay, Exeter, Exmouth and Newton Abbot are all in South Devon and relatively close to each other. Barnstaple is out on a limb, and is nearest to

Exeter – 40 miles (64km), or at least an hour's journey away on a winding road – so it has had to be self-sufficient for goods and services.

## Eggesford Forest

Before leaving this rural part of Devon – discussed in general at the beginning of the chapter – one should visit **Eggesford Forest**, which flanks the A377 near Chudleigh, halfway between Exeter and Barnstaple. It was at Eggesford that the newly-formed Forestry Commission planted its first tree on 8 December 1919, a fact commemorated by a stone unveiled by the Queen in 1956, to mark the planting of 1,000,000 acres (400,000 hectares) by the Forestry Commission. An information office, picnic site and car park are near the stone (on the east side of the road), and two walks of a mile each, the **Home Valley walk** and the **Hilltown trail**, are routed through the trees. Another walk in **Heywood Wood** across the valley can be either 1 mile or 2 (1–3km). Red deer live in the forest.

The town's pre-eminence in North Devon goes back to Norman times; in 1086 it was one of the four Domesday boroughs in the county. Pilton, a nearby village, but now a pleasant part of Barnstaple, was the original settlement in the early tenth century, but the *burgh* was surrendered to Barnstaple a few years later, possibly because it was closer to the ford across the Taw, later bridged

## Exmoor Zoo

Where the road levels out on Bratton Down, on the left is the **Exmoor Zoological Park** at South Stowford. Penguins, tropical birds, waterfowl and rare poultry are on show, together with a collection of small mammals and a pets' corner.

about 1280. The present bridge was built about 1437, but is much altered. A much needed bridge over the Taw was opened as part of Barnstaple's western bypass in 2007, and has greatly eased traffic conjestion in the town centre.

The **Castle Mound** (dating from about 1100) can be seen near the Civic Centre and is now an environmental study area. Once surmounted by a wooden keep or look-out tower, it now grows a mixture of trees, shrubs and flowers, and birds are encouraged by nest boxes. Early in the twelfth century, the town was walled around, but nothing remains of that era, and all the gates have gone.

Barnstaple's early prosperity was built on wool, and much was exported. Later, it began to import Irish wool and yarn, which was carried inland to factories in east and mid-Devon. But when the Taw began to silt up, this trade was transferred to Bideford. A sea-going trade survived, however, and, even today, coastal vessels put in with building materials and other bulk cargoes.

Pottery was an important industry for hundreds of years, and still is, and shipbuilding kept the maritime links going. Other trades were cabinet making, glove manufacture, machine-made lace and industries associated with farming, such as milling and the making of agricultural implements.

**Queen Anne's Walk** near the bus station is Barnstaple's most outstanding building, and a reminder of its former importance as a trading town. It was built in 1708 as the exchange for merchants but now houses **Barnstaple Heritage Centre**. One thousand years of history are brought to life here with interesting, interactive displays. Nearby is the **Museum of Barnstaple and North Devon** including the Tarka Gallery and the Story of North Devon.

Barnstaple's **parish church** is more interesting for its monuments than for its architecture, though its broach spire is worth a second glance, twisted as it is by the warp of time and temperature. Throughout the town there are quiet courts and alleys. Perhaps the best are the **Penrose Almshouses** in Litchdon Street (1627). The granite-pillared arcade recalls a similar style (of 1637) at Moretonhampstead.

Barnstaple is best visited on a Tuesday or Friday when the **pannier market** is at full stretch. Stalls selling fruit, vegetables, dairy produce, antiques and clothing jostle each other; perhaps the dark North Devon delicacy, laver bread, may be on sale. Sold as a wet pappy hcap, it is a kind of seaweed found in these parts and is highly regarded when cooked with bacon.

Standing at the south end of the bridge is the modern **North Devon Leisure Centre** which caters for most popular indoor sports, and has a bar and cafeteria. It is a good place to visit with the family on a wet day.

From Barnstaple, drive west along

the A361 to Braunton, passing, some 3 miles (5km) from Barnstaple, the one-time Chivenor Air Station on the left, now a Royal Marine Base. The hill on the right has the prominent tower of **Heanton Punchardon** church, which has a well-kept plastered interior, with many interesting monuments.

# Around Barnstaple

**Braunton** is sometimes spoken of as the largest village in Devon, but it has the aura of a small town. How many villages possess a good art gallery? It is one of those places which shows its least pleasant face to the casual visitor but the church and its surroundings give a very different impression. The church itself is a delight, with a lead-covered broach spire, stockier than Barnstaple's, but right for the building. Inside, the roof bosses, bench ends and Jacobean woodwork catch the eye. The small **local museum** nearby reflects the traditions of farming and seafaring. For Braunton was once a port; small coasting craft sailed up the Pill (the creek) to Velator on the west side of the main road. This is the way to come to see **Braunton Great Field** (shown on the 1:50,000 Ordnance Survey map), one of the few remaining open field systems to be seen in England. The strips in the area are divided one from another by grass balks 1ft wide.

Beyond (south of) the Great Field is the extensive sweep of Braunton Marsh, a bit of Fenland scenery dropped into Devon, and buttressing this low-lying area from the Atlantic is the largest expanse of sand dunes in the West Country, **Braunton Burrows**, big enough to contain a nature reserve, a firing range and golf course.

The southern tip of the Burrows looks out on to the confluence of the Taw and Torridge Estuaries. North Devon differs from South Devon in not having such a dissected coastline. To travel the South Devon Coast Path from Plymouth to Lyme Regis requires the walker to negotiate nine estuaries. North Devon has only two, which come together before the sea is reached, but what a mighty obstacle they are! One further house remains to be seen in the Barnstaple area – **Arlington Court** (National Trust), some 7 miles (11km) north-east of Barnstaple on the A39. There are usually peacocks on the approach path, and Shetland

## The Gravel Trade

A local trade of some antiquity involves the collection of gravel from tidal banks opposite Appledore, where the Rivers Taw and Torridge meet. Barges from Barnstaple arrive on the banks on an ebbing tide, allow themselves to go aground, and the crew wait for the tide to go out and expose the gravel. In former days the gravel was shovelled into the barges – a taxing task as the barge coamings were 7ft (2.5m) high! Now, the work is done mechanically, but the wet gravel has still to be shovelled on to the elevator. The barges float off on the flood tide – 'fleeting' is the term used – and set off back to Barnstaple, to be unloaded by a grab crane.

# Places to Visit

## Near the North Devon Coast

### Baggy Point (N.T.)

Croyde
Mighty headland with easy circular walk.

### Morte Point (N.T.)

Mortehoe
Gorse and grass-covered rocky head-land with many walking possibilities.

### Ilfracombe Museum

Wilder Road EX34 8AF
☎ (01271) 863541
devonmuseum.net/ilfracombe
Small museum showing the rise of Ilfracombe in the nineteenth century. Open: 10am–5pm daily, except 10am–1pm Nov–Mar.
℗ (Nearby)  &  👪<Family Ticket  ☂

### Torrs Walk (N.T.)

Ilfracombe
Gentle, well-engineered path up the cliffs west of Ilfracombe.

## Tunnels Beaches

Ilfracombe EX34 8AN
☎ (01271) 879882
www.tunnelsbeaches.co.uk
Give access to Ilfracombe's tide-washed bathing pools. Beaches, play area, restaurant. Open: 10am–6pm daily Easter to Oct. Longer hours in mid-summer. Victorian pool visible 3 hours either side of low tide.

## Chambercombe Manor

Ilfracombe EX34 9RJ
☎ (01271) 862624
www.chambercombemanor.co.uk
Delightful old house containing contemporary furniture. Thought to be one of the most haunted dwellings in the UK. Open: 10am–5.30pm Mon to Fri, 12–5.30pm Sun, Easter to Oct. Also 12–5.30pm Sat in Jul and Aug.
℗  & (Lior Floor Only)  👪<16 Child Rate
☂ (Except Gardens)

## Hele Corn Mill

Hele Bay, Ilfracombe EX34 9QY
☎ (01271) 863185
www.helecornmill.com

ponies in the paddock. There is much to see at Arlington, including the National Trust's largest collection of horse-drawn carriages, and it is worth buying a copy of the leaflet map about the estate (which incorporates a nature trail) and the catalogue of ship models in the house.

The present house was built in 1820 and succeeded two others. The Chich-

esters owned the estate for over 500 years, and the Trust received it on the death of the last member of the family, Miss Rosalie Chichester in 1949. She had lived there for 84 years, and the house and its contents reflect her acquisitive interests during a long life.

The nature trail conducts the visitor down to the lake, with its wildlife hide and waterfowl. Jacob's sheep will be

Working water mill. Can produce wholemeal flour and muesli. Pottery and tea room. Open: times vary

Ⓟ ♔♔♔ <14 Child Rate ☂

## Watermouth Castle and Family Theme Park

Combe Martin EX34 9SL

☎ (01271) 867474

www.watermouthcastle.com

Comprehensive tourist attraction in pleasant surroundings. Open: Apr–Oct, Sun–Fri 10.30am–3pm. Closed Sat. High season open: Sun–Fri 10am–3.30pm. Closed Sat. Closed some Mon and Fri out of school holiday times.

Ⓟ ♿ (Steep Paths) ♔♔♔ <Family Ticket ☂

## Pack o' Cards

Combe Martin EX34 0ET

☎ (01271) 882500

Pub shaped like a house of cards

## Combe Martin Wildlife and Dinosaur Park

Higher Leigh, Combe Martin EX34 0NG

☎ (01271) 882486

www.dinosaur-park.com

Family attraction with play area and restaurant. Open: from 10am–5pm (last entry 3pm) daily, mid-Mar to Nov.

Ⓟ ♔♔♔ <16 Child Rate & Family Ticket

## Lyn and Exmoor Museum

St Vincent's Cottage, Market Street Lynton EX35 6AF

☎ (01598) 752225

Fascinating ephemera collection. Open: 10am–4pm, Mon to Fri, 2–4pm Sun, Easter to end of Oct.

## Lynton and Lynmouth Cliff Railway

Esplanade EX35 6EQ

☎ (01598) 753486 or 753908

www.cliffrailwaylynton.co.uk

An effortless and exciting way to travel between the two places. Open: 10am, daily. Closing times vary during season. Open until 9pm in Aug.

♔♔♔ <12 Child Rate

## Glen Lyn Gorge

Lynmouth EX35 6ER

☎ (01598) 753207

www.theglenlyngorge.co.uk

Privately owned valley of the West Lyn River. Open: Easter to Oct. daily 10am–4pm. Power of Water Exhibition during the main season. Gorge also open Nov–Mar, weather permitting during winter. Please call.

Ⓟ (Nearby) ♿ (Exhibition Only)

♔♔♔ <16 Child Rate ☂

seen in the park. Carriage rides along the drive give an idea of what road travel was like before the internal combustion engine. The estate woodlands are extensive, and the nature trail only nibbles at the edges. A full and happy day can be spent at Arlington, and the meals in the restaurant are both delicious and sustaining.

Near the stables is the brick and timber granary which was brought here from Dunsland House near Holsworthy after that building was destroyed by fire in 1967.

East from Barnstaple for a final flirtation with Exmoor, for the National Park boundary is only 1 mile (1.5km) from Brayford, a village on the A399 just past a succession of quarries.

## Watersmeet (N.T.)

Nr Lynmouth
☎ (01598) 753348
Open: Information Centre/
Restaurant/Shop: Mid-Mar–Oct, daily
10.30am–5.30pm (4.30pm Mar &
Oct). The valley is open all year, daily.

## Countisbury Hillfort

(National Trust)
Massive earthwork on Wind Hill.

## Glenthorne Estate

Contains many walks, from County
Gate (at an altitude of 1,000 ft) down
to sea level.

# Away from the coast

## Quince Honey Farm

North Road, South Molton EX36 3AZ
☎ (01769) 572401
www.quincehoney.co.uk
The production of honey from plant
to pot is described. Open: Shop all
year, exhibition and café from Easter
to Oct, 9am–5pm (6pm in summer).
ⓟ ♔ <16 Child Rate ☂

## South Molton Museum

EX36 3AB
☎ (01769) 572951
www.southmoltonmuseum.org
A typical small town museum in
the Guildhall. Open: 10.30am–4pm
Mon, Tue, 10.30am–1pm, Thu, Sat
10.30am–1pm, Wed, Fri from Apr to
Oct.

## Eggesford Forest Walks

Forest walks among the earliest
Forestry Commission plantations.

# In and around Barnstaple

## Chittlehampton Church

Devon's finest church tower. The
pulpit and monuments are worth
seeing too.

## Cobbaton Combat Collection

Chittlehampton EX31 9RZ
☎ (01769) 540740
www.cobbatoncombat.co.uk
Collection of military vehicles. Open:
10am–5pm Sun to Fri, Easter to Oct;
most weekdays in winter. Phone first.
ⓟ ♿ ☂

## Swimbridge Church

Splendid furnishings. The Rev Jack
Russell is buried in the churchyard.

## Barnstaple Market

One of Devon's premier pannier
markets. Local produce.
Tue, Fri and Sat.

## Castle Mound

Barnstaple
Remains of Norman motte, now an
environmental study area.

## North Devon Leisure Centre

EX31 2AP

☎ (01271) 373361

www.leisure-centre.com

Seven Brethren Bank, Barnstaple

All the popular indoor sports under one roof. Open: Mon–Fri 6.30–10.00am (Sat 8.30am–5.30pm; Sun 8.30am–8pm).

Ⓟ ♿ ♛<16 Child Rate ☂

## Barnstaple Heritage Centre

Queen Anne's Walk EX31 1EU

☎ (01271) 373003

www.thelocalchurch.co.uk/barnstapletowncouncil

Exhibition of the history of Barnstaple. Open: 10am–5.30pm Tue –Sat, Apr to Oct; 10.30am–5pm Mon to Fri, 10.30am–3.30pm Sat Nov to Mar.

♿ ♛<7–16 Child Rate ☂

## Museum of Barnstaple and North Devon

The Square EX32 8LN

☎ (01271) 346747

www.devonmuseums.net/barnstaple

Local antiquities from the Barnstaple area. Open: 9.30am–5pm Mon to Sat, all year, not Christmas week.

Ⓟ(Disabled Only) ♿ (Limited) ♛<FREE ☂

## Braunton Great Field

Unusual medieval survivor of the open fields once common in England.

## Braunton and District Museum

Bakehange Centre EX33 1AA

☎ (01271) 816688

www.devonmuseums.net

Small collection reflecting the town's seafaring and farming history. Open: 10am–4pm Mon to Sat; 10am–5pm Good Fri to end of Oct.

Ⓟ(Public Car Park) ♿ ♛<FREE ☂

## Arlington Court

near Blackmoor Gate  EX31 4LP

☎ (01271) 850296

nationaltrust.org.uk/arlingtoncourt

Stately home containing collections of different kinds. Stands in a lovely park with a lake. Carriage collection and rides. Open: House, carriage collection and Victorian garden – 11am–5pm daily, Apr to Oct.

Park – as house plus footpaths open from Nov to Jan during daylight hours.

Ⓟ ♿ ♛<Family Ticket ☂

## Exmoor Zoological Park

South Stowford, Bratton Flemming, EX31 4SG

☎ (01598) 763352

www.exmoorzoo.co.uk

Over 150 species, many hands-on opportunities. Open: 10am–5pm daily in summer, 10am–4pm (or dusk) daily in winter.

Ⓟ ♿ (Tarmaced Hill Paths ) ♛<Family Ticket ☂

---

## Steamer Excursions

### Ilfracombe

☎ 0845 1304647

www.waverleyexcursions.co.uk

Occasional cruises and excursions on restored steamers *Waverley* and *Balmoral*.

---

# 6. North-West Devon

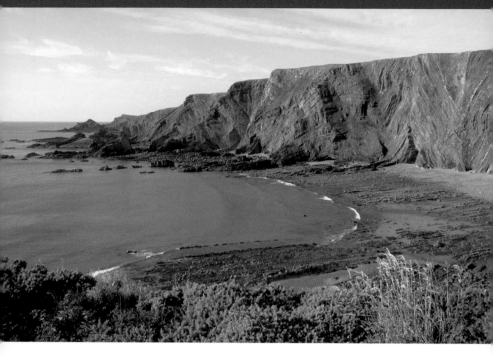

The apologia at the beginning of the chapter on North Devon is equally appropriate here. The wide east-to-west rural corridor bulges across the whole of North-West Devon except for the lower Torridge Valley where commerce, industry and tourism have become established.

If the visitor first approaches this corner of the county from Barnstaple, as many will, along the busy bungalow-lined B3233 through Bickington, Fremington and Yelland, this backwoods character is not obvious. The Atlantic Highway, the A39, connects Barnstaple with a high-level bridge downstream from Bideford.

## Instow

Some 6 miles (9.5km) west of Barnstaple, **Instow** is reached, and can be swiftly bypassed if a distant destination beckons. But that would ignore a village of considerable distinction. Sited in a similar position on its estuary to that of Starcross on the Exe in South Devon, Instow preserved its character by having the railway pass behind the seafront, and not in front as at Starcross. Also, it has splendid sands. Presumably a trick of the tides determines that some estuaries have muddy verges, and others have sandy beaches. Starcross is indisputably muddy, as indeed is Appledore, just across the Torridge from Instow. Mud is fine for wading birds and fishermen digging for worms, but not much fun for family beach parties.

The small seventeenth-century pier hints at an early history, but major events have passed Instow by. An 1838 promotion, advertising 'newly erected' baths, replete with water, hot and cold, and shower bathing', seems to have come to nothing, for no trace remains of the baths. Not the least of Instow's charms is its position facing Appledore.

A mile south of Instow is **Tapeley Park**, an undistinguished house with a fine garden. Originally built in the eighteenth century, it was Gothicised in the 1880s, and finally altered in 1901. The Christie family own Tapeley – John Christie founded Glyndebourne in 1931 – and still live here. The house and garden are open to the public in the summer; the furniture is well worth seeing.

# Bideford

**Bideford** is, by common consent, the most attractive town in the northern half of Devon, and is reached by an ancient bridge from East-the-Water. The bridge probably dates from the end of the fifteenth century when a previous wooden bridge was used as a framework for the stone structure. Because the timbers of the old bridge were of different lengths, the stone arches inherited this uneven characteristic. Several widenings and rebuildings later, the bridge at last failed in 1968, when two arches at the west end collapsed. During the months that elapsed before restoration was complete, all traffic had to travel round narrow lanes to the south, though a footbridge was strung across the gap for pedestrians. A high-level bypass road bridge, some distance downriver, was opened in 1987.

The history of Bideford can be explored at the **Burton Art Gallery and Museum** whilst also viewing both permanent and temporary art exhibitions. A craft gallery showing innovative local work adds to the interest of a visit here.

The eighteenth-century wars and the collapse of the Devon woollen industry killed off overseas commerce, leaving a coastal trade which has survived to this day. In the nineteenth century, Bideford was a trans-shipment port for goods going further up the Torridge. Cargoes were unloaded into barges, which continued upstream to Weare Gifford or, between 1836 and 1871, up the Rolle Canal from above Bideford to upstream from Great Torrington.

## The Grenville Family

Bideford's business throughout history has been the sea and shipbuilding, and the town owes much to the Grenville family, who first acquired land there in Norman times, an interest they retained until 1744. Trade with Sir Richard Grenville's colonies of Virginia and Carolina continued until their independence, and in the meantime a wool trade had developed with Spain, Holland and France. Bideford was involved at an early stage with Newfoundland.

Bideford is now once again the port of embarkation for Lundy.

The town rises steeply from **the Quay**, and there are many corners worth seeking out. Bridgeland Street, at right angles to the Quay, is the street with most architectural pretensions. At the north end of the Quay is Charles Kingsley's statue. This nineteenth-century writer was born at Holne, on Dartmoor, and wrote at least some of his famous book *Westward Ho!* at the Royal Hotel in East-the-Water.

# Appledore and Westward Ho!

**Appledore** must next be visited. Bideford and Appledore are inextricably linked and are only 10 minutes apart by car, though there is a pleasant 3-mile (5.5km) walk along the estuary edge footpath. The shipbuilding industry at Appledore is a present-day success story. The yard has moved with the times, is under cover and turns out ships of considerable size. Furthermore, the yard has not spoiled the town. It is therefore appropriate that the **North Devon Maritime Museum** is sited here in Odun Road above the town. Models, tools and photographs tell the story of the area's long maritime tradition.

Appledore is in two parts: the southern part behind the Quay, and Irsha Street beyond the church. This is a long narrow street, just wide enough for a car, with tempting little cobbled courtyards and slipways. Halfway along are three waterside public houses, and, at the far end, a pleasant open space with views across to Bideford Bar, the treacherous sand-shifting channel through which ships have to make their way in and out of the estuary, and only negotiable for 3 hours around high water. Imagine running for the 'safety' of the Bar in the days of sail, in failing light, and on a falling tide!

**Westward Ho!**, the self-catering holiday resort just 'round the corner' from Appledore is probably the only place to take its name from a book and the only place I know to include an exclamation mark. A nineteenth-century development company used the interest evoked in Kingsley's book to create a watering place at the southern end of **Northam Burrows**, a 650-acre (260 hectares) stretch of sand dunes, salt marsh and pasture. A hotel, church, a few terraces and villas were built, followed by a golf course on the Burrows - even a promenade-type pier, but the waves demolished it very quickly. Kipling was educated here in the United Services College, and later wrote up his schoolboy experiences in *Stalky & Co*. Last century, Westward Ho! expanded as a chalet, caravan and camping resort. The beach, of course, is wonderful; 2 miles (3km) of golden sand, backed by the Pebble Ridge which protects the Burrows from the Atlantic breakers, though now and

again it has to be repaired. Northam Burrows is now a Country Park, administered by Torridge District Council, where the pursuits of riding and golf can be carried out, whilst also being a site of special scientific interest.

South-westwards from Westward Ho! the cliffs rise gradually and curve in a parabola towards Bucks Mills. But North-West Devon extends many miles to the south, and this vast inland district should be described before ending at the Cornish border.

# Great Torrington

**Great Torrington** is a hilltop town, the more attractive parts of which motorists normally miss. A long street of dull buildings ensures that the casual passer-by goes on his way oblivious of its charms. Visitors are strongly advised to penetrate to the heart of the town and explore for themselves. From one of the car parks on Castle Hill the land falls away down a steep slope of bracken and gorse. Round three sides of Great Torrington is an open common. Indeed, Great Torrington is sometimes spoken of as being the English Jerusalem by those who have visited the Holy Land. The slopes are contoured by many well-kept paths, and a walk round the circuit probably takes 1 hour. The town is focused on **the Square**, where the Town Hall stands, with the **Market House** at the bottom end. The **museum** is in the Town Hall (but temporarily closed). Nearby is **Torrington 1646** heritage centre recreating an experience of life in the seventeenth century. Round the corner in Fore Street is the **Plough Theatre, Cinema and Arts Centre**,

165

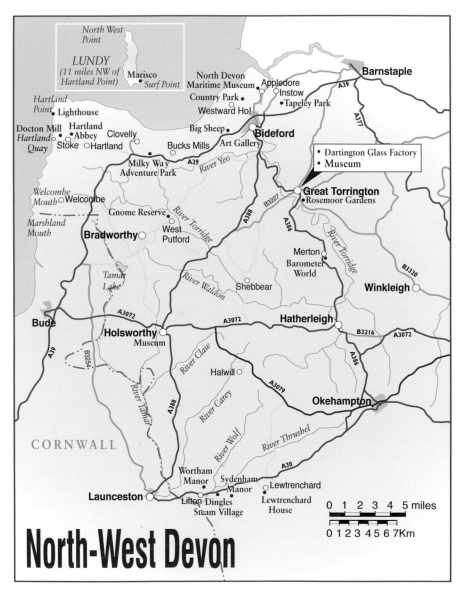

# North-West Devon

a lively community entertainments complex where something is going on most days.

Great Torrington has several thriving industries including the **Dartington Crystal factory**, which opens its doors to visitors and glass is also on sale.

During the Civil War, in 1646, the church, which had been used as a powder magazine, was crowded with Royalist prisoners when the powder exploded, killing several hundred men. A mound in the churchyard may be the mass grave.

*Docton Mill garden*

Just south of Great Torrington, beside the A3124, are the **R.H.S. Rosemoor Gardens**, well worth visiting for the variety of shrubs and plants growing in this sheltered valley.

The A386 going south towards Hatherleigh soon reaches **Merton** where **Barometer World** is a museum of the history of barometers in a workshop where barometers are still crafted. The A386 now continues through the ball clay area round Meeth and Petrockstowe. This deposit matches up geologically with the ball clay beds in the Bovey basin in South Devon.

# North of Dartmoor

**Hatherleigh** is a small market town whose market days are a wonderful gathering of rubicund farmers.

South of Hatherleigh, bestriding the A30 west of Okehampton, are three country houses of more than usual interest. The first is **Lewtrenchard Manor** near **Lewtrenchard** village. This seventeenth-century house, now a hotel, was much altered by its famous nineteenth-century occupant, the Rev Sabine Baring-Gould (1834–1924), the author, folk song collector, antiquarian and hymn writer (the author of 'Onward, Christian Soldiers').

The second house, **Sydenham Manor**, about 4 miles (6km) away along narrow lanes, is perhaps the finest Jacobean house in the county, but is not open to the public.

About 7 or 8 miles (11–13km) north-west of Sydenham, beyond the A30 and **Lifton**, is **Wortham Manor**, an even earlier house, of the late fifteenth or early sixteenth century, somewhat reconstructed inside in the seventeenth. This splendid stone house was deteriorating when the Landmark Trust purchased it in 1969, and it has been converted into three holiday flats. The project received a Civic Trust Award in 1975. Despite being apparently at the back-of-beyond, this house has the new A30 passing nearby.

A very large reservoir to serve North Devon and Plymouth at Roadford on the River Wolf, just 4 miles (6km) to the north-east, offers fishing, sailing and picnic opportunities. Also close to Lifton, at Milford, is **The Dingles Fairground Heritage Centre**., which houses an amazing array of old fairground rides and steam machinery. There is also a village store selling souvenirs, and a childrens' play area.

The part of Devon around **Halwill** has a number of large Forestry Commission plantations, and several walks through the trees are laid out. As forestry operations can alter these arrangements, visitors are advised to contact the Forestry Commission office at Cookworthy Moor, near Beaworthy (☎ 01409 221692).

At **West Putford**, not far from Bradworthy, is the **Gnome Reserve and Wildflower Garden**, where, in a woodland setting, over 1,000 gnomes may be seen living their immobile lives in a 'natural' environment. **Bradworthy** is an interesting village built round an enormous open space once used as a market. The well-stocked shops are worth seeking out.

Not far away, and literally on the border with Cornwall, are the **Tamar Lakes**, two reservoirs straddling the infant River Tamar, the county boundary. In a part of Devon where there are few stretches of water, the lakes are much frequented by waterfowl and ornithologists. Sailing and boardsailing are possible, and there is a picnic area

## Holsworthy

Holsworthy is a market town serving a wide area of rural Devon, and is best visited on Wednesdays, when the Square swarms with traders and shoppers. Once a year, in July, the ancient St Peter's Fair is held in the town – as it has been since 1185! – and one of the charming traditions is the Pretty Maid Ceremony. This began in 1841 when a sum of money was left so that a local single woman under thirty, noted for her looks, quietness and attendance at church, should be given a small financial award. A seventeenth-century manor house contains the town museum.

and water's edge footpaths. The upper lake is stocked with trout and the lower lake is a coarse fishery.

To the west of Bideford the A39 heads towards Clovelly, soon passing the **Big Sheep**, a farm experience. Children can touch the animals or try the adventure playground. Beyond, **Bucks Mills** is soon reached. The village has many similarities with Clovelly, our next stop; a steep, cottage-lined road, in a valley leading to a final drop to the beach. Bucks Mills is small and has a free car park at the top of the village. At the bottom a massive lime kiln is built above the beach.

From here the white buildings of Clovelly can be seen spilling out through the woods like a frozen coastal waterfall. For those arriving on foot with some time to spare, go via Hobby Drive, (foot access only). This leaves the A39 a mile (1.5km) west of Bucks Cross and follows the contours of the wooded slopes for 3 miles (5km) to Clovelly. The name Hobby was given to it as its construction was the hobby of Sir James Hamlyn Williams, the landowner in the nineteenth century. Close to Bucks Mills, the **Milky Way Adventure Park** is the largest indoor children's adventure park in the south-west, with all the usual entertainments plus a few novelties – laser rifles and commando-type nets and swings.

# Clovelly and Hartland

**Clovelly** is the ace in the North-West Devon pack. There is nothing else like it in Great Britain. A very steep cobbled street lined with attractive flower-decked cottages occupies the entire width of a narrow north-facing valley. All cars are kept at the top, and supplies for properties in the valley have to be carried down or manhandled on sledges. The donkeys which once provided transport are retired, and there is a back road Land Rover service (Easter to October) to the Red Lion on the Quay which takes people back up the hill. The **Visitor Centre**, modeled on a traditional Devon long barn is the ideal place to start your visit. Don't miss **Clovelly Court Gardens**, with ancient manor house and church. A beneficent landowner ensures that the place remains unspoilt, and despite the many thousands of visitors it receives annually, Clovelly has the strength of character to rise above the tourists. The tiny quayside has a period air about it. Fishermen are busy with their tackle and a lifeboat is stationed there.

The 8 mile (13km) walk along the **North Devon Coast Path** to **Hartland Point** is highly recommended, particularly in spring when the bluebells and primroses are in bloom. As there is no public transport at the far end, however, one must either backtrack or arrange to be met by car. The first part, as far as **Mouth Mill**, is in the Clovelly estate, and passes various small summerhouse follies, such as Angels' Wings and Miss Woodall's Seat, an incredible clifftop viewpoint. The path descends to sea level at Mouth Mill, and there is another valley a short distance further on at Windbury but, having passed these, the path stays high all the way to Hartland Point. Just before the Point is reached, a truly beautiful beach will be seen, **Shipload Bay**, a rarity in these parts – a sandy beach, at least at low tide. The National Trust rebuilt the path down to the beach as the previous one had been swept away in a landslide.

The 3-mile (5km) clifftop walk from the Point to Hartland Quay is another fine walk, and is short enough for a there-and-back ramble. But most people will arrive at **Hartland Quay** by road.

In the days when England had an extensive railway network, **Hartland** boasted it was further from a railway than anywhere else in the country. Cars have made a difference, of course, but it is still remote, and the inhabitants are more than usually self-reliant. The architecture is not outstanding, but the main street has charm, and to enter the shops or public houses is to experience old-fashioned service and courtesy. Inland from Hartland town are extensive commercial tree plantations.

*Hartland Church*

*Hartland Point
Lighthouse*

*Clovelly*

# Hartland Point

However one returns, on foot or in a car, **Hartland Point** must be visited. This is Devon's own Land's End, a 90-degree turning point on the coast of the West Country, and here the scenery changes dramatically. Left behind are the gentle slopes and wooded combes of the Bristol Channel, for the cliffs and shoreline take on a malignant savagery not often seen even on an Atlantic-facing coast. Fretted reefs of black rock reach out like teeth on a saw.

There is a large car park (small fee), but no beach. Strongly recommended is a short stroll onto the west-facing coast, not visible from the car park. Walk along the coast path beside a wall outside the Trinity House gate as far as the first stile, from where the lighthouse can be seen. Beyond looms Lundy, 11 miles (17.5km) away, and this is the nearest point to it on the mainland.

# Hartland Quay

If Clovelly is the ace in the pack, **Hartland Quay** is the trump! On a calm day in summer everything appears benign. But a struggle to the Quay in a force nine gale in January is a very different matter. Enormous waves crash on this harsh and uncompromising coast. Yet, for over 250 years, a small harbour served this remote corner of Devon and gave a name to the spot. Skilfully sailed small boats edged

in through the reefs, bringing coal, lime, slate, planks, nails and numerous domestic supplies. The record of the arrival of lead for the church roof is still in existence.

The last ship to discharge cargo was the *Rosamond Jane* in 1893, and by then the harbour had already begun to break up under the relentless battering of the Atlantic. By the 1920s it had all gone, and a major effort of the imagination is required to see where it stood. An excellent, well-illustrated 48-page book *Hartland Quay: The Story of a Vanished Port* is obtainable from the **Shipwreck Museum** in the hotel giving the full history of this fascinating place. Two small rows of buildings at the Quay face the 'Street', where there is a hotel with a bar, a shop and lavatories. On the cliff to the north is a ruin which as it stands is probably an eighteenth-century folly, but may have been built from an earlier lookout.

*near Hartland Quay*

## Tarka the Otter and the Tarka Trail

Henry Williamson settled in Georgeham, a village inland from Croyde, after his return from the First World War. There he wrote a book dealing with the life and death of an otter among the otter hunts in the Land of the Two Rivers, as the country between the Taw and the Torridge is known. The book – *Tarka the Otter* – was published in 1928 and won the Hawthornden Prize. Though Williamson lived to the north of the Torridge it was that river that he loved and he had his animal-hero born in a holt near the canal bridge on the river between Weare Gifford and Landcross, two hamlets about 3 km (2 miles) apart, Weare Gifford being about 5 km (3 miles) downriver from Great Torrington. At the end of the book the waters of the Torridge close over the heads of Tarka and Deadlock, the otter-hound, as they fight their last battle close to Landcross.

*Tarka the Otter* is a book which arouses differing emotions: is it an indictment of the hunting of a beautiful creature by a man appalled by the casual slaughter of the trenches, or a glorification of country values, including otter-hunting?

Williamson wrote further books, several of which also document animal lives – *Salar the Salmon*, *Chakchek the Peregrine* – each of which, and most especially *The Lone Swallows*, evokes the atmosphere of North Devon in the first half of the twentieth century. He briefly moved to Norfolk, but when he died in 1977 he was buried at Georgeham.

An interesting project that takes its name from Williamson's otter hero has set up headquarters in Great Torrington with the aim of promoting conservation as well as recreation and tourism in North Devon. One aspect of the Tarka Project is of interest to walkers, as it involves the waymarking of the Tarka Trail, a 180-mile (290 km) walk. The walk is a figure-of-eight based on Barnstaple, going east and then north to Lynton and returning via Ilfracombe, and south through Bideford and Great Torrington to Oke-hampton, returning on a route to the east.

Hartland's great treasure, apart from the coastline, is its parish church at **Stoke**, 1 mile (1.5km) back from the sea, and over 2 miles (3km) from Hartland town. The tower combines strength with grace. Inside, the main features are the late fifteenth-century rood screen, bench ends and wagon roofs. The church is worth cycling 30 miles (48km) against the wind to see, not only for the building but for its setting in a wind-torn landscape. Trees bow before the westerlies, gravestones lean, and there is a timeless aspect about everything which makes a mere mortal feel uplifted by the permanence of the place.

**Hartland Abbey**, a family home since 1539 with its furniture, porcelain and other family collections, is nearby. The Abbey was built in 1157 and dissolved by Henry VIII who then gifted it to the Seargeant of his Wine Cellar. Today visitors can also enjoy a beautiful woodland walk to the beach or wander the gardens, part of which was designed by Gertrude Jekyll.

A walk of about a mile (1.5km) southwards leads to **Speke's Mill Mouth** and the finest waterfall on the north-west Devon coast – a sheer 54ft (19m) drop. This walk is well worth doing, passing on the way the sliced-off hill known as St Catherine's Tor. Speke's Mill Mouth is the second valley going south. In Speke's Valley, **Docton Mill** is a working mill with Saxon origins set in delightful grounds. Its garden, either side of the mill leat is open to the public.

There is one further place on the coast that drivers can visit – **Welcombe Mouth**, though the lanes are narrow and there is little provision for parking. The church is a couple of miles inland. A sandy beach is exposed at low tide and the place is unspoilt, except for the cars. To escape one can climb out of Welcombe Mouth up the coast path to the south and as steeply descend to **Marsland Mouth**, a kind of replica valley, but devoid of vehicular intrusion, and briefly pretend that the twenty-first century doesn't exist, for Marsland Mouth is untainted by technology. What is more, it is only half Devon; beyond the stream is Cornwall, but that's another story…

# Lundy

The island of Lundy lies 11 miles (17.5km) north-north-west of Hartland Point. It is about 3 miles (5km) long and roughly half a mile wide. The MS *Oldenburg*, the island's own ship, sails from Bideford several times a week, though not in winter. Occasional pleasure trips by the paddle steamer *Waverley* are not to be relied upon, but are worth enquiring about. They usually go from Ilfracombe.

A pier has greatly improved disembarkation. There is then a steep climb up the beach road to the southern end of the 400ft (140m) plateau where most of the buildings are sited. The island was purchased in 1969 from the last of the private owners, the Harman family, by the National Trust, but the Landmark Trust leases it from the National Trust and is responsible for its day-to-day running.

For those who want to stay on the island there are 23 letting units of various types and a small campsite. There is a small shop, a public house – the Marisco Tavern – and a church. There are no other artificial attractions; the beauty, wildlife and history are delights enough. The cliffs have a rugged grandeur unspoilt by any buildings.

The Old Light on the plateau dates from 1819, but as it was frequently obscured by fog it was replaced by the north and south lighthouses, which were built lower down the cliffs in 1896. A fog gun battery on the west side is still *in situ* and is a fascinating place to observe seabirds and the interaction of waves and rocks. Both lighthouses are now automatic. (On a personal note the author's great-grandfather was the penultimate principal keeper of the Old Light. He left the island in 1893, and the author's grandfather spent his boyhood on Lundy).

Lundy should never be referred to as Lundy island. Lundy is Norse for 'puffin island'. The 'y' is the same suffix as is found in Guernsey, Alderney, Orkney, Anglesey, and so on.

Lundy is now linked to the mainland by telephone and a wind-powered electricity generator has been built to harness the winds that sweep across the island and to save fuel.

# Places to Visit

## In and around Bideford & Appledore

### Tapeley Park
Instow EX39 4NT
☎ (01271) 860897
www.tapeley-park.co.uk
House can only be viewed as part of a pre-booked party. Gardens at their best from May to Oct. Tearoom. Open: 10am–5pm daily except Sat, late Mar to Oct.

### North Devon Maritime Museum
Odun House, Appledore EX39 1PT
☎ (01237) 422064
Models, tools and photographs in an attractive display. Open: times vary please ring.

### Burton Art Gallery and Museum
Kingsley Road, Bideford WX39 2QQ
☎ (01237) 471455
www.burtonartgallery.co.uk
Open: 10am–4pm Tue to Mon, 11am–4pm Sun all year.
Ⓟ(Opposite)  ♿  ♟<FREE  ☂

### Northam Burrows Country Park
EX39 1SX
☎ (01237) 479708
An expansive salt marsh and sand dune area near Westward Ho! Small park centre. Open; 11am–5pm Easter to Oct.

## Away from the coast in North-West Devon

### Castle Hill
Great Torrington
A beautiful open space beside the town, with miles of contouring paths.

### Dartington Crystal
Linden Close, Great Torrington EX38 7AN
☎ (01805) 626242
www.dartington.co.uk
The public may see quality glass being manufactured. Opening times vary, please call to confirm.
Ⓟ  ♿ (Most Areas)  ♟<Family Ticket  ☂

### The Plough Arts Centre
Fore Street, Great Torrington EX38 8HQ
☎ (01805) 624624
www.plough-arts.org
Theatre, cinema, arts centre and community enterprise.

### Rosemoor Gardens
Great Torrington EX38 8PH
☎ (01805) 624067
www.rhs.org.uk/rosemoor
RHS gardens offering a great variety of settings and plants, shop and restaurant. Open: 10am–5pm (6pm in summer) daily, all year.
Ⓟ  ♿  ♟<16 Child Rate

### Barometer World
Merton EX20 3DS
☎ (01805) 603443

www.barometerworld.co.uk
World's largest specialists in barometers. Museum and showroom. Open: 9am–5pm Tue to Fri and 1st and 3rd Sat in month, all year. Call to confirm times.

ⓟ ዼ ☂

## Holsworthy Museum

EX22 6DJ
☎ (01409) 259337
A small town museum of considerable charm. Open: 11am–1pm Mon to Fri, Mar to Sept closes 3.30pm on Wed.

## Dingles Fairground Heritage Centre

Lifton PL16 0AT
☎ (01566) 783425
www.fairground-heritage.org.uk
Large coll., of old fairground rides and steam machinery. Open: 10.30am–5.30pm Thu to Mon, Mar to the end of Oct (last entry 4pm). Sat–Sun only in Nov–early Dec

## Gnome Reserve and Wildflower Garden

West Putford EX22 7XE
☎ (01409) 241435
Hundreds of gnomes in a 'natural' environment. Open: 10am–6pm daily, mid Mar to end of Oct.

## Tamar Lakes

Bradworthy EX23 9SB
☎ (01288) 321712
Fishing, walking and watersports, visitor centre and cafe.

## The Big Sheep

Abbotsham, Bideford EX39 5AP
☎ (01237) 472366
www.thebigsheep.co.uk
Themed farm with all-weather attractions. Open: 10am–6pm daily, Apr to Oct. 10am–5pm weekend and half-terms only, November to Mar.

ⓟ  ዼ  ẘ <3feet Child Rate  ☂

## Great Torrington Heritage Museum

Town Hall
☎ (01805) 624324
Temporarily closed.

## Torrington 1646

Castle Hill, South Street, Gt Torrington EX38 8AA
☎ (01805) 626146
www.torrington-1646.co.uk
Displays show how the Civil War affected the town. Open: 10am–5pm Mon to Fri, Apr to Sep; Sat 10am–3pm Jul & Aug. Last entry 2hrs before closure.

# The North-West Devon Coast

## Milky Way Adventure Park

Clovelly EX39 5RY
☎ (01237) 431255
www.themilkyway.co.uk
Voted one of the best 50 theme parks in the world. Open: Easter–Oct, daily 10.30am–6pm. Also open weekends and school holidays in

# Places to Visit

| | |
|---|---|
| ℗ | Parking Available |
| ♿ | Disabled Facilities |
| ♁ | Family Attraction |
| <№ | Concession for under certain ages |
| ☂ | Suitable in Wet Weather |

winter, 11am–5pm.

℗  ♿  ♁ <1.2Metres Child Rate  ☂

## Bucks Mills

A narrowly confined valley village leading down to a beach that disappears at high tide.

## Clovelly

A beautifully-kept village with an extremely steep main street leading to the harbour.

## Hobby Drive

Clovelly
A winding, wooded, private, pedestrian-only unsurfaced drive from which you have glimpses of the sea.

## Mouth Mill

Clovelly
Only to be reached by walking. A deep valley usually devoid of people.

## Hartland Abbey

EX39 6DT
☎ (01237) 441264
www.hartlandabbey.com
Sixteenth-century family home, gardens, dairy, museum. Open: 2–12pm Wed, Thu, Sun, bank holidays in Apr and May, also Mon and Tue Jun to Sep. Gardens open Sun to Fri 12.30–5pm, Apr to Sep.

## Hartland Church

Stoke
Wonderful tower, screen, bench ends and roof in bleak setting.

## Hartland Point/Lighthouse

Savage turning point on coast where the Bristol Channel ends and the Atlantic begins.

## Hartland Quay

The quay has gone, but the place remains. The small museum in the hotel should be visited.

## Speke's Mill Mouth

Hartland
Has the finest coastal waterfall on the northern coast of Devon.

## Docton Mill Gardens and Tea Room

South of Hartland Point EX39 6EA
☎ (01237) 441369
www.doctonmill.co.uk
Gardens around a working mill.
Open: daily 10am–6pm Mar to Oct.

℗  ♁ <Children FREE

## Travel to Lundy

Details from Lundy Shore Office, The Quay, Bideford EX39 2LY
☎ (01271) 863636
www.lundyisland.co.uk
The Landmark Trust have several properties to let daily or weekly for holiday accommodation.
MS *Oldenburg* sails several times a week, Mar to the end of Oct.

℗ (£2.50)  ♁ <Family Ticket

# How to get to Devon

## By Car

M4/M5 or M25/M3/A303/A30 to Exeter. A38 Devon Expressway links Exeter to Plymouth with access to all destinations in between. For north Devon leave M5 at J27 to Barnstaple.

## By Rail

Direct services from London (Paddington), the Midlands, North of England, South Wales and Scotland. Contact National Rail Enquiry Office ☎ (08457) 484950 for further details or website, www.nationalrail.co.uk

## By Coach

National Express runs regular services to Devon from most areas of Britain. ☎ (08717) 818181 for details or website, http://www.nationalexpress.com

## By Air

Direct flights to Plymouth from many British airports. Connecting flights from other UK destinations. Contact Plymouth Airport on ☎ (01752) 204090 or website, www. plymouthairport.com

## By Sea

To Plymouth from Roscoff, Brittany and Santander, Spain. Contact Brittany Ferries, ☎ 0871 244 0744 or website, www.brittanyferries.com

# Accommodation

There is a very wide range of accommodation available throughout the area, from hotels, guest houses, farmhouses, bed and breakfast establishments, inns and youth hostels, to caravan and campsites, self-catering in all types of property and camping barns.

## Hotels, Guest Houses, Bed and Breakfast, Inns

Details of this type of accommodation can be obtained from the appropriate local Tourist Information Centre. These are listed towards the end of the Fact File.
The Dartmoor Tourist Association issues a comprehensive guide to both serviced and self-catering accommodation in the Dartmoor area.
☎ (01837) 52200
or write to Dartmoor Parnership Limited,Unit 6, Okehampton Business Centre, Higher Stockley Mead, Okehampton EX20 1FJ
E-mail: info@discoverydartmoor.com
www.discoverdartmoor.co.uk
www.dartmooraccommodation.co.uk

## Farm Holidays

### Devon Farm Holidays

☎ 0870 225 0079
www.devonfarms.co.uk

### Farm and Cottage Holidays

☎ (01237) 479698
www.holidaycottages.co.uk

### North Devon Farm Holidays

☎ (01288) 341215 for B&B;
☎ (01769) 560796 for self-catering
www.north-devon-farm-holidays.co.uk

## Youth Hostels

Details of YHA hostels in the area from Youth Hostel Association:
Trevelyan House, Dimple Road, Matlock, Derbyshire DE4 3YH.
☎ (01629) 592700
website: www.yha.org.uk

## Caravan and Campsites

Contact nearest Tourist Information Centre for details of sites.

## Self-Catering

Local Tourist Information Centres and the following agencies will be pleased to supply details of properties available:

### Helpful Holidays

☎ (01647) 433593
www.helpfulholidays.com

### North Devon Holiday Homes

☎ (01271) 376322
www.northdevonholidays.co.uk

### Salcombe Holiday Homes

☎ (01548) 843485
www.salcombe.com

### South West Holiday Cottages

☎ (01752) 260711
www.southwestholidaycottages.com

## Specialist Holidays

For details of Activity Holidays, go to:
www.devon-online.com

# Birdwatching Sites

### Berry Head Country Park

Brixham

### Dawlish Warren

east of Dawlish.

### Exe Estuary

reserves on east and west shores.

### Fernworthy Reservoir

approx. 6 miles west of Moreton-hampstead.

### Lundy

10 miles off north Devon coast.

### Prawle Point

south of Kingsbridge.

### Slapton Ley Nature Reserve

nr Torcross.

### Tamar Lakes

north-west of Holsworthy.

### Yarner Wood

between Bovey Tracey and Manaton.

### Taw Estuary

near Barnstaple.

# Boat Trips

### Riverlink
Dartmouth
Cruises and private hire.
☎ (01803) 834488
www.pdsr.co.uk

### Estuary Boat Trips
Salcombe
☎ (01548) 844475
www.salcombeboathire.co.uk

### Plymouth Boat Cruises Ltd
☎ (01752) 408590/ 0781 398 0833

### Rivermaid
Salcombe
☎ (01548) 853525/853607
Kingsbridge to Salcombe ferry cruises and scenic creeks and coastal excursions.

### Tamar Cruising
Plymouth
☎ (01752) 822105
www.tamarcruising.com

### Tarka Cruises, Appledore
☎ (01237) 477505

# Cycling

Devon County Council publishes a number of leaflets on cycling routes in Devon covering long and short distances and including some off-road routes.
☎ (01392) 383223/382104
www.visitdevon.com
The Dartmoor Way is a circular route around Dartmoor of 90 miles (145km). In addition Dartmoor National Park Authority publishes a guide to cycling on Dartmoor and a map showing off road cycle routes. They are available from all National Park Information Centres or ☎ (01822) 890414.
There are leaflets available about cycling in the Exmoor National Park.
These are available from Exmoor National Park Visitor Centre, Dulverton, TA22 9EX
☎ (01398) 323841.
Remember cycling is only allowed on public roads, byways open to all traffic, public bridlepaths and Forestry Commission roads. Cycling is not permitted on public footpaths, common land or open moorland.

## Facilities for the disabled

The English Riviera Tourist Board publishes a free leaflet Access for all, which details facilities, specialist equipment hire, transport, hotels, restaurants, tourist attractions, car parking etc and also local organisations and associations which can offer help and advice. Contact the Tourist Centre, Vaughan Parade, Torquay, TQ2 5JG
☎ (01803) 211211 or e-mail: holiday@torbay.gov.uk
website: www.englishriviera.co.uk
For information on accessible areas on Dartmoor contact ☎ (01822) 890414.
Accessible Exmoor – a Guide for Disabled People is available free of charge, from TICs or National Park Information Centres. ☎ (01398) 323665
www.whatsonexmoor.co.uk

# Ferries

## Bideford (and Ilfracombe in summer) to Lundy on MS Oldenburg.

☎ (01271) 863636
March to October, several times a week.

## Dartmouth to Kingswear

Operates all year, approximately every 10 minutes, vehicles and passengers.
☎ (01803) 832580
Two vehicle ferries, higher and lower (both carry foot passengers as well). Higher connects with the A3022 Torbay ring road at Kingswear. Lower connects with the B2305 at Kingswear. Foot ferry operates from Kingswear station on the Paignton and Dartmouth Steam Railway. All services run daily at frequent intervals until late evening.

## Salcombe/East Portlemouth Ferry

☎ (01548) 842061/842364
Runs all year to and from Salcombe and East Portlemouth.

## South Sands Ferry

☎ (01548) 561035
Runs South Sands to Salcombe between Easter and the end of October half-term.

## Western Lady Ferry Service

☎ (01803) 842424 (Brixham) and (01803) 297292.
www.westernladyferry.com
Runs from Torquay to Brixham and return.

Details of other ferry services that are useful when walking the coastal paths may be found in the South West Coast Path Association guide.
☎ (01752) 896237.
www.swcp.org.uk

# Fishing

For detailed information on fishing opportunities in Devon contact:

## South West Lakes Trust

Coarse and fly fishing
☎ (01566) 771930
www.swlakestrust.org.uk

## Mid-Devon District Council

Produce a guide to fishing in the heart of Devon
☎ (01884) 255827

# Golf

There are several golf courses in the area which accept non-members on payment of green fees.  A selection only is given here.

### Ashbury Golf Course
Okehampton
☎ (01837) 55453

### Bigbury Golf Course
nr Salcombe
☎ (01548) 810557

### Dainton Park
Newton Abbot
☎ (01803) 815000

### Dartmouth Golf and Country Club
☎ 0800 043 3669

### Ilfracombe Golf Club
☎ (01271) 862176

### Woolacombe and Mortehoe Golf Club
☎ (01271) 870343

### Royal North Devon Golf Club
☎ (01237) 473817

### Saunton Golf Club
☎ (01271) 812436

### Teign Valley Golf Club
☎ (01647) 253026

### Teignmouth Golf Club
☎ (01626) 777070

### Torquay Golf Club
☎ (01803) 314591

### Gt Torrington Golf Club
☎ (01805) 622229

### Wrangaton Golf Club
nr South Brent
☎ (01364) 73229

# Guided City Tours

Exeter City Council Red Coat Guides offer free guided walks around the City, on a variety of themes, all year round.  Most walks last 90 minutes and there are usually between 4 and 6 a day to choose from. Between November and March there is a reduced programme of 2 tours per day.
☎ (01392) 265203 for full details
www.exeter.gov.uk

# Guided Walks

Dartmoor National Park Authority offers a programme of guided walks.  They vary from gentle half-hour strolls to full days on the high moors.  All walks have a theme whether it be wildlife, archaeology, sketching, navigation skills, strolls by moonlight or picnic walks. A small charge is made for participants unless they arrive by public transport (ticket to be shown to walk leader) in which case the walk is free. Full programme available from local Tourist Information Centres and published in the annual free

information newspaper issued by the Park Authority.
☎ (01822) 890414 for further information or www.dartmoor-npa.gov.uk
Exmoor National Park Authority offers guided walks. Contact Exmoor National Park
Authority, Exmoor House, Dulverton, TA22 9HL, ☎ (01398) 323841 or any National
Park information centre for details, or www.exmoor-nationalpark.gov.uk

# Local events and festivals

## Ashburton
Early July, Carnival; early
November, Winter Carnival

## Bampton
October, Charter Fair

## Barnstaple,
Late May, Jazz Festival;
September, Fair and Carnival week

## Bideford
September, Carnival and Regatta

## Chagford
August, Agricultural and Flower Show

## Exeter
Mid-May, Devon County Show; late May/
early June, Exeter Festival

## Great Torrington
First Thursday in May, Torrington May
Fair

## Hatherleigh
November, Carnival

## Holsworthy
May, Agricultural Show; July, St Peter's
Fair; November, Carnival

## Honiton
July, Fair with Hot Pennies ceremony;
August, Agricultural Show; October,
Carnival

## Ilfracombe
June, North Devon Festival; all summer,
Evening Entertainment on the seafront;
July/August, Sea Fishing Festival

## Kingsbridge
July, Fair Week

## Modbury
May, Carnival

## Moretonhampstead
August, Carnival, Horse and Flower
Show

## Newton Abbot
May, Merrymakers' Day; July,
Carnival; September, Cheese and Onion
Fayre

## Okehampton
August, Show; October, Carnival

## Ottery St Mary
November, Carnival and Tar Barrel
Rolling

## Plymouth
August Bank Holiday weekend, Plymouth
Navy Days

## Sidmouth
August, International Folk Festival

## South Molton

Last Wednesday in August, Sheep Fair

## Tavistock

May, Show; June, Annual Art Exhibition; July, Carnival; October, Tavistock Goose Fair

## Torbay

July/August, Torbay Carnival, August, Regattas at Paignton, Dartmouth, Torbay and Brixham; December, Torquay Christmas Carnival

## Totnes

Every Tuesday morning May-September, Elizabethan Market

## Widecombe-in-the-Moor

September, Widecombe Fair

**Many more events both large and small happen throughout the region and details will always be available at TICs and in the free tourist newspapers which are readily available.**

# Maps

The following Ordnance Survey maps cover the area included in this book:

**Explorer Series, 1:25 000 scale (4cm to 1km or 2½in to 1 mile)**
108 Lower Tamar Valley & Plymouth
110 Torquay & Dawlish
112 Launceston & Holsworthy
113 Okehampton
114 Exeter & the Exe Valley
115 Exmouth & Sidmouth
126 Clovelly & Hartland
127 South Molton & Chulmleigh
139 Bideford, Ilfracombe & Barnstaple

**Outdoor Leisure Series, 1:25 000 scale (4cm to 1km or 2½in to 1 mile)**
9 Exmoor
20 South Devon - Brixham to Newton Ferrers
28 Dartmoor

**Landranger Series, 1:50 000 scale (2cm to 1km or 1¼in to 1 mile)**
180 Barnstaple & Ilfracombe
190 Bude & Clovelly
191 Okehampton & North Dartmoor
192 Exeter & Sidmouth
201 Plymouth & Launceston, Tavistock & Looe
202 Torbay & South Dartmoor, Totnes & Salcombe

# Public Transport

There is a network of public transport throughout the area, enabling visitors to travel in comfort without the strain of driving and the problems of parking. Everyone can enjoy the view and linear walks become possible as there is no need to return to the car at the end of the day. Fewer cars on the roads will make this lovely area a pleasanter place for everyone to enjoy. Local TICs will always be delighted to supply up-to-date information.

## *Traveline*

All public transport enquiries in the south west :-
☎ 0871 200 2233 or www.traveline.org.uk

## *Devon Bus Enquiry line*

Timetable information for all local bus services - ☎ (01392) 382800 Mon–Fri 8.30am–5pm. www.devon.gov.uk/buses

In addition to the main railway line serving the south coast, the Tarka Line runs between Exeter and Barnstaple. There are also a number of private railways in the area. All rail enquiries to ☎ 0845 748 4950. www.nationalrail.co.uk

In the Torbay area Stagecoach South West operates local services which include rover tickets for use throughout the Torbay area. Open top buses run along the routes in the seafront area and by taking the bus to Paignton Zoo visitors receive a discount on admission. Combined tickets are available for journeys using the Paignton to Kingswear Steam Railway, the Dartmouth Ferry, a cruise from Dartmouth to Totnes and return from Totnes by bus. Contact Stagecoach: ☎ (01392) 427711 www.stagecoachbus.com, call Traveline (see above) or enquire at the Tourist Information Centres for more details.

There are regular interlinking bus services to and across Dartmoor. Trains run along the Exeter to Plymouth line, the Tamar Valley line, the Dartmoor Railway, and on Sundays the Exeter to Okehampton line. These give access to towns on the edge of Dartmoor and, by connecting buses, to areas further afield. Anyone joining a Dartmoor National Park Guided Walk who arrives by public transport will not have to pay a fee for the walk. The Exmoor Moor Rover ia a flexible transport service that operates in July, August and September,but must be booked at least 24 hours in advance. ☎ (01643) 709701 or download a leaflet from http://www.exmoor-nationalpark.gov. uk/moor_rover_leaflet.pdf

# Swimming Pools (Indoor)

## *Brixham Pool*
Higher Ranscombe Road
☎ (01803) 857151

## *Holsworthy Leisure Centre*
Western Road
☎ (01409) 254013

## *Ivybridge Leisure Centre*
Leonards Road
Ivybridge
☎ (01752) 896999

## Quayside Leisure Centre
Rope Walk
Kingsbridge
☎ (01548) 857100

## Torbay Leisure Centre
Paignton
☎ (01803) 522240

## Central Park Leisure Pools
Plymouth
☎ (01752) 566410

## Plymouth Pavilions
☎ 0845 146 1460

## Plympton Pool
☎ (01752) 348459

## Meadowlands Leisure Pool
Tavistock
☎ (01822) 617774

## Waves Leisure Pool
Chestnut Avenue
Torquay
☎ (01803) 299992

## Swim Torquay
Plainmoor
Torquay
☎ (01803) 323400

## Torridge Pool
Northam, nr Bideford
☎ (01237) 471794

## Torrington Leisure Centre
School Lane
☎ (01805) 623085

# Tourist Information Centres
Those Centres marked with asterisks are open in the summer only.

## Ashburton
☎ (01364) 653426

## *Axminster
☎ (01297) 34386

## Barnstaple
☎ (01271) 375000

## Bideford
☎ (01237) 477676

## Bovey Tracey
☎ (01626) 832047

## Braunton
☎ (01271) 816400

## Brixham
☎ (01803) 211211

## Buckfastleigh
☎ (01364) 644522

## Budleigh Salterton
☎ (01395) 445275

## *Combe Martin
☎ (01271) 883319

## *Crediton
☎ (0800) 0187720

## Dartmouth
☎ (01803) 834224

## Dawlish
☎ (01626) 215665

## Exeter
☎ (01392) 665700
www.exeter.gov.uk

## Exmouth
☎ (01395) 222299

## Great Torrington
☎ (01805) 626140

## Hartland Peninsula
☎ (01327) 431504

## Haytor
☎ (01364) 661520

## Holsworthy
☎ (01409) 254185

## Honiton
☎ (01404) 43716

## Ilfracombe
☎ (01271) 863001

## Ivybridge (South Dartmoor Tourist Information)
☎ (01752) 897035

## Kingsbridge
☎ (01548) 853195

## Lynton/Lynmouth
☎ (01598) 752225

## *Modbury
☎ (01548) 830159

## *Moretonhampstead
☎ (01647) 440043

## Newton Abbot
☎ (01626) 215667

## *Okehampton
☎ (01837) 53020

## *Ottery St Mary
☎ (01404) 813964

## Paignton
☎ (01803) 211211

## Plymouth
The Barbican
☎ (01752) 306330
www.visitplymouth.co.uk

## Plymouth Discovery Centre
March Mills
☎ (01752) 266030

## Princetown (High Moorland Visitor Centre)
☎ (01822) 890414

## Salcombe
☎ (01548) 843927

## Seaton
☎ (01297) 21660

## Sidmouth
☎ (01395) 516441

## *South Molton
☎ (01769) 574122

## Tavistock
☎ (01822) 612938

## Teignmouth
☎ (01626) 215666

## Tiverton
☎ (01884) 255827

## Torquay
☎ (01803) 211211
www.englishriviera.co.uk

## Totnes
☎ (01803) 863168

## *Woolacombe
☎ (01271) 870553

# Walking

There are a number of walking trails in the area. Contact any TIC for a free leaflet *Walking Trails in Devon* outlining the routes ☎ (0870) 608553.
The Dartmoor Way is a 90-mile (145km) walking route around the moor, or download from www.devon.gov.uk/ddwalking.pdf

Additional information about walks on Dartmoor can be obtained from High Moorland Visitor Centre.
☎ (01822) 890414 or www.dartmoor-npa.gov.uk

For information about walking on the 700-odd miles of footpaths and bridleways on Exmoor contact the National Park Office:
☎ (01398) 323665 or www.exmoor-nationalpark.gov.uk

The South West Coast Path runs for part of its 630 mile length along the South Devon coast. The South West Way Association produces a guide to the route with details of accommodation, transport, ferries and tide tables. South West Coast Path Association
☎ (01752) 896237, www.swcp.org.uk

# Watersports

All forms of watersports can be enjoyed around the coast of Devon. For up-to-date information on facilities, tides, weather etc. contact the nearest TIC.

# Weather

For one to ten day forecasts for Devon call Weathercall
☎ (09068) 500404.
For coastal forecast for sailors use Marine Call ☎ (09068) 500458

# Websites

The following websites provide useful information on local facilities etc.

Dartmoor and west Devon – www.dartmoor.co.uk
Devon Tourist Board – www.visitdevon.co.uk
Exeter, east Devon and mid Devon – www.exeterandessentialdevon.co.uk
North Devon – www.northdevon.co.uk
South Devon – www.visitsouthdevon.co.uk
Torbay, (Torquay, Brixham and Paignton) – www.englishriviera.co.uk

# Index

# Index

Published in the UK by:
**Horizon Editions Ltd,**
**Trading as The Horizon Press**
The Oaks, Moor Farm Road West, Ashbourne, DE6 1HD
Tel: (01335) 347349
E-mail: books@thehorizonpress.co.uk

**6th Edition**

ISBN 978-1-84306-493-0

© **Brian Le Messurier 2010**

British Library Cataloguing in Publication Data:
A catalogue record for this book is available from the British Library


**Printed by:** Gomer Press Ltd,Llandysul
**Cartography:** Mark Titterton & Sarah Labuhn
**Design:** Michelle Prost & Sarah Labuhn
**Edited by:** This edition was updated by Ian Howe

**Front cover:** Beer
**Back Cover top:** Sidmouth
**Back Cover bottom:** Mol's Coffee House/ Bookshop, Exeter

**Picture Credits:**
The images below are supplied by Shutterstock with copyright to:
**Juneisy Q. Hawkins:** p.166b & front cover; **David Hughes:** p.102, p.138
**Mark William Penny:** p.59TL; **Russ Du Parcq:** p.14
**Martin Garnham:** p.20; **Peter Elvidge:** p.18; **Catherine Jones:** p.18

**Devon Tourism:** p.10t, p.10b, p11b, p.34m, p.50, p.86b, p.125 & p.166tr

**All other images: Lindsey Porter**